ENYWAY... A JUMP IS A JUMP

For our sons

Guy, Ben, Jo and Sam

and also our daughter, Kim,

who died in 2006.

All shared some part in Giles's life.

With love and many amazing memories.

The Spirit of man is nomad,

his blood Bedouin,

and love is the Aboriginal tracker

on the spoor of his lost self:

and so I came to live my life

not by conscious plan or prearranged design,

but as someone following the flight of a bird.

Sir Laurens van der Post

ENYWAY... A JUMP IS A JUMP

A FAMILY TRIBUTE

TO

GILES THORNTON

1966 – 1998

COMPILED AND EDITED
BY
ALAN HOE

THORNTON & THORNTON PUBLICATIONS

Copyright © Brian Thornton 2008

First published in 2008 by
Thornton & Thornton Publications
PO Box 120
Waterlooville PO8 0WZ

Distributed by
Thornton & Thornton Publications
PO Box 120
Waterlooville PO8 0WZ
www.ajumpisajump.com
email: thornton@starlings.org.uk

The right of Alan Hoe to be identified as the author and editor
of the work has been asserted herein in accordance with
the Copyright, Designs and Patents Act 1988.

British Library Cataloguing in Publication Data
A catalogue record for this book is available from the British Library.

ISBN 978-0-9559639-0-2

Printed and bound by T J International Ltd, Padstow, Cornwall, UK.

All proceeds from the sale of this book
will be donated to the registered charity
Save the Rhino

Contents

Acknowledgements

Brian and Verity Thornton and Alan Hoe would like to record their
deepest appreciation to the following people who assisted
in the compilation of this memorial to
Giles Thornton

Richard and Tara Bonham, Clare Boscawen, Christina Bryant,
Emma Campbell, Tony and Rose Dyer, Michael and Nicky Dyer,
Charlie Dyer, Sally Dudmesh, Simon Dugdale,
Tony Fitzjohn OBE, Sally Higgin, John and Penny Horsey,
William Kupe, Belinda Pinkney, Roland and Zoë Purcell,
Alan Root, Jackson Sacimba, Inés Sastre, Alexandra Stancioff,
Mary Sykes, Ben Thornton, Guy Thornton, Jo Thornton,
Sam Thornton, and Geoffrey Wheating

Throughout the research stages all of you gave generously of
your time, offered great warmth and hospitality and gave
candid opinions. For some of you the memories were
painful and this was particularly appreciated.
Thank you

Brian and Verity would also like it to be known that
all proceeds from this work will be donated to
the registered charity
Save the Rhino

LARGE SCALE VIEW OF
MAP INSET OPPOSITE

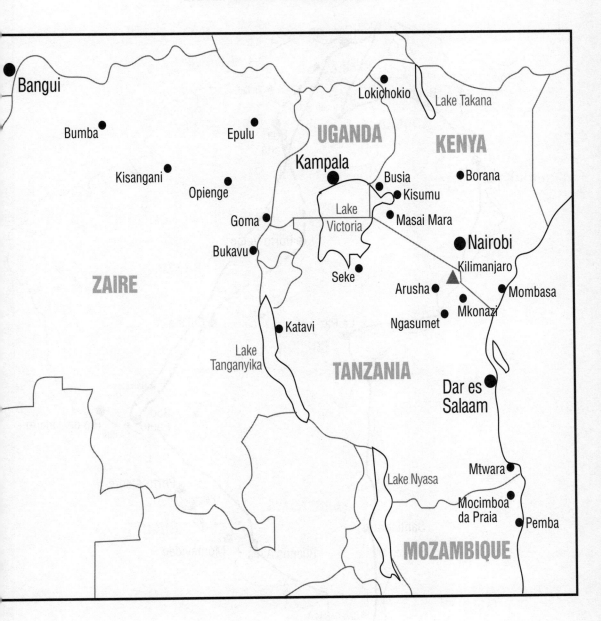

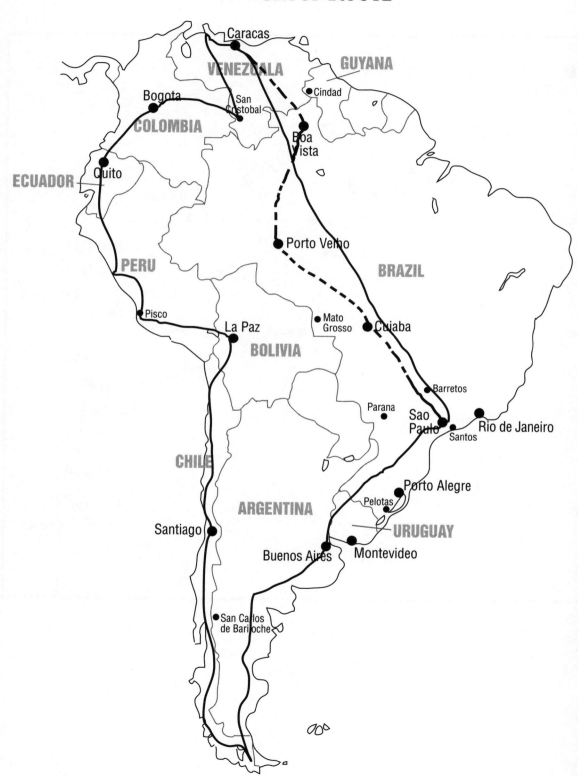

- - - - GILES'S ROUTE TO JOIN BEN, TESSA AND FLOYD
—— GROUP ROUTE

Caracas

VENEZUELA

GUYANA

Cindad

Bogota

San
Cristobal

COLOMBIA

Boa
Vista

ECUADOR

Quito

PERU

Porto Velho

BRAZIL

Pisco

La Paz

Mato
Grosso

Cuiaba

BOLIVIA

Parana

Barretos

Sao
Paulo

Rio de Janeiro

Santos

CHILE

Porto Alegre

ARGENTINA

Pelotas

Santiago

URUGUAY

Buenos Aires

Montevideo

San Carlos
de Bariloche

Prologue

Roland Purcell's Eulogy
Offered At The Cremation Of Giles Thornton

What kind of man is it whose death can bring together so many people
from around the world to a remote ridge in Northern Kenya?
A young man who left no will, no home, no children, none of the
conventional baggage of twentieth century life. Just a motorbike,
a paraglider, saddlebags and a Walkman. A man who rarely spent more
than three days in one place and never washed his hair.

To me he was an enigma: part Englishman, part Comanche — birdman, gaucho. I
never met a truly free spirit — but Giles came pretty close.

He was a man perpetually on the move. Before Africa, he'd travelled through South
America. When he arrived in Kenya, he was on his way to Cape Town.
But seven years later he was still here. He knew a good thing when he saw it.

In those seven years he saw more of this place than most of us will see in a lifetime.
On safari through the Congo, Tanzania, Ethiopia, Mozambique.
And yet he mostly worked his way. The list of employers is impressive:
Danny McCallum, Alan Root, Richard Bonham, Tony Fitzjohn, Gilfred Powys.
He cut roads, trapped animals, broke cars, made friends, moved on.

But it was here in Laikipia, he felt most at home. He had an uncanny bush sense:
no Latin names but a poacher's eye. It was typical of Giles that he should
be the first white man in a generation to see the Congo peacock. It was also
typical that he should pluck and eat the bird for supper when it died. He had
none of the usual piety attached to conservation, more of a farmer's approach
to the natural world. He preferred the Africa to be found outside the
National Parks, a dry landscape where thorns and cattlemen prevailed and
where the game was clever. Such truly wild places, the Northern Frontier
Department especially, were food to his soul. I never once saw him sentimental.

His years of travelling had left him with a minimalist approach to luggage:
extravagantly ruined clothes, bike parts, a camera in a sock, that sinister
sponge bag: these made up his visible belongings. He kept a journal throughout
and took truly original photographs. I'm sure they'll be kept intact for
he had stories to tell in that unique dyslexic way of his.

We took up paragliding together on a particularly medieval skiing
holiday through the French Alps. Our base was a Harringay Council
Gas van that Giles had refurbished with an old pair of his mother's
curtains. Breakfast was kept in our ski boots.

The paragliding was a defining moment for Giles. He seemed almost
visibly to grow feathers. No safari was now complete without an evening
ridge soar with the buzzards. Free-fall parachuting followed and some
highly unorthodox jumps. He once amazed the Maasai world by
dropping out above the Chuylu Hills in full Morani regalia.

Giles was a natural gymnast and tended to bounce if things went wrong.
Nevertheless it could be unwise to imitate some of his manoeuvres. He had
a laugh, not easily forgotten, that preceded moments of mildly mortal danger.
But that was exuberance. For Giles knew his risks; he would finesse
them in his deceptively offhand way. There was no death wish.
He had too much life stuffed into him for that.

He was a brave man in a casual Elizabethan sense, that I suppose
passes for recklessness in our pale vicarious times. But courage for him was
something assumed both in him and in others. Against that the waste of
his killing is suddenly intolerable, insane; a blackness that will not go away.
Emma was with him when he died – I hope he knew that.
At least in her he had found a match in courage and love.

It was Giles's wish to be burnt and scattered here on Borana (with his
family and friends about him). His element was the wind and that is where
I shall always imagine him – a young man gliding over these hills and
ridges with the whole of the distant north beneath his boots.

Giles, you were a dear, mad, beautiful man.

Fly well.

Introduction

Giles Thornton was an excellent communicator with a great capacity for giving love and warmth; he stormed his way through modern Africa touching the hearts and lives of everyone he met. He was living a dream. To capture his essence in words is like trying to catch one of the feathers he loved so much bobbing and weaving in a thermal current; as your hand approaches the dancing object so the movement of air in front of it sends it whirling off in another direction.

Many of the things that Giles achieved; his overland journeys, his paraglider and free-fall flights, his charity work and his long periods of solitude in the bush had been done by others but he tackled all these things in a different way. The well-funded, well-planned and well-supplied safari was not for him. His minimalist instincts required only water, a small bag of biltong, a few bike parts, a camera, a map and the compass his grandmother had sent to him. He was a risk-taker (and sometimes a show-off) but he did not, as Roland Purcell said in his Eulogy, "have a death wish." In the air, on his motorcycle or on foot in the mountains, rain forests and deserts he understood the nature of the dangers and faced them head on with a chuckle of anticipation.

Giles, though highly intelligent, was a physical man rather than an academic. Higher educational qualifications were denied him; dyslexia, during the early years of his schooling, was largely unrecognized by the teaching fraternity. But the resolutions to these problems gave an indication of the tenacious spirit which characterised his life. When, academically, his back was against the wall he was able to knuckle down and force himself to work hard.

Giles was also a great charmer. Handsome, well-built and athletic, he had a natural, easy going allure that allowed him to smile and beguile his way out of situations with ease. An irrepressible sense of humour and boundless energy, won him a huge number of friends and earned him an enviable reputation with the fairer sex. These qualities also took the stinging effect out of his need to speak his mind.

A fiercely independent man; he did not sponge off others; no task was too menial if it was going to fund his travels. He often knew fear but he was able to control it and even enjoy it as part of an adventurous lifestyle.

He was at home in the company of others but he also enjoyed solitude. Days and nights alone in the African bush hunting rare species of animal life; free-fall parachuting; paragliding, wild, solitary motorcycle rides over rough terrain and confrontations with restless lions are not for the faint-hearted and these activities show his penchant for calculated risk taking. Above all, he was a romantic and his thoughts often went back to the early days of explorers such as Livingstone, Stanley, Speke and Burton who had seen the 'Dark Continent' in a pre-colonial age. How fantastic and daunting it must have been to be one of the first white men to set foot in the great rain forests, mountains and deserts of Africa? Living a dream can only have one outcome – dreams have to end and it is doubly tragic that just a few weeks before his untimely death, Giles was beginning to think long and hard about his future – a future that would certainly have been based upon life with the woman he loved.

What forces shaped the course of life of this adventurous young man? Some of the answers to that question can be found in Giles's letters and the diaries which he maintained from late 1987 and upon which this book is based. His dyslexia shows in his words but some of his descriptive passages show a restless, romantic spirit. He was a superb photographer with a natural appreciation of light and composition and through his collection of photographs it is easy to detect his love of the environment in which he spent his happiest days.

Chapter I

The Young Giles

Born on 8th July, 1966 at St. Mary's Hospital, Paddington, Giles Thornton was little more than a year younger than his brother, Ben, and the fourth child of the Thornton family whose home was at Stansted, Essex where they had built a new house that was large enough to accommodate a close, loving family that grew to consist of five sons and a daughter. At an early age Giles realised that his beguiling smile could extricate him from the scrapes that he got into with Ben. Brother Ben recalled an incident that showed another aspect of Giles's personality – he was full of curiosity as was evidenced by his reaction to getting a wristwatch for one of his birthdays. The manufacturers had stamped the word 'Shockproof' on the case and, of course, the veracity of this had to be tested – a test which the boy conducted by throwing the watch from his bedroom window then dashing down to check the result!

Education for Giles began at the age of four years when he entered Miss Cornell's Kindergarten at Bishop's Stortford who included in her end of year report: "He could write quite well when he liked to and showed some ability in his number work. He was a boisterous member of his class, but so long as he was kept occupied was *usually* a good boy." He progressed to Farnham Primary School at which his dyslexia was not properly identified and his reading difficulties were misinterpreted. Mrs Winch, the headmistress, remembered Giles "…as a popular, happy little boy who arrived at school with a smile, even when we decided he should arrive an hour early for one-to-one reading practice."

And on to preparatory school at Wellesley House, Broadstairs: "He is not unlike an untrained puppy, with a great sense of fun and with tremendous enthusiasm. However, he is not resentful when he is corrected and recently there have been signs of a more disciplined approach." The dyslexia made things difficult. Always in a terrible rush to complete an exercise, he wrote the first thing

1

that came into his head and spelt it however it sounded to him on the day. He was a bold and courageous player of team games but lacked the skill of ball control.

In the summer of 1977 the Common Entrance examination was looming fast and in order to achieve a place at Gordonstoun, Giles had to suffer special lessons and holiday tuition. Knowing that 'the chips were down' he made a huge effort and managed to obtain a place; even though it took a display of the Giles Thornton charm at the required interview to swing the day.

In Round Square House he was under the custody of Anthony Jones when he arrived at Gordonstoun at the age of 13 years. Jones later reported: "Giles attacked his first term with great vigour and enthusiasm. He tore into everything, work, games and expedition training; he swept the floor as though he were charging the Russian guns with the Light Brigade." He developed a good relationship with his Housemaster and did quite well during his first two years. A typical comment that runs as a theme through many of his school reports at this time is: "Giles is genuinely concerned to do well and there is nothing forced about his enthusiastic response, but he could begin to exercise restraint and sit and think just a little bit more before rushing in with a quick answer. He needs to temper his headlong approach somewhat, but I hope he will never lose his enthusiasm."

Sadly Anthony Jones died in July 1980 and Giles did not strike the same rapport with the new Housemaster, Angus Miller. As time went by matters improved but some quotes from letters written by the Headmaster, Michael Mavor, and Angus Miller will give an insight into the difficulties they were having with this hyperactive and exuberant pupil:

12th May, 1981, from the Headmaster: "The breakage of Richard Gregory's calculator occurred when Giles threw Gregory's bag of books, which contained the calculator, across the room. Giles was seen by his Housemaster and told that the cost of this breakage would be added to his end of term bill."

From his Housemaster, in 1982: "Last night, well after lights out, Giles was making outrageous noises out of his dormitory window, clearly audible all around the Round Square, while supposedly he was in charge of the dormitory. I hope that this time Giles might learn his lesson. I might add that I have already had to talk to him about his language this term. I am afraid that I have had to strip him of his status as a duty senior."

Again from the Headmaster, in 1983: "Giles was sent to me by his housemaster for again letting off fireworks in the vicinity of his house. The house is in the process of having a major refurbishment and it has been made very clear to the boys that the improvements must be treated with respect.

"Only the day after these points had been made to Giles he was found repeatedly kicking a football at the ceiling of the locker room. When I saw Giles I displayed to him a light fitting, which he had decorated with graffiti and which was only fit for the dustbin. At the end of term Giles left his mark on the newly painted wall of his study with the words 'Fred was here'.

"I have made it clear to Giles that if he behaves in this sort of way again it is likely that his Housemaster will say to me that he no longer wants Giles in his house. It will then be for me to decide whether I can persuade any other Housemaster to take him in." In his final report the headmaster, Michael Mavor, said: "Fred was undoubtedly here. I greatly enjoyed his verve and enthusiasm, but he certainly did not know the time and the season for everything. His heart is in the right place, however, and I think that he will do very well; I'd like him to."

During the holidays Giles benefited from his father's interest in creating a pedigree herd of Charolais cattle on his smallholding. Giles worked hard on this project and formed a good close relationship with Joe Reed, a farm manager-cum-stockman. Giles began to acquire the arts of animal husbandry and came to realise that he had an affinity with animals. This aptitude was instrumental in his making the decision to study agriculture when once again he had to make a huge effort to qualify for Writtle Agricultural College. He decided that he would not take a 'gap year'.

At Writtle Giles made good friends who stayed in touch with him for the rest of his short life. The second part of the three-year course was a period of practical experience which he started by working at Hampton near Farnham, Surrey, where his grandfather's cousin has an estate with a pedigree herd of Guernsey cows. Giles was in his element and though he thrived in the hard working environment his headlong approach got him into trouble! Tractors and other farm machinery became bent and unusable at regular intervals and, despite the pleas of the farm management, his determination to complete tasks faster than anyone else never left him.

For his second six months of practical work he was employed by the Earl of Mansfield on the Scone Palace estate. He loved the freedom of the wide-open spaces of Scotland where his mentor was John Mitchell who became a life-long friend.

In 1986 Giles achieved his coveted OND and having not had a 'gap year' he spent some weeks skiing with old friends at Val d'Isère and Tignes. He perfected his monoski technique which he was most adept at showing off to the cameras. On returning home in the spring of 1987 he worked on farms in East Anglia for friends he had made at Writtle and during this time his maternal grandmother, Mrs. Rhoda Lawrence, made a decision that she was not to know would change the course of Giles's life. Rhoda had a small farm in Hertfordshire and by 1987 she was finding it a burden and she decided to sell. Thus a possible commercial basis for Giles to use his newly gained knowledge and experience disappeared.

Chapter II

Adventures In Brazil

By late 1987 Giles was in a quandary. There was no place for him on what had been his grandmother's farm. With his Writtle qualifications, his lively, likeable character and his propensity for hard work he would never have been short of employment in Britain but he was unsettled. He wanted a challenge and when he began to think about his options, his restless spirit came to the fore. The weeks spent on the ski slopes had given him a taste of freedom. He wanted to stretch himself in a way that would not be possible in Britain – the one area in the country where he felt truly happy was Scotland. His love of the Scottish Highlands was inspired by the open spaces and wide horizons.

The Scots were imbued with a true sense of history and this had been one of Giles's favourite subjects: the ideals of the early explorers, colonialists and empire builders were close to his heart. The romantic side of his nature was burgeoning and the world beckoned him. It became clear that in order to satisfy his yearnings he would have to look outside Britain. Some of his romantic notions were temporarily killed off by the acceptance that whatever he wanted to do – he would have to earn his living. He wanted to use the skills that had been so hard to acquire. Brazil, with its huge cattle ranches, arable farms and wide open plains was the ideal destination. Through Sir Edmund Vestey[1] he was introduced to Union International and he decided to learn Portuguese in order to become employable on one of the company's farms in Brazil. There were only two problems for Giles to consider at that point: he had never ridden a horse and he was in love! With the optimism of youth he saw the riding problem as being easily resolved – he took a course at Elaine

---

1   *By the late 1980s the Vestey family dominated the UK meat trade and had large investments in Brazil.*

Braekman's riding school. The same youthful wisdom told him that the love that he and 'Floyd' had for each other would survive a year of separation.

In late November 1987 Giles's diary shows that preparations for his new life were well under way.[2]

23 November, 1987: Last week of Portuguese lessons starts. My thoughts for Floyd were strong as we had a rather odd week-end, where we seemed very distant. I bought this diary at Dillons, off the Tottenham Court Road. Went to the cinema with Floyd, "Roxanna", got very well drunk in cocktail bar, had a fine night of little sleep, talked well into the morning about life.

24 November: Interview at Union International at 9.00 a.m., went well with much laughter and information about Guarriroba Fazenda [farm]. Left their office for language studies, a day of much talking in Portuguese and little writing. Phoned Floyd – wished her luck with tonight's meeting with her parents about last weekend. Gran and Grampy, Kim and Geoff and me went out to dinner at Gran's old club. A great evening talking about ignorant relatives. Grampy on good form.

27 November: Short morning of Portuguese. Finished at noon and went to Union International to pick up tickets and get my insurance. Got my stuff ready for Scotland. Rang Floyd. Went to get brake lights on car mended. Set out for Edinburgh at 3.00 p.m. Floyd hit a Rolls Royce near Lord's cricket ground. Bad journey to Scotch Corner with queues on the A1. Charlie Millard on good form. I drove from Scotch Corner, but Tessa found the A68 did not agree with her and was carsick. Went to Mary Rose at midnight, when we arrived. Ben welcomed us with, "F*** off."

29 November: Got up at 10.00 a.m., after a night of very little sleep with Floyd! Set off with Ben in Whiplash to Tully Murdoch to see Johnny Mitchell and the crew. Arrived at 11.30 a.m. Met Johnny and his Mum; Johnny McKay and Helen arrived later. After lunch went to see Johnny's farm at the Beach Hedges. Very impressive as they got all the crops in early. Went to see George and Lynn at Aberbothrie. Had dinner at John and Helen's at Rosewell. James came down as well.

30 November: Went to meet Tessa, Katie and William Sporborg at Leith waterfront wine bar. Set off for London at 5.00 p.m. I drove to Scotch Corner, where

---

2   *It was at this time Giles began to keep a diary. He was to make entries almost daily for the next two years. Subsequently it became more in the form of intermittent journals describing particular events or projects.*

we stopped for supper. Floyd drove to Grantham. I drove the rest in thick fog, behind a maniac in a BMW who was going at 85 mph. Arrived London at 11.30 p.m., and went to bed. Slept very well with Floyd on my arm all night.

1 December: Woke up at 9.30 a.m. Floyd went to work after a row with her sister. Got the wheel off my bike (puncture) and then got a train from Liverpool Street home for lunch. Mum and I packed my bags and got ready for Brazil. Guy came around in late afternoon. Guy, Diana, Grandma, Mum and Dad for dinner. Drank a bottle of champagne and became plastered. Went to bed at 1.00 a.m., after long dinner.

2 December: A morning of rushing about. Boots the chemist, M&S, socks, records. Also went to the Green Man to get my diary and put £10 behind the bar for the boys. Riding lessons in the afternoon were most interesting, must have been a good gallop of at least 50 yards without falling off. Went to London at 4.00 p.m. Dumped my kit at Kim's [Giles's sister] house and rang Floyd. Met Tessa, Floyd, Rodney, Will Sporborg, Charlie Mitchell at Floyd's house. Buck's Fizz and beer and pizza. Went to Feelings, then to Café des Artistes. Great evening.

With his goodbyes behind him Giles embarked upon his first adventure. By way of Paris, Recife and Rio de Janeiro he made his way to the teeming, polluted city of São Paulo. The journey to Rio Preto, where he was met by Richard Turnley, the ranch manager, took an hour. The next day, 5th December, he was driven to the ranch at Guarriroba and shown his quarters. If he had expected to spend some time acclimatizing and getting to know the lay of the land – he was wrong! At seven o'clock the next morning, he was presented with a horse and a saddle and sent off into the country to meet up with a team of gauchos. It was a long hard day. After rounding up 300 head of one-year-old Zebu/ Simmental cross-bred cattle and moving them three kilometres to a corrall, they took on the back-breaking task of branding. It was exhausting work in the airless humidity – never having the time to break off to drink water. When the long day ended at about five o'clock he was able to take a swim before heading gratefully to his bed.

During the run up to his first Christmas away from his family, Giles endured many similarly exhausting days but he soon got used to it and during periods of light relief he began to meet new people and enlarge his circle of friends though thoughts of Floyd were never far away:

9 December: God knows how I got out of bed, but I did – man or mouse? – whichever made me move. Spent the whole day roaming the farm, checking cattle and horses. Played my harmonica for the first time, also tied up my first bois [young bull] on a lasso. Had a good day, swam in the evening and got some writing paper and envelopes from Richard. Wrote home and to Floyd, I went a bit OTT with her letter. I look forward to her reply in a month's time. First shave tonight.

12 December: Saturday. Got up at 7.00 a.m., and went to ask Richard Turnley if I can borrow a car or be driven into town to get some boots. No problem, he said, but Monday. I changed a $50 bill with him into crusados [local currency]. Finished reading the book that morning and I went to play tennis with Rod, Ian and Richard [students who came around from their farm]. Played until 2.30 p.m., had a big lunch called a Fayshwader. Went to Rio Preto for big piss up at the Anglo workshop. There, Richard Turnley [the boss], Gloria Turnley and I went to a night club at 11.00 p.m. Danced with some Brazilian girls. Had fun. Got back to the farm at 3.00 a.m., not too late.

25 December: Merry Christmas at Barretos. Got up at 11.00 a.m. Went with Simon and Rupert to Ian's and CA's for champagne breakfast. 2.00 p.m. Went to club house and played water polo for two hours with the boys. Went to Jim and Sharon Bennett's house for Christmas lunch. Started at 6.00 p.m., finished at 8.30 p.m. with a good fight. Very good food. CA and Sharon are superb people. Dave the Rugby Argy man was there with his wife. Rang home. Four minutes of quick talking to Ben, Guy, Mum and Dad. Got to my bed at 12.15 a.m.

26 December: Went over to Richard Turnley's house at 10.00 a.m., he was having a churrasco[3] for 30 friends. I helped cook the beef, lamb, sausages, piglet, goose and chickens. Never in my life have I seen people eat and drink so much. They were quite fat – no – very fat. Live band and tape music, great fun, messing around with Brazilian girls. They think I'm crazy. CA is super, reminds me of Floyd – look out Giles – she is married.

Christmas passed and the New Year dawned: Giles was now a cowboy in South America. The daily routines described in his diary are typically misleading. He makes no mention of the fact that he had to hold his own with South American

---

3   *Churrasco: in the towns this is predominantly pork but in the country it is a feast of all meats usually cooked barbecue-style over open fires.*

gauchos, born to the saddle and as tough as whipcord. They are amongst the finest horsemen in the world! He was spending whole days in the saddle, riding over rough terrain on horses bred for working with cattle; they could turn and stop as quickly as polo ponies. A far remove from a couple of hours of genteel cantering on the green fields of England under the tutelage of Elaine Braekman! The fact that he coped so well speaks volumes for Giles's physical agility, stamina and capacity for hard work. A hard life breeds hard humour and Giles would have been ridiculed at any early ineptitude he may have shown before he first earned the grudging respect and then the friendship of the ranch hands.

23 January: 7.00 a.m., in the office. Went with Nick and John to count caterpillars on soya plants. We had a 30-metre chain with one-metre intervals marked on it. We crawled on our hands and knees counting and calling out how many caterpillars we had seen every metre. Rod Paxton came over in the afternoon; he had a video of the Tyson v. Holmes fight. I went to Voltaparanga with Nick. We visited a very busy bar where there were plenty of women. I danced from 1.00 a.m., until 5.00 a.m. Met an absolutely stunning girl. I did not know whether to chase her up or not, she was really stunning, but not a good dancer and rather boring like most Brazilians.

24 January: Went over to Richard's when I got up at 1.30 p.m. Had a barbecue and played tennis until 7.00 p.m. Four sets, really sweaty tennis. In the evening had a big pot of tea with Nick and shared the large piece of Christmas cake that Mum had sent me which arrived yesterday. Also wrote to Mum and Dad. I don't know what to do. The Clare Floyd problem will become big unless we do something.

2 February: Went to the office at 7.00 a.m. Told I was tractor driving. Went down to the work shop and was told that my tractor, the Miller, was broken down. Had a letter from Floydie, my heart raced, it was beautiful, Floydie's best yet. Got on the Miller at 10.00 a.m., disking. Disked all afternoon and evening until 7.00 p.m., then the night driver took over. Put myself to sleep reading Floyd's letter, too lovely for words. Oh! How deep I am, but still – so far...

5 February: 7.00 a.m. Went to Cede Velka with John to weigh calves. My job was to get hold of the calf's head, while someone else read the number in the ear. In the afternoon went to watch the killing of some pigs (illegal). Then got a horse and went off with the boys, did some rodeoing and fell heavily on my coccyx. Ow! Does it hurt! Wrote a huge letter to Floydie. Went to bed with very sore arse at 12.30 a.m. I feel for Floyd.

The two months or so that he had been working in Brazil wrought some changes in Giles. In a short space of time he had been absorbed into a hard-working, hard-playing environment which was full of new experiences. Holding his own on horseback with some of the world's finest rough riders, he was learning about the problems of rearing cattle and sheep on the remote open rolling sierras. He tackled with gusto some of the less pleasant tasks associated with farming – cleaning out corrals and pens did not disturb him in the least. He was learning the widely disparate arts of machinery maintenance, motorbike riding in rough terrain, animal husbandry and basic veterinary skills, horsemanship, gaining agricultural experience in varying weather conditions and last, but not least, the art of getting on well with people of a very different culture.

Giles's frequent references to beautiful landscapes perhaps show that his love of open spaces was still growing but he was gaining another sort of experience. Expatriates in South America, particularly those who are subjected to hard physical working conditions, tend to play hard and drink hard. Giles was well able to hold his own with them and there is no question that he was a popular member of the team on the farm. On many occasions he would have had to converse solely in Portuguese (not an easy language) and this would impose stresses of another kind. Giles took smoothly to Brazilian rural transport: horses and motorcycles have one common aspect which appealed to him – the independent nature of both modes of travel. In each case it is one man in control of one machine (or beast) – there is no-one else to help, interfere or criticise.

His work ethic was impressive. Many times he suffered minor injuries and fevers but he never used these as an excuse for taking time out. Throughout these first few weeks the young man who had such a huge capacity for work and life in equal measures, was suffering from one of the more common tribulations of youth. His first real love! The diaries clearly show his swings between high humour and mild depression as he first cautiously acknowledges his love of Floyd and then begins to question it. A liaison between young lovers that is dependent on a slow postal process and an occasional telephone call is not satisfactory at the best of times but to an impatient lad it must occasionally have seemed almost unbearable. Beautiful women abound in South America and there must have been many a temptation for such a handsome and sociable fellow.

Giles carried on working hard at Guarriroba and occasionally entertaining doubts about his love for Floyd but he was heartened that along with his brother, Ben, and Floyd's friend Tessa, Floyd was planning a visit to South America later in the year. His diaries show a now-established pattern of life on the ranch.

21 February: (Back at Guarriroba.) Caught a lorry going there at 7.00 p.m. He was going to pick up cattle for the next day's kill at Barretos. Two new English chaps to stay for two weeks aged about 18–19 from Eton. Got a handful of letters from the office, went home and read. Ah! A letter from Floydie. She sounds desperate and low, needs a phone call. I will try tomorrow. Oh! Floydie – why so low?

22 February: 7.00 a.m., to the corral. All the men very pleased to see me. Gosh it's so good to know you are wanted! Loaded lorries all morning with bois to go to Barretos. The two English chaps, Ed and Jaque, are good guys and helped. The rest of the day was spent vaccinating bois and vacas. A good day's work which passed very fast. Phoned Floyd in the evening. What an experience! I realised then that I had lost her. She sounded so distant, as though she wanted to escape out of my lock. Wrote to Floyd. Ciao Floyd! I give you two weeks to reply and then – Ciao!

24 February: 7.00 a.m., at the corral. Got given a lovely horse. First, blood testing some horses that were being sold, also writing up their pedigrees. I named a beautiful Egua filly, Floyd. I felt like hell for two good reasons: 1. I was tired. 2. A certain girl had gone. Lunch at noon, I got a letter from Floyd. It must have been sent before I telephoned her. Fantastic! Very deep and thoughtful. I will ring her on Monday or Tuesday night next week. Sent my self to sleep reading Floydie's letter.

8 May: (Sunday) Bob's wife and daughter arrived yesterday. The daughter, Jua Vahna, is pretty, only 15 going on 20 (these Brazilians mature early) and is obviously interested. I woke at 8.00 a.m., had breakfast: peanut butter and marmalade, much to the horror of Bob's wife, she doesn't look good, but is kindly in an odd way. Went for a two hour burn on the Agrale bike, listening to Bruce Springsteen. Shades on, good stares from people I passed. Went for a churrasco, one and a half hour drive to the nearest town, outrageous. It is very beautiful scenery. Jua Vahna coming on strong now, leg brushing etc. Watched Johnny Cougar on the TV, sat and talked to Jua Vahna for a couple of hours – no – I want Floydie, I want YOU! Phoned home and said "Hi" to everyone. Ben says he is coming out with the girls. Wow! My dream has come true after all. Everyone sounds in good shape.

17 May: At Bob's flat in Campo Grande. 8.00 a.m., got up after very little sleep, the bed was too small. Cup of coffee then Bob, Maria and me went shopping. Bought black jeans, blue denim shirt and George Harrison tape. Noon – picked up Jua Vanha from school and went back to the apartment for lunch. Jua Vanha coming on strong again, lots of rubbing against me and holding my hand. Oh well! Looked for more tapes but there were none that appealed. Went to the supermarket. It took Maria one and a half hours to collect all that she wanted. Jua Vanha snogged me in the corner of the supermarket, back at the apartment more kisses. Home at 11.10 p.m. Floydie it's just physical – only that.

30 May: (Public holiday in Brazil) heavy rain and a cold wind, really miserable. Read my book for a couple of hours and then contemplated what to do. Bob went down to the office so I phoned Floydie, she was in great spirits, staying at her father's house for the bank holiday. She said that she, Tessa and Ben will be out before 1 September, but she has to find the money! I still don't really know if she will make it. I know that Ben and Tessa will. It's that she's going to have to work to get the money. I day dreamed about Floydie out in South America. Is it really possible?

Chapter III

A Break In Argentina

Giles enjoyed his break from the rolling plains of the Guarriroba. In the highlands of Mato Grosso he was experiencing another of Brazil's many faces. There is a majestic beauty in Mato Grosso and the air is sharper and cleaner. He was still able to keep up his sporting activities as most farms, in a peculiarly English fashion, had tennis courts and swimming pools and cricket was still a hugely popular game. He was adding to his collection of bumps and bruises as he took falls from horses (and cattle) and split a finger with an awkward cricket ball catch; the knee (injured during a jet ski session in April) continued to trouble him. He took all of these minor setbacks with good humour and if other people laughed at his antics – well – that only seemed to add to his own innate sense of the comic.

The long range affair with Floyd continued to bring mental highs and lows. Having heard on 30th May that Floyd expected to be in South America by 1st September, he was disheartened when he spoke to her again on 22nd June to hear that it could be mid-September or later.

On 1st July Giles returned to Guarriroba and a warm welcome. Over the last few days he had been making preparations for a visit to Argentina. He decided to work his passage as far as Santos (the sea port closest to São Paulo). There would be a constant stream of trucks departing from the refrigeration plant in Barretos carrying frozen meat for export to Africa. From Santos the trucks would be continuing on to Uruguay.

He started his journey on 6th July reporting to the refrigeration plant at 7.00 a.m. Dressed in white overalls he spent the whole morning loading frozen meat onto three lorries. It was very hard work: *...we worked very fast today. After the first lorry I was sweating, also my left shoulder began to ache, no worries, we finished working at noon. The blokes were excellent fun, built like brick shithouses, but a*

13

really good laugh when they knew you could swear. Lunch back at Jim and Sharon's. Jim went back to work and Sharon went to a book club. I went and saw Magnum, who told me that my lorry was leaving at 6.00 p.m. I phoned Floydie and she rang back. We chatted for a while, but she was in a bad mood. She was upset that she had to work while me and her other friends were free to travel the world...

The driver, José, was humorous and easy to chat with. At 7.30 p.m., they stopped to have a nap on the hills overlooking the city. The truck made slow progress through the dense, stinking traffic of São Paulo but it was even slower as it crawled down the steep hills from the city into the port of Santos where they were told that they would have to wait until 3.00 p.m., before they could move alongside the Cuban ship to off-load the meat which was destined for Angola. Unloading took three exhausting hours and after a poor dinner in a dingy dockyard café, Giles, smelly and dirty, crawled into his sleeping bag on the floor of the lorry cabin.

Progress was good the next day in the now empty lorry and even though it was pouring with rain Giles was enjoying the journey along the hilly roads that wound their way through the banana and tea plantations. As they entered the state of Parana the sun burst through and it was then that Giles realised what had been nagging at his mind. It was 8th July – his birthday! Much to the amusement of José he opened the one and only card that he had been saving for the occasion.

The scenery changed as they entered the state of Santa Catalina. The hills were heavily forested but soon they descended onto the coast road and Giles looked out over the cold, grey vista of the South Atlantic Ocean. It was extremely cold. Giles's birthday night was spent in the car park of a roadside garage-cum-restaurant.

The next morning they tackled the 300 kilometres to Port Alegre. Sitting high in the cab of the lorry Giles absorbed the changing scenery. The countryside was flattening out into a sort of fenland with lakes and marshes and the weather was getting ever colder. On through Port Alegre and Pelotas for a night stop at Santa Vitoria close to the Brazilian–Uruguayan border, before moving on the next morning to Chuy where the free travel ended. Giles decided to take the bus into Montevideo. Passing through the Brazilian customs without any problems he was surprised to find that the line on the map separating Brazil from Uruguay also meant a sudden switch in language – he was now confronted with Spanish.

Using the hydrofoil to cross the estuary of the famous River Plate into Buenos Aires he took a further bus to Bariloche. In his usual affable manner Giles struck up a conversation with Tom who was a Dutch skiing instructor also headed to Bariloche. He was full of hope that his new-found friend may be able to help him to find work and lodgings. Giles was determined to enjoy his skiing but equally set on earning money in order to stay as long as possible. The following diary extract shows his mind set.

12 July: I woke after a little sleep. The bus was in the middle of a huge arid, freezing expanse. The mountains of the Andes began to loom up, white and shining in the morning sun. I got Tom's telephone number and he told me that he goes to the Status bar in the evenings. We arrived at Bariloche at 5.30 p.m. I went to the tourist office and was given the names and addresses of cheap hotels and the places where jobs are advertised. I went job hunting. There was nothing advertised that was any good. I went into one restaurant and asked about washing up. The going rate is US$60 per month and that's for working all day long. Also there are no jobs available at the moment. The ski lifts pass costs US$20 a day, so the only way I am going to be able to stay is by finding a ski job. Otherwise it will have to be a two week holiday and then back to Buenos Aires. I went over to Yvonne's hotel and had dinner at a pizza place. It did cheer me up to be with friends. After I went to the Status bar with Marianne and met up with Tom.

13 July: 10.00 a.m. Out of bed after a huge sleep. Went down to Yvonne and Marianne's hotel. Hopped on a bus to the ski lifts. Inquired about surfing and met a chap who hires out boards. Yvonne and Marianne are amazed by snow, because they have never seen it before – really amusing. Afternoon back at the village. I went to the First Aid Pisteur's office to inquire about work. They took my particulars and said they would contact me, which sounded good. Went to the hire shop to get skis and kit for Marianne as I hope to teach her tomorrow. Met some Brazilians in the shop, who said they wanted a teacher, so tomorrow I may be earning some money. Delicious dinner that Yvonne very kindly bought me. I went to the Status bar late on in the hope of finding Tom. He wasn't there. No worries; I will have to hire some skis tomorrow.

20 July: I walked up to Tom's house to pick up my board, then I hitched a lift to the mountain, bought a ski pass and onto the chair lifts. It was ice surfing and very fast and exhausting, but great fun. As the snow became softer and wetter, the surfing improved. It was easier to 'edge' and fly down the mountain. I did some huge wipe-outs, followed by the wipe-out of them all! I flew down the mountain; it was the best run of the day so far at 3.00 p.m. I headed towards a group of people with a large mound of snow in front of them. Oh well! Why not? I flew over the hump, showing off, a big air wipe-out. My knee goes – ouch! Lots of applause from the crowd watching. I had to take the chair lift down the mountain where I tried to sell my ski pass at the bottom, but I was taken in by the police and given a good bollocking. I played the innocent gringo!

27 July: Out at 11.00 a.m. I went down to the shop to pick up the leaflets. I met Steven and had a chat over some coffee. I spent the morning giving out leaflets and had lunch back at the Victoria. Then out again to give out more leaflets, mainly to car drivers and smarter tourists, who are shopping. By 4.00 p.m., my feet were hurting, so back to the Victoria for a smoke. Went out again giving out leaflets, then at 9.00 p.m., to the cinema ... back to the Victoria at 2.30 a.m., to bed, wet and sad. Will it be snowing at the top of the mountain? Is it love with Floydie? Has she drifted on? Will Steven pay me?

In fact Steven paid Giles US$50 per day and though the leaflet distribution job was done energetically and thoroughly it did not seem to significantly increase custom. Giles managed to get in some very good skiing with various new friends from different parts of the world. He found that he preferred the snowboard and was becoming very adept even though he managed some more incredible wipe-outs that gave him yet more knee problems. He realised that he would be hard pressed to earn sufficient money to relax and enjoy much more of the carefree life but he was to have one more adventure before decision time. On 6th August he woke to a dismal, cloudy day. Eventually the mists began to rise and the wind dropped so he took a walk during which he ran into his friend, Gilbert and they decided to go the slopes.

After some sluggish boarding in heavy, damp snow Gilbert suggested that they should head off to a place where he had enjoyed some good skiing a few days previously and they set out into the now thick, wet fog. Giles, concerned about the direction they were taking, asked Gilbert if he was sure of his route. Gilbert confidently stated that there was no problem. But, as they headed down into and beyond the tree line, the snow got very sparse and after more pointed questions from Giles, Gilbert finally admitted that he was lost. Committed to the descent, they were concerned when the snow eventually disappeared and the trees gave way to bushes and scrub. When Giles reached the bottom of the first descent he realised that Gilbert was no longer following him and there was no response to his loud calls.

Dusk was rapidly approaching. Should he retrace his footsteps in an attempt to link up again with Gilbert or should he continue downhill? Giles decided to press on until he came to a fast-flowing river swollen with the icy waters of melted snow. He crouched down and entered the foaming water. The strong current immediately whipped his legs from under him. The snow board went flying and he was suddenly immersed in the near freezing mountain waters. He struggled to the surface and, fixing his eyes on the opposite bank, and fighting the current at every faltering step as he gasped for air, he bulldozed his way forward. At times he thought he would be swept away but with teeth chattering, semi-frozen diaphragm allowing only short, sharp gasps and clothes heavy with water, he managed to haul himself out to the safety of the far bank. The snow board had wedged in the rocks and after another quick dunking he was able to retrieve it. He was now seriously cold and he knew that if he didn't get his blood circulating quickly he would begin to suffer from hyperthermia and lose his judgement.

He set off fast, his limbs were jerking and difficult to control and he opted to follow tracks that he was able to recognise as a horse, a man and a dog. They must surely lead to habitation. It soon turned out that Gilbert, though still on the 'wrong' side of the river, had seen Giles and so they were able to maintain loose contact by shouting to each other. By then it was dark. Cold, wet and clumsy he stumbled onwards branching off onto a more promising looking track. He shouted to attract attention but there was no reply and he was beginning to worry when he heard a dog barking. His calls were then answered by a man. With his help Giles was put onto another track which, after an hour-long walk, took him to the main road where he finally met up with Gilbert. After dinner at the Mirador Hotel it was a happy young man who climbed into his bed thanking his lucky stars for their help in a dramatic situation that could so easily have become a tragedy.

Giles decided to return to Buenos Aires and from there he made the train journey to Hurlingham to stay with his friends the Harrisons. At Hurlingham Giles was very much at home. The weather was temperate and he held his own in a number of tennis, rugby and cricket matches. He found a strange beauty in the low-lying 'wetlands' with the long avenues of eucalyptus trees and the wide variety of flamingos and other water birds.

Communications with Floyd during this period seem to have been sparse but he did find out that her new plan was to arrive at Venezuela along with brother Ben and Tessa. This suited Giles's plans admirably. On 24th August he left for Montevideo.

Conditions in Uruguay were the worst he had yet encountered. The poor grazing resulted in thin, undernourished animals. There was little regard for the rules of good husbandry and much of the machinery was poorly maintained. He worked through a few long, tiring days with the sheep shearing crews. During this hard, dirty labour tempers often became frayed and harsh words were common though a few beers at the end of the day was usually enough to restore tranquillity. He found time to fit in a few solitary motorcycle excursions into the countryside and began, after all, to appreciate that the lowlands did have a particular beauty of their own. He loved being alone astride his bike and at those times his imagination took him wherever he sought to go in his mind as he roared along the rough tracks.

He eventually made contact with Floyd and got the good news that she, Ben and Tessa would be flying to Venezuela on 6th or 7th October. He also called 'friends of a friend' who lived in Caracas and he was given a warm invitation to stay with them. It was a light-hearted Giles Thornton who left Uruguay on 16th September. He was planning to return to Brazil and Rio Preto to collect his gear and make his farewells to all his mates there before he set out for Caracas.

1. Giles aged three already turning on the charm for Bimbo Stancioff

2. With his eldest brother Guy in Scotland, 1972

3. Sailing on Loch Coalisport, Argyll. Verity, Brian, Giles, Ben and Sarah Slight, 1978

ROUND SQUARE, 1983

Photograph by   Studio Tyrrell

P. Wynn-Jones, J. Campbell, R. Pritchard, C. Thomson, R. Potter, B. Burdett, S. Jahan, C. Lamont, E. Shanks, S. Wright, A. Cook, F. Kreutzer, M. Pritchard, J. Knapp, S. Dunn, P. Kreutzer, J. Armstrong, S. Khalil, T. Withall, C. Darby, R. Lightfoot.

A. Kleinman, H. Allanby, D. Kirkup, S. Roberts, E. Bishop, P. Momber, G. de la Roche du Ronzet, M. Gibbs, B. Scholten, N. Fletcher, F. Lorentzen, P. Williams, M. Carling, C. Armor, J. Sharp, G. Smith, J. Ellis, C. Idowu, S. Ogilvy, W. Mason, E. Sutton, C. Taylor, F. Lamont.

G. Thornton, D. Wright, L. Alexander, Mr Spooner, G. Magnuson, Dr Pickering, A. Myerscough, Mr Miller, D. Smailes, Mr Waddell. A. Mason, Dr Thomson, K. Mordue, C. Mason, M. Halbert.

R. Berry, L. Muncaster, J. Spooner, R. Austey, A. Bartlett, S. Johnston, A. MacGillivray, R. Zahid.

4. Round Square, 1983

5. Giles collecting his athletics cup at Gordonstoun, July 1983

6. Brian, Giles and Jo Reed with the Charolais bulls at Stansted, 1983

7. With the Gauchos at Fazenda Lageado, Brazil 1988

8. Giles, Floyd, Tessa and Ben at Cuenca, Equador, Christmas 1988

9. The team at Colca, Peru, a long way down

10. Clare Floyd,
Santiago,
February 1989

11. By Lake Llanquihue with Huequi beyond

*12. With
Bimbo Stancioff
at Dunlugas,
Banffshire, 1989*

13. Sam, Giles, Jo, Guy, Verity, Kim, Tara and Ben, at Stansted House, July 1989

14. Leaving home for Africa,
Boxing Day 1990

15. En route at
Yaounde, Cameroun, 1991
(Photo: Jeremy Matthews)

16. With a young gorilla at Ratshuru, Zaire

Chapter IV

Backpacking In South America

To a well-heeled traveller the journey from Montevideo to Venezuela's capital city, Caracas was simple. Giles had a shoestring budget to cover the 3,500-mile road route. The bus from Montevideo took him to São Paulo on 17th September where he reached his friend Anthony's house on Jardin Paulista.

The Venezuelan Embassy was closed at weekends but he was told that a visa was no problem and to collect it as he passed the official border-crossing point at Boa Vista in Northern Brazil. Giles made phone calls to his mother (to wish her a belated 'Happy Birthday' for the previous week) and to Floyd, who told him that her group would arrive at Caracas on 8th October. He decided to go back to Rio Preto to wangle a ride on a truck to Manaus which straddles the junction of the Rios Negro and Amazona, the main ferry crossing point for heavy vehicles. At Rio Preto, Giles got the bad news that it was an eight-day journey to Manaus. Time was short and he would need a great deal of luck to reach Caracas on time. Luckily there was a lorry scheduled to leave on 25th September.

He was concerned when he viewed the transport. The dilapidated Fiat lorry was loaded with 30 tonnes of clay drain pipes! Nonetheless the vehicle seemed to perform well under the tender care of the driver, Domingus, and they got off to a good start. But, this was Brazil, and about half an hour into their journey the Fiat was overtaken by an overloaded estate car which promptly crashed. Domingus and Giles had to spend some unscheduled hours giving assistance. They took their first sleep at midnight. Eventually they arrived at Rhondo Napolis where half of the load of clay pipes was to be delivered. They were told that the pipes would have to be unloaded by hand that evening so Giles decided to strike out on his own. After a long, hot wait he caught a bus to Cuiba. It was an unpleasant journey; at midnight the bus broke down and there was another lengthy delay whilst it was replaced.

27 September: Went through a yellow fever clinic. I showed my London clinic receipt. No worries. Went through a vast area of burnt forest and small fires still alight. Then into a big electric rainstorm. Morning came and revealed a horror: a sight that resembled the Battle of the Somme. No trees, just a few bits sticking up here and there. All of the towns were dusty, hot shanties of the same design. Each had a big sawmill and coffee warehouses. At one stop I rushed to the supermarket and bought bread, tomatoes, cucumber etc. When we got going again I had lunch. I am drinking the most incredible amount of water. Two litres so far today. The towns became smaller with more shacks and were now about one and half hours apart but there was still much deforestation with huge burnt out areas. We arrived at Porto Velha as the sun was setting. I did not have enough crusados to buy a ticket to Manaus. I changed $10 at a bad rate with a chap and then found that the next bus did not go until 10.00 a.m., the next morning.

28 September: The bus left on time. Asphalt surface, then over the river on a ferry, more asphalt and then into the jungle. The forest has been cleared for 500 yards on either side of the road. Subsistence farming is taking place on the road margins, some cattle and corral ranches. I started talking to some of my Brazo fellow travellers. The woman beside me was a big, dark Indian, five months pregnant and with a four- year-old kid. After lunch he sat on my lap and gazed out of the window. The road deteriorated into 10 yards of asphalt followed by 20 yards of terra, with very bad ruts in both. The bus broke some leaf springs but the driver carried on regardless. Bang – bang – bang went the suspension at every hole. There were ferry problems at two ferries during the night. Lorries could not get up the bank because of the mud therefore we could not get on the ferry. Much pushing and towing of the lorries. Then there was another ferry wedged between the ramp and our ferry. Eventually it was pulled out of the way by another lorry. The little boy pissed on me. My God! Was I angry! I washed my trousers in the river.

29 September: We arrived at the big Rio Negro ferry point to Manaus and while crossing, I saw the meeting of the two rivers. Clear black water. The next bus to Boa Vista is at 9.00 p.m., tonight. The bus left on time. It was full of blacks all on their way to Boa Vista to hunt for gold, including my friend Manuel. Apparently there is a great deal of gold to be found out in the jungle.

30 September: I woke at 6.00 a.m., when the bus stopped for breakfast. I had coffee and bread and looked at my South America handbook. It looks as if I have made a big mistake!...

They reached Boa Vista in the late evening and, as the Consulate would be closed, Giles teamed up with Manuel and some of the other gold-seekers for the weekend. He was grimy from the uncomfortable travelling over the past six days but despite the presence of a shower in the hotel he joined the others and did his laundry with a bar of soap in the Rio Branco. The weekend was spent in pleasant company, cleaning up, resting, writing letters, doing a little drinking and eating and generally exploring Boa Vista.

At the Venezuelan Consulate the clerk told him firmly that he could not be given a visa without an onward air ticket from Venezuela. He had been misinformed in São Paulo! Through a travel agency with cheap fares on offer he was able to book a flight to Caracas (via Ciudad which sits on the delta of the impressive Rio Orinoco in Guyana) followed by an open ticket from Caracas to a small Dutch island to satisfy the visa requirements.

In Caracas he made contact with the friends he had called from São Paulo. The Armstrongs made him very welcome. Their house, in the expensive residential area of Los Palmas Grandes, was large and imposing with a swimming pool, large garden and domestic staff. Whilst he was exploring Caracas, Giles had an unexpected encounter: *At Altimira I was told to take off my Walkman by some official. Sod you! I got off the bus after two stops at Chaciara. I intended to buy some bread for lunch to go with my tomatoes, so I went into a bakery and who did I bump into? Gilbert the Frog!* [His friend from the Argentina skiing session.] *We just roared with laughter, embraced and started talking. We were pulled off the pavement by the police and searched for drugs at gunpoint. When they saw my rolling tobacco, they thought they had caught a druggy. No way! I played my harmonica all the while, which caused a laugh. Back at the Armstrongs' house it was tea time, a swim and into my book. We had wine and cheese for dinner with Parma ham and a great conversation with two wonderful people. William said: No worries for putting up Ben and the girls.*

9 October: 5.15. a.m., and the Avianca 'jumbo' landed and I went down to 'Arrivals'. I watched them going through Customs. My stomach went tight with adrenaline. Ben's height stuck out a mile. Big hugs for Floydie. We took a bus into

Caracas and the metro to Los Palmas Grandes. We walked up the hill and into the house. Floydie went to bed. William and Mary Frances got up and I introduced everyone around. Then I went and jumped on Floydie. Wow! Hello! We had a swim then I cleaned the pool, sun bathed and talked and talked. Ben and I went for a pizza and chatted about everything and nothing. By 6.00 p.m., everyone was getting tired. I made a salad and went out to buy some chicken at the next door take-away. Dinner, wine and bed – we were all very tired due to lack of sleep and too much sun.

The happy group spent the next few days exploring Caracas and enjoying the hospitality of their friends as they celebrated Floyd's 22nd birthday and planned the route they were going to follow around South America for the next nine months. Before departing for Colombia they decided to spend a few days camping on the Terreros Islands. They would travel by bus to Valencia and then to Tucacas at which point they would take a boat to the islands – but – there were no boats so they decided to camp on the beach. It was a mistake.

...After two hours we arrived in Valencia and boarded another small bus for Tucacas... when we arrived it was very hot. We had a snack lunch and went to the port to ask about a boat. No one was going due to the high winds. Shit, but no worries, we went to a hotel – full. We saw a pier sticking out into the bay with a shelter half-way along it. We sat in there and had a swim and then put our hammocks up. A man told us to take them down again so we did that. An Italian man came by and Floydie chatted him up and we put the hammocks up again. It was a lovely evening with no wind – so much for the fisherman's forecast. Mosquitoes and sand flies started biting but I couldn't be bothered to put up my net.

16 October: The mosquitoes bit, I had slept little, so on with the next insect repellent. Then it started to rain. The girls carried out some precarious loo activities off the end of the pier and the rain continued. What are we to do? I lay in my hammock under my sleeping bag with Floydie. We wrapped ourselves together and watched the rain. At last it stopped and the sky began to clear. There were still no boats going to the islands – shit! We bought some food and went into the National Park. Oh dear! There were hundreds of grockles, buses, and cars everywhere. So we sat down amongst them and had a swim in the very clear water with good coral. Tessa sulked, Ben laughed, we played cards, Floydie was cool. The sun came out and Ben went red. As the afternoon went on the grockles left and at 5.00 p.m., we went to find a place to sling our hammocks. *Hell! The mosquitoes were really bad. We ran away and got a lift in a pick-up truck to a cheap hotel. Air con, three beds at 100B each...*

...we got a boat to Cayo Sombrero. What a beautiful place it was. Palm trees, sand, coral and see-through sea. In the afternoon Ben and I made a camp using bamboo, four trees, driftwood and our sheet. At 5.00 p.m., everyone else left and we slung our hammocks...

18 October: I had just wrapped myself in a ball and then woke to find Floydie shivering. I rubbed her warm and then the rain stopped. Hell! Out came the 'gehenes' [a minute sand fly with a painful bite]. *And so began the worst night of my life. Thousands of millions of 'gehenes' descended on us along with mosquitoes. Soaking wet, we put on trousers, socks, shoes and long shirts and covered our heads. I covered my ankles with my cafir and we went through hell while the sand flies devoured our hands, ankles and bellies. Ben walked up and down the beach from midnight until 6.00 a.m., and dived into the sea at dawn. I joined at various times during the night. We just itched, slapped and prayed for wind. At 9.00 a.m., there was a slight breeze and we hung everything up to dry. When the first boatload of people arrived we quickly packed up and jumped into the boat for the return journey to Tucacas and away from the God forsaken place. We boarded the bus to Valencia with loud Venezuelan music blaring. From there to Caracas in a comfortable bus. Floydie and I chatted while Ben and Tessa slept. At the Armstrongs' we told our sorry tale and had a shower and a swim.*

After travelling to San Cristobal, high in the Venezuelan Andes the next stop was Cucuta in Colombia from where they flew to Bogotá, the capital. A typical diary entry is:

7 November: I woke at 8.30 and had a shower and went to see Floydie and Tessa only to find that Floyd has a severe tummy problem! We decided we could not go to the Gold Museum without her, but that we would go to town anyway and leave her in the house... we alighted at Plaza Bolivar... there were many police and soldiers around toting their guns... the President of Colombia came past and walked into the cathedral... Ben and me were spread against the wall and searched but all very good natured.

They travelled by coach and train through the mountain passes stopping off at many towns and villages to take in the local culture. Over the months they journeyed through Colombia, Ecuador, Peru, Bolivia, Chile, Argentina and Brazil before completing the circuit by returning to Venezuela for the flight back to England. Along the way there were many high spots and low spots for Giles as his relationship with Floyd became strained at times. Some diary entries show times of sheer enjoyment, frustration and tensions:

2 November (Caracas, Venezuela): We woke early. It was an effort for Floydie to get out of bed... then on our way to the telerifiico, stopping for a coffee in a café where there were horrible women serving. Up we went – a fantastic view on a beautiful, clear day. The altitude did not seem to affect us much. We became a little breathless throwing snowballs. The wind was very cold so we had hot chocky and returned down the mountain. We walked around the town. On our way back to the hotel we passed some students walking the other way shouting, some of them threw stones at a bank. We were about to go to the park but when we entered the street there was a battle raging about two blocks away – students v. police. There was tear gas and plastic bullets flying from the police and stones from the students. In the park we sat for a while but on our way back we could hear explosions and the tear gas was really bad. Ben took some photos from the top of the hotel and our eyes were running sore from the tear gas...

27 November (Esperanza, Ecuador): Ben, Nissan, Chaski and me went off for a mushroom experience. We took the bus to Ibarra where we bought some bread and then onto another bus to Esperanza up the other side of a huge volcano. Chaski had a small map of the location of the field to which we were to walk down to in the valley. When we arrived at the field full of cows we started picking yellow and orange mushrooms with a nipple on the top and a black ring around the stem. They were good. I ate six, Ben four and Nissan three. The remainder we gave to Chaski who was drying them to make coffee. The effect of the mushrooms was startling. It hit Nissan hard, quite amazing: the valley was beautiful! We walked back up while we were still intoxicated through a village called Buenos. A mad priest gave us a lift back to Ibarra where we caught the bus to Otavalo. When we arrived back at the hotel we found that the girls had gone to Quito so we packed and checked out. On the bus we slept for two hours and on arrival went and checked in at the hotel the girls had found. We went out to eat and got to bed at midnight. What a fine, fine day!

28 November (Quito, Ecuador): Moved to the Marsella which was a better place and Floyd and I had a room to ourselves. Two English girls, Gill and Kate are with us. We had an English lunch in an English pub and picked up our mail from the British Embassy. Floydie was in a real wooze because she only got one letter... after a few hours we walked back to the hotel via a hot banana stand. Floydie seemed quite ill. She did not want to go out for dinner, so we cuddled up while the others went out. Later I went out and bought bananas and bread. Then back to bed for intermittent sleep. I felt odd. What's this relationship? We go up and down, round and round. But all is cool when we are in each other's arms.

2 January 1989 (Pisco, Peru): We boarded the bus for a four and a half hour trip along the coast. It was desert all the way with the sea on our left. The others decided to stay in Pisco and meet us the next day in Parocas for a boat tour. When we arrived at the Hotel Mirador the girls were already there to give us the good news that a dog on the beach had bitten Floydie. Oh Shit! Sure enough it was true and she was sick with worry and a bit of shock about rabies. We had dinner and chatted. The bite did not look bad but a bite is a bite so it had to be off to the hospital the next day – after the boat trip I reckon.

3 January: We boarded the boat along with some other English, Germans and Americans – the boat was only 28 feet long and skippered by a really cool guy. In the bay there were many sea lions and Jay and I jumped into the sea. The sea lions swam with us... it was a fantastic experience! We got back to the mainland and gave the skipper a good tip. Then Ben, Floydie and I went off into the town to the hospital. Floydie was whining on and on. They cleaned the wound and gave her antibiotics and told us to return the next day to see the doctor. Floydie was really whining now because they had done nothing about the rabies. We went back to the others and it was whine – whine – whine. It's just so annoying.

11 January (Arequipa, Peru): We went high up onto the pass which was covered in snow, passed the llamas and down into Arequipa arriving at 1.00 p.m., fair knackered. Ben and I stopped for a coffee and the girls went back to the Guzman... then we heard this shriek from Floydie and Tessa – there goes her body belt! Floydie was just so angry! She had put the belt in her pocket and it was snatched with her passport and 6,000 intis. Shit! Shit! The loss of the passport is really bad shit. I was raging inside with the stupidity and inconvenience of it all but I was sure that was not what she wanted to hear at that moment. It was hard not to show it. We went to

the police and were given the document that shows that she has lost her passport and she can travel in Peru.

27 January (La Paz, Bolivia): We awoke at the deathly hour of 4.00 a.m., and it was a huge effort for Floydie to get ready but we managed. We took a taxi to the bus terminal and arrived in time for coffee. We then saw the state of our jacked up old yellow bus. Inside the seats were old and rocking. The road we were about to travel on must have been in some state. Oh shit! We remembered it was a 24 hour trip. So we piled the rucksacks onto the roof – inside I sit in the aisle on a sack of Floydie's clothes. Then we notice that all the other passengers have an abundance of blankets and food. What could this mean? We took out some jerseys and I retrieved my poncho. After one and a half hours we stopped for breakfast which meant bread and tea for us. What a windswept, rainy damp place it was. We set off again in pouring rain and I noticed that we were crossing many rivers by ford – there were no bridges and there was no concrete on the river beds. We came to a great queue of stationery lorries which we overtook and went to the front where there was a large swollen river with mud on both sides and no visible place to cross.

Nobody seemed worried so we got out of the bus and went to have a look around. They said it would be a four hour wait if and when the rain stopped. It did eventually stop and slowly, slowly the river went down. While we waited men waded out into the water to try the bottom over and over again. Some two and a half hours later we set off, the first to try it. We slipped and slid, with the wheels spinning and splashing and we were across. There was jubilation on the bus. From then on it was river after river, just making it each time. There were numerous lorries stuck in the mud up to their axles. One driver, a Chilean, joined us on the bus. As time went by the passengers became a happy family. We so nearly became stuck so many times but the maestro driver kept us going. We arrived at an army garrison at 5.00 p.m., where they wanted to see our passports. As night fell it was onwards into the darkness and the snow, passing more lorries stuck in the mud. It was white everywhere. We sang, spoke Spanish and nodded off.

28th January 1989 found the young adventurers in Chile. They were excited by the prospects of sandy beaches, high mountains, culture and wildlife that Chile had to offer but, even more eagerly anticipated, was the planned visit by Brian and Verity Thornton. Giles and Ben's parents were taking a holiday and they were breaking their journey in Santiago to meet up with their wandering sons. The rendezvous was planned for 12th February and the intervening days were spent exploring the country whilst trying to eke out their dwindling supply of cash by using the cheapest hotels. The arrival of Ben and Verity changed that for a few days:

12 February: I went into town and bought three Valentine cards for Tess, Mum and Floydie and then went back to the Hotel Florida for hugs. We packed the rucksacks and set off for the Sheraton. What a hotel! At £65 per night excluding food and drink! Ben and I set off for the airport... we saw the flight arrive. Greeting them was lovely – a super moment. They had a car waiting with a "Welcome to Santiago" guide who never had the chance to say anything as we talked all the way back to the hotel. We went for a swim and chatted by the hotel pool and then met up with Tess and Floyd in Mum and Dad's room where the champagne flowed as we told them about our trip and showed them the photographs... Wow! We were living well!

Brian and Verity continued on their journey to the Galapagos Islands. Giles's relationship with Floydie continued to fluctuate:

29 February: For lunch we had fresh conger eel done in a cheesy number sauce – delicious! After I went back on deck for a while as it was so beautiful. Then the ship stopped. One engine had failed but we carried on slowly on one engine. After that it was hugs with Floydie while we watched a film. Love is so good – wow how do I feel for her now.

Slowly and amicably they worked their way into Argentina, across Uruguay and into Brazil. The journey was uneventful except for an incident at the bus station in São Paulo which typifies the hazards of South American travel:

7 April: We arrived at the São Paulo bus station feeling a bit lethargic but ready to try and sort out our hotel problem. First Tessa and I went and phoned Jim but he had gone into town. So I went off to the tourist information office in order to find out in which area of the town the cheap hotels were located. I rejoined the others who were sitting with all our clobber. We picked up our stuff to go – "Where the fuck is my small rucksack with my Walkman, camera, hat, tapes, undeveloped films etc?" "I don't know" they say. Fuck, fuck, fuck, the stupid fools had been robbed. They explained how a man had come and sat beside them and started to talk and getting their attention off the bags. An accomplice picked up my bag and walked off with it.

Shit! Well – I was furious for two reasons: my stuff had gone and worst of all was the undeveloped film. Also I had been robbed while the three of them had been sitting there. Ben, Tessa and Floyd. All so-so, I didn't know what to think... I was fuming with frustration... Floyd was being so kind and loving and she and I found a grim, but cheap abode, so we checked in. We had one huge round bed, mirrors and another bed and a dirty bathroom. We discovered in fact that we were in a whorehouse where the prostitutes bring their customers. We slept three in the bed that night – Ben, Floyd and me.

At this point Giles took a break from the group and went back to the farm where he had worked in order to pick up some of his gear and to say farewell to his old friends. A couple of days later he met up with Ben, Tess and Floyd in Rio de Janeiro. Then on to Venezuela where they arrived on 22nd June. At the time Giles was suffering from a malarial type of fever and took to his bed; Floyd soon followed with the same bug and so their last week in South America was not especially pleasant. A shortage of space on the aircraft meant that Giles had to return to England the day before Ben and Floyd but it was a happy homecoming.

Chapter V

Itchy Feet And The Sahara

Giles flew back to England – *3 July, 1989: I woke with the sun blazing in but I felt ruff. Breakfast made my tummy hurt. Anyway Cornwall came up below us, it was a beautiful day in England. We landed at 1.25 p.m., and my bag came through quickly and I went on through customs. I was not stopped – I went straight through. Mum and Dad and Sam were there waiting. It was wonderful to see them again. Sam had changed completely – a different one! Both Mum and Sam had tears in their eyes – "Oh how sweet!" Into the BMW we went and off to Sunningdale School to take Sam back, then all the way round the M25, onto the M11 and home. Jolyon was there. "Hi boyo!" I had a swim and went round the cattle with Dad. Home is wonderful – this was a very special moment. Jo went off to see a friend in Suffolk, so it was just Dad, Mum and me for supper – super! I unpacked my crates and bags and fell into bed. I wonder how Flow is?*

He spent the winter of 1989 working on farms in East Anglia and a period in Scotland working for his old friend, John Mitchell, during which he visited his beloved cousin, 'Bimbo' Stancioff. He was able to maintain his financial independence and keep his ageing Ford Fiesta on the road. For the whole of the winter Giles took a job as a representative in Flims for 'Powder Burns', a specialist skiing holiday company. He returned home in the spring of 1990.

The semi-nomadic life as a jobbing farm worker and ski holiday representative was very enjoyable but there was something missing. Coaxing tractors into life and ploughing a furrow on the East Anglian fens on a bitterly cold winter morning were not activities that could satisfy the urges that Giles was beginning to feel. His work as a cowboy on the wide open rolling plains of Brazil and his travels in and along the majestic Andes had left him with a yearning for more adventure. He recognised in himself the need for personal challenge and it was a desire that was becoming stronger. He simply had to travel.

The well-documented, romantic (but often tragic) tales of early British explorers and adventurers; the hugely differing population and the descriptions of deserts, rain forests, mountains and vast rolling fertile plains made Africa the perfect choice. He would go the hard way! Autumn was eaten up as he planned his trip and practised on his new Yamaha XT600ZE. On 26th December, 1990, he set out on his journey to the Dark Continent. His plan was to travel the length of Africa stopping off in Kenya to visit family friends and then to move down to South Africa.

In his diary Giles recorded that fear, trepidation and uncertainty were his companions as he drove to Dover but these emotions were part and parcel of any great adventure. On arrival in Calais his journey got off to a bad start. High winds and lashing rain made him opt to take his bike by train to Marseilles where he arrived with only 30 minutes to spare before boarding a boat for Algiers. He struck up a conversation with two German bikers. Dieter and Andy had begun as a party of three but one of them had an accident and damaged his bike beyond repair. So there they were – two bikers with food for three! *Well – I slotted in perfectly didn't I...* is the note in his diary. Dieter and Andy were old hands at this and the passage through Algerian Customs was fast and flawless and soon the trio were roaring their way through and out of Algiers and up towards the beckoning ancient Atlas mountains.

...so out of Algiers we went and up over the Atlas. The seaward side of the Atlas is very fertile and green with regular rainfall, but, as you go up, over and down the other side heading for Bou-Saada, it is an arid, flat and rocky sand plain with just a few bushes. This was where we spent our first cold, damp night. There was a good cook up of bratwurst and sauerkraut (real Germans these chaps) and we were fine.

We woke to a thick mist and damp. A morning bowl of muesli and coffee and we roared off getting soaking wet – not rain – just a very damp mist full of water. As you drive through it you get soaked. I had every piece of clothing on. At around 10.00 a.m., the sun burnt through but it was by no means hot. I kept all my clothes on: T-shirt, rugby shirt, Patagonia jersey, leather jacket, DryserBone, long johns and Belstag bike trousers. All day through I needed to keep this on.

From Bou-Saada the companions dipped into Biskra and then headed south to Touggourt. The roads were excellent and it was possible to maintain high cruising speeds. Giles was a little worried about the impending Gulf War and Arab reaction to a Briton but it was never mentioned by any of the people they met. His schoolboy French ensured that he had no communication problems with the Algerians. He also discovered that changing his money and buying petrol on the black market gave him a much better deal.

The ground was flat with rocky outcrops and sparse vegetation. After Touggourt the dunes and shifting sands began to appear and Giles felt that at last he was closing with the great Sahara Desert. From Hassi Messaoud they headed south into the huge sand dunes of the Grand Erg Oriental. Recent heavy rains had formed a hard crust on the dunes which easily supported the bikes allowing them to leave the road and follow a compass bearing through the virgin dunes. Giles loved the strange new vista that was set before him.

We filled up with petrol and off we went along the tarmac towards Tin Fouye and Ohanet. Here the road runs along the top of a large escarpment. On the left is a rocky plain with dome-like hills and the Erg Oriental on the far side. On the right is a 200 metre high cliff falling down into a huge sea of dunes called the Erg Issaouane. The view over these cliffs is unreal – you just see dunes for miles and miles. This is what I imagined the desert to be like when I was in England. Here we spent New Year's Eve. We had cheese fondue, schnapps, white wine and fireworks. The hills were all around us – not a speck of life, no plants, no animals to be seen and a full moon overhead. We could have been on Mars or Jupiter – anywhere but Earth. We got very merry and I changed the oil in my bike. The moon was so bright it was like daylight.

Next day down the tarmac road, heading south to Illizi, the colour of the sand dunes has changed from yellow to orange-red. On experimenting the dunes were very soft and the bike got stuck easily so we stayed on the road. As we travelled south along the road, overlanders on bikes and in jeeps roared past heading north and going home. They were covered in dust and looked exhausted. What is there in front of us? The next two weeks are going to be hard; no tarmac; no petrol and water only at certain places. The real desert; the real adventure; the real test of endurance was about to start and I could not have been in better company. Andy and Dieter are two super chaps, 28-30 years old, a dentist and an architect, very straight in their ways, cool and collected. I was feeling very good and full of enthusiasm.

Illizi is the end of the tarmac until we reach Agadez in Niger some 2,000 kms away. I changed my tyres and went onto the big knobbly ones. I tied my bald English ones onto the back of the bike for use in Niger. From Illizi to Djanet (next major port of call) is 700 kms so the jerry cans had to be filled and some extra water was required... the road was rocky and I used only first and second gears... then, all of a sudden we came to the edge of the plateau and we were looking over a 500-metre cliff and across mile after mile of desolate landscape – no sand – just dry river beds, scrub and more rock as far as the eye could see, the road wound down the cliff – it was most precarious and would be rather scary for a vertigo-infected person like you, Papa. My bike was becoming very bouncy and the suspension very soft so I adjusted it to make it stiffer but this made no difference, I did not say anything to the others as the bike continued to travel well over the bumps. After about 150 kms from Illizi we arrived at a tiny village called Iherir – it is a Taureg settlement – set at the bottom of a mountainous area that looked like the Grand Canyon. Here a whole community survives on a river that flows along the valley floor for one kilometre and then disappears. Palm trees, dates, fruit and maize all flourish, along with goats. We saw rock paintings and the spring where the small stream wells up and flows off down the valley. We stayed there for three days recovering from the Fadnoun Plateau and enjoying washes in the river. My first wash and shave of the trip!

The main reason why we had travelled through the desert quite so quickly was that Andy and Dieter had only four weeks holiday and, therefore, had to keep on the move. It suited me because of the 15 January deadline in the Gulf. The next day we began the onward trip to Djanet. The road was appalling but very, very beautiful. I took a big fall and the frame carrying the jerry cans snapped. We tied it up with cords and bungies and carried on to the village of Fort Gardel and there was a welder there so I stopped and told Dieter and Andy that I would catch up with them either on the road or at Djanet (I thought it was only 80 kms away). They agreed and took off. It was 11.45 a.m., and the man started welding, but at noon the electricity supply to the town was shut off and not turned on again until 2.30 p.m. Oh Shit!

Giles had lunch with the welder and studied his map. To his horror he discovered that he was not 80 kms from Djanet but 164! There was just about three hours of daylight left and he made the dangerous decision to move on alone in an attempt to keep his rendezvous with Dieter and Andy. The main track was a nightmare; corrugated sand criss-crossed with many ruts. The virgin sand would not support the bike and so he had to stay with one of the parallel tracks. He accelerated far too fast for the conditions and the inevitable happened! With 80 kms to go to Djanet he got into a rut from which there was no escape. The bike cart wheeled and Giles was thrown into the air and landed heavily on his left foot. His bike was still driveable but the weld had broken. His left foot would not support his weight but he managed to right the bike, repack the scattered jerry cans and set out again. The stretched tendon of his foot went into rebellion and he was unable to change gear with his toes. He eventually worked out a technique by using his heel and it was at this point that the foolhardiness of his decision struck home. What if his accident had been more severe? He had been 500 metres away from the main track and out of sight of fellow travellers. Nonetheless he made it to Djanet late that evening to find Andy and Dieter still waiting for him. Overnight he got the frame welded once more.

Thanks to the analgesic contents of Dieter's medical pack and a tight bandage Giles was able to continue. They headed for Tamanrasset, some 350 miles away as the crow flies to the south west of Djanet. There was no road and they knew that they faced a hard drive over huge dunes. The diary shows a typical problem:

The dune was about 400 metres high and the loaded bikes could not cope. Four times I went up and then back down the dune with my jerry cans and bags... then came the final crunch – will the bike get up? Dieter and Andy were still carrying their stuff up the dune when I turned the bike around and faced the slope: "OK you son of a bitch!" I felt like Evel Knievel or something; revving my engine with this huge dome in front of me. Out went the clutch – first gear – second gear – third – fourth and then top. I mounted the dune at 60 k.m.h., and then started changing down through the gears as the revs dropped. I needed to keep the revs high but the last gear you want to be in is first. The wheels just dig in. Three quarters of the way up and I was into second gear and the engine was dying on me. But it began to gain revs and power as I hit some harder sand. Up – up – up and then – there I was within arm's reach of my baggage. I was at the top of the dune and what a view! Looking west was a great open plain stretching as far as I could see. Looking east the dunes were turning red as the sun was dying in a blaze of fire. We had a great feeling of achievement as we ate hungrily after the huge effort.

The first part of the journey to Tamanrasset was good and they were able to drive at high speeds over a smooth, hard surface. It was a wonderful experience as they sped along never seeing another vehicle in the vast desert. Giles marvelled at the apparent insignificance of man in the scheme of nature – he was just a tiny speck on the surface of this seemingly endless expanse of sand and gravel. They hit the main track at an abandoned French Foreign Legion post at Serouenout. Conditions deteriorated and progress was much slower. They chose one of the tracks from the many that criss-crossed the area and took a gamble in striking south. It worked – they found the main track and soon they were buying black market petrol at Ideles to the north of the Hoggar mountain range.

The route through the Hoggar is incredible: beautiful and hazardous. Sheer cliffs reach awe-inspiring heights with no pattern; huge volcanic 'plugs' that can rise to 1,000 metres, some bent and twisted are scattered around like a young giant's discarded playthings. There is little vegetation in this barren, dry place and it is a marvel that the place the travellers visited next has continued to exist. L'Ermitage is a tiny French monastery perched on the top of a plateau commanding marvellous views and housing only three monks who offered some welcome tea before they faced the descent. It was a touching little act of hospitality in a wild and lonely place. At Tamanrasset Giles had to say a reluctant farewell and God Speed to Dieter and Andy who had made his initiation into desert travel so much more enjoyable

He soon found companions for the next leg of his journey. Norman and his partner, Angie, were both on one bike and also there were Martin and Gerhardt. It was Norman who sat on Giles's bike that evening and told him that his shock absorbers were suspect and, on stripping them down, was proved correct. Giles calculated that he could continue for a while. He did, however, take advantage of the fact that he was in civilisation and sent a fax to his father asking him to arrange for a new shock absorber and two tyres to be delivered to Douala Airport or Yaounde in Cameroon.

Soon after departure from Tamanrasset, Giles lost contact with the others and decided to just go it alone. There was not so much risk at this point because the track was being well-used by other travellers. He met up with a Frenchman, Dominique, who was a veteran at crossing the next difficult stretch of desert. Dominique had made the journey 30 times! He was taking advantage of the fact that he could buy a Peugeot car in France and sell it in Niger for three times the price he had paid for it. He knew a good route and asked Giles if he would care to follow him the next day. Giles readily agreed to take advantage of Dominique's great experience.

The next morning I awoke early – 5.30 a.m. I linked up with Dominique and we roared out of camp before the others had even started to wake up. Now Dominique had not been kidding me! He left the main route (marked by bollards) and went wide travelling at 80-90km/hour. His route was excellent – no soft sand and no big rocks... speed – I was enjoying this. He then came to a stop. I drew up alongside him; in front of us was chaos. Cars were stuck in every direction, wrecked hulls, sand-blasted black by storms in the summer were strewn around like a battlefield scene. There was every different make that had come here to die. "This," said Dominique, "is loony dunes. This is where you find out if you really can drive in the desert and whether you bought a decent car in France or a wreck. Once you enter this area, you must not stop, you must keep moving. I will see you at the other side." He roared off going wide to avoid the confusion of struggling overlanders labouring with sand ladders and shovels. I went through a little wide of him, the sand was indeed soft, very soft, but – no worries – the bike pulled herself through while Dominique cruised over the top with low tyre pressures and no luggage in his car.

It was 15th January when Giles, Dominique and others they had collected along the way, reached In-Guezzam, the gateway into Niger. Two days later the convoy reached Arlit where Dominique sold his car and asked for a lift to Agadez, the Tuareg capital of Niger. On arrival they reported to the police as required by Niger law. Giles was told with some glee that the bombing had started in the Gulf.

The onward journey continued with no real problems except the continued need for minor bike repairs. Giles began to understand the lure of Africa. The harsh, burning deserts of Algeria and northern Niger and the lush, rich cultivations of Nigeria and Cameroon all had their different forms of beauty. He was greatly pleased with his decision to stop and visit the Parc National de Waza in Northern Cameroon where he revelled in the abundance of animal life. In Garoua he had a mishap. He was having his bike and jerry cans filled with black market petrol when the bag containing his passport and all of his travel documents was snatched. He reported to the police and the next day he was summoned to the police station where he very reluctantly witnessed the brutal beating of the boys who had taken his bag. Giles was never to forget the inhuman treatment of the youngsters and he made many references to it over the following years. After three or four days of solitary travelling he arrived at Douala, the commercial centre of Cameroon.

Douala is a big city. My guidebook told me that the cheapest place to stay was the Catholic Mission. There I met up with Norman and the gang who had arrived the day before. I went to pick up the tyres and shock absorber from Socarno Airport and went through a nightmare with Customs. They wanted £300 in import tax! After much debate and after I went to see the Chief, I proved that I was a tourist and that the tyres were not going to be sold but put on my bike. In the end I got my equipment without paying a red cent. The next day was motorbike service time at a Yamaha garage in Douala. Two days of sweat, grime, oil and grease and there was a gleaming, smooth running Yamaha XT600ZE with a new shock absorber and fit to go through Zaire's[4] mud and on to Kenya.

A good rest was in order and where better to take that rest than at Tara on one of Cameroon's lovely beaches. Tara is a bay about one kilometre across and it is also the site where a clean, fresh water river discharges into the sea. There are fish in abundance from the local fishermen and to Giles it was Paradise. The village was well supplied with beer and fresh bread and it was the ideal place to rest up and put on some weight.

He reached an agreement with three Frenchmen who were building a beach restaurant – they would "feed and water" him in return for his labour. He persuaded one of the local fishermen to take him out in his *pirogue*[5]. The craft is only about 18 inches wide and not particularly stable and it required a muscular effort to launch it through breaking surf. So, at 3.00 a.m., the next morning Giles was introduced to the life of a coastal fisherman. The row out to sea seemed endless and it was still dark when they finally shipped paddles and the fisherman stood up in the narrow bobbing canoe to cast his 50-foot-long net. As dawn

4   Zaire. Since 1971 this has been the Democratic Republic of Congo
5   A pirogue is a dug-out canoe fashioned from a single tree trunk. The word is Central American in origin but seems to have crossed the oceans to Africa.

broke Giles was perturbed to note that he could not see land! He was comforted though by the fact that there was a huge flotilla of fishing canoes just like the one he occupied. In the silence of the pre-dawn he had assumed that they were alone. The net was pulled in to reveal a mass of sardines and other multi-coloured little fish. These were immediately put on hooks with 20-feet lines and cast overboard. Then there was a period of constantly pulling in larger fish including many barracuda. At about 9.00 a.m., the boat was full and it was time to return. They rowed back over the horizon to beach comfortably on a warm rising tide.

Chapter VI

"The Africa I Had Dreamed Of"

Soon Giles was feeling ready to face the next part of his adventure. He made a visit to the Mission Prespitorean where many overlanders tend to stay and there he found a rather dour Australian who was heading in the same direction. This part of the trip was really a three-day dash during which they followed a major logging route from Yoaunde to Abongmbang, Bertoua, Batouri, Berberatti, Carnot and on to Bossembele. Along the way Giles saw all the signs that Africa's rain forests were being raped in the same ways as South America – deforestation was taking place at a manic pace.

Arriving at the border post with the Central African Republic they got their first real taste of African police corruption! "Where are your sidelights?" "Where are your mirrors?" "Where is your warning triangle?" The questions were endless along with an oblique hint that money would ease their way through these minor infractions of the law. They refused to pay and sat down in the shade. After two hours the officials became so bored with the two Bolsheviks that they waved them through the barrier. After that it was a case of constant and unwarranted police checks. At each they were asked to pay a 'fine' – this they always evaded. This was the pattern of events all the way to Bangui. Though Giles was the sort of man who could make himself at home virtually anywhere he was ill at ease in Bangui. The campsite was full of travellers with tales of horror to tell. There were constant 'fines' from the police for non-existent breaches of non-existent laws. Giles was told that the policemen were not paid a salary – they were given a uniform and had to survive on the wide variety of fines they imposed on the travellers and locals alike. A policeman going off shift would hand his uniform over to a relative who wanted to supplement his salary. Many of the travellers had been robbed and it was generally an unhappy town. Some of the adventurers went down with malaria. After a few days Giles teamed up with three Dutchmen who planned to travel through Zaire in the same direction as himself. A day later and they were crossing the River Ubangi into Zaire Zongo.

Giles's companions now were two brothers, Shef and Franz, aged 30 and 43 years, who had been all around South America on their motorcycles and Ep, aged 40 who had hardly ridden a motorcycle before. *...these three lunatic, middle-aged Dutchmen were excellent company and perfect travel companions...* Giles's main concern was that the rains were due to start any day and the dirt tracks would become a muddy morass. Tracks of indifferent quality and some chaotic ferry crossings took the intrepid group to the town of Bumba from which point they planned to take a boat along the River Congo to Kisingali.

Bumba was a malaria-ridden, humid sweltering rainstorm of a town but beer was plentiful and cold. There were some things that brought me down to earth; one month before we arrived in town a New Zealand girl had died of malaria. So we went to her grave to check it out only to find American, Australian, English and French graves there also! All had died of malaria. Zaire has absolutely no form of communication internal or external. If you get ill here or your vehicle goes crook then you have to suss it out with your own wits. As I travelled through Zaire this was always in the back of my mind. What good is insurance here? It's the survival of the fittest aided by a dollop of good luck.

Since the departure of the Belgians, any traveller through Zaire has suffered. The shipping line that runs the boats between Kinshasa and Kisingali has no right to the title now. Where once there had been three boats there was now only one. One boat had been sunk and the other burned and wrecked. The remaining boat was expected at Bumba in about three days. The locals were in a festive mood as it had been three months since the boat's last appearance. Giles and his group awaited the arrival of the vessel with great anticipation.

On the third night in Bumba we were sitting in that bar at about 2.00 a.m., just talking about this and that. It was quiet apart from the sound of the frogs. Suddenly these small sounds were eclipsed by the deafening blast of a ship's siren that was broadcast over the whole town. We looked at each other and grinned – our boat had arrived. As the boat came closer the bright harbour lights were turned off and we could see the vessel – or should I say the vessels. There were six barges, each about 100 metres in length, lashed together with a big power unit tug at the back. Each barge was two decks high and covered with a mass of humanity. The tug itself was in the same condition. Now there was a flotilla of canoes going out to meet it in order that the vendors could offer their goods before the people on dry land could do so.

The next morning was pure African chaos. There were 11 Land Rovers and 10 motorcycles to be loaded onto one of the barges. How and when this was to be done was a mystery. Both the paperwork and the bribery involved were immense. The huge throng of people on and around the boat was overwhelming. I began to have second thoughts. "Was I doing the right thing?" "Will I have everything stolen?" "How will I be able to move around on a boat like that?" "Where will I stay?" We were reassured by a local who told us that the reason why there were so many people aboard at that time was because they were from Bumba buying and selling.

The loading of cars and bikes commenced using a crane. All the vehicles were placed together on the roof of the front barge. Thus all the vehicle owners were placed together making security less difficult. Thus began the most weird, bizarre, unreal, wonderful and outrageous boat trip of my life. Each barge had second-class cabins, bars and a maze of passages that were turned into 24 hour markets. Because the river is very shallow in places there is no room for holds so everything is stored on deck making it very difficult to move around. Apart from transportation the function of the boat is commerce and everyone becomes involved including the captain and the crew. There were merchants who live on the boat (out of 3,500 people on board, 500 were full time traders). They do business in a variety of manufactured goods including pharmaceuticals along with the products of the river and forests which are brought to the boat as it moves back and forth. Everyone is looking to make a profit. All day there was loud Zairian music issuing from the different bars and the merchants selling tapes. All day and all night canoes came with smoked carcasses of monkey and fish, freshly butchered or live caiman crocodiles ranging in length from one to 12 feet. They were kept alive, thus fresh, by being strapped to long poles and muzzled with twine. Turtles, tortoises, and monitor lizards were tied beneath taps to keep them cool. There were bats, river snails and large palm nut grubs along with many, many different species of fish and, of course, pigs and goats.

The boat's progress is communicated by bush telegraph so the hunters ashore are able to anticipate its arrival. The boat has no schedule; even the anticipated departure date is useless because, as in our case, we had to spend two hours tied up alongside *for the funerals of those who had died on board since the last stop! The boat also stops alongside other vessels so that the captains can have a chat. There was a smoke box for monkeys. Every now and then the smell of burning hair and flesh was foul if the wind was in the wrong direction. The whole boat stank of smoked fish, cooking food in palm oil, BO from the unwashed bodies and their dung. Fortunately, up on the roof with the bikes there was a cool breeze and it was very pleasant. Washing was done by chucking a bucket over the side with a rope attached, hauling it up and over the head, applying the soap and then the rinse. Right beside you, a goat or a pig was being slaughtered and there would be barbecued meat for sale 30 minutes later. At any one time 300-400 canoes would be tied up alongside. Business was done and money was made, clothes were bought or swapped for monkeys, oil or bananas etc.*

The trip took five days and actually that was about right. Kisangani is the town at the end of the cruise. The boat can go no further because of the rapids followed by the Stanley Falls. It was good to be off the boat and onto dry land again. Great to be on my bike again but I was so glad that I had witnessed and experienced the Zaire river boat.[6]

Kisangani had a faded grandeur but it was beyond redemption. The post office in the old Belgian colonial town had neither telex nor telephone. The unloved houses were falling apart under sagging roofs and the grass in the old gardens, parks and roadside verges was long and unkempt. It was a happy place though and thousands of smiling people bustled around the old town square where the huge market offered every imaginable vegetable, fruit and cut of meat. Fuel was in short supply, however, but now Giles was a semi-seasoned African traveller. He urged his companions to find fuel before lodgings. The sudden influx of travellers would send the price of the limited petrol soaring. They found sufficient for their needs and heard later that the price had risen by over 40% after they had made their purchases.

The only good road out of Kisangani led to the east through Batama, Epulu and on to Mount Hoyo but Giles heard that a German construction company had already completed 150 kilometres of road to the south of Labutu. The snag was that when the road finished there would be a further 54 kilometres of jungle

---

[6] *Anyone wanting a haunting description of this journey should read Joseph Conrad's "Heart of Darkness".*

footpath and rivers to be negotiated. The road to Labutu was old and in parts it had been reclaimed by the jungle but progress was good and they made it to the town and new road in one day. Driving on a new perfect road was a bizarre feeling and they enjoyed high speeds up to their next camp just before the end of the construction.

Here the road was replaced by a surveyor's track which was still quite easy driving but the track soon became little more than an overgrown footpath, muddy and slippery. Giles was undaunted when they arrived at the banks of a murky 30-feet-wide river. He unpacked his machine and waded across the waist-deep river with his baggage. The Dutch partners cheerily exhorted Giles to go first. In he went – water up to his navel but the Yamaha engine scarcely missed a beat as its exhaust burbled away willingly under the water. The mud got worse and the footpath became less distinct. Then the biker's worst nightmare happened! The engine of Franz's bike suddenly stopped with a loud cracking noise. The piston had seized and there was massive crankshaft damage. With no easy solution to the problem they took the chain off and roped the damaged bike to Shef's machine. They were going to have to tow the big Italian Cagiva.

The next 18 kilometres were horrendous. Shef kept falling off his bike as it slipped and skidded under the immense load it had to tow. Ep and Giles became very tired and filthy as they pushed and pulled to get the bike out of the endless potholes and boggy patches. They were forced to continue long after it was dark and they finally arrived at Walikali at 8.00 p.m. They had reached the road head. Lady Luck smiled again in the form of a Danish missionary who offered them shelter, showers and a hot meal. He told them that there would be a lorry leaving Walikali for Bukavu in two days' time and that it could easily take the men and the bikes. The bad news was that the 160 kilometre journey would take six days by truck. The priest had no idea how long it would take by motorcycle. He said that rain erosion had washed away roads and bridges resulting in thick, treacherous mud. But Giles was eager to get going and he decided once again to take his chances on his own. He donated a few dollars to the church, said his farewells to Shef, Franz and Ep and left on a cloudy, damp morning.

He had a hair-raising journey! It was completely exhausting as he had to constantly pull himself and his machine out of mud holes. If he was lucky and there were locals around they would happily render laughing assistance to him but much of the time he was on his own. One particular incident amused him:

At Bun Yakiri I came to a bridge without any decking, just the iron frame with gaps about two feet apart. "What now?" I thought. But, yet again, people came running from a nearby village, carrying planks to lay across the gaps. However, these were not the 'happy to help you' kind of people. They wanted money. So we struck a deal and while I rode 10 feet at a time, they walked back and forth with the planks. An amazing spectacle and I guess these folk take a toll from all the traffic that passes that way. The last two obstacles before reaching the 20-kilometre-stretch of tarmac running into Bukavu were two enormous holes in the road, 50 metres long and five metres wide. The ruts were deep and I struggled for at least 10 minutes in each hole, pushing and wrestling to stay upright with the mud around my ankles. Then I came to the tarmac and arrived in Bukavu at about 6.00 p.m.

Bukavu was a town that President Mobutu enjoyed visiting and so it was not quite as run-down as the other places since Mobutu donated cash to the owners of the various businesses. There were French patisseries, nice cafés and restaurants and shower facilities. Giles fed and rested but decided that even though he was tired he would carry on early the next day. He was keen to reach Goma and to climb the Nyiragongo volcano.

On the tarmac he was able to travel at about 70 k.p.h., an exhilarating speed after all the mud. Roaring round one corner he spotted a man in the middle of the road walking away from him. He braked hard and swerved to the left – of course – the man also moved left. Giles swerved again – to the right. The panicking man moved right also and there was the inevitable collision. The bike crashed to the road and careened off into a ditch, Giles hit the road hard and the man flew over him to land with a loud thud onto the hard surface. As Giles picked himself up the thought was running through his head that he had done the worst thing possible in Africa – he had run over a pedestrian! Assuming that he had killed the unfortunate, Giles ran back to him dreading what he would find. There was a cut on his head and he was moaning – but – he was alive!

Not wanting to move the man and possibly cause more damage Giles decided to wait for a passing car. A jeep with two nuns on board came round the corner and stopped. They acted swiftly putting the man into the jeep and telling Giles that he should follow them as they would take the injured person to hospital and then inform the police. Only about three minutes had elapsed since the accident. Giles's arm was bleeding. He dragged the bike back onto the road and found that there was a hole in the petrol tank. He treated the injury to his arm with TCP and filled the hole in the petrol tank with soap. Giles thought of his options. Should he try to find the hospital? Should he go to the corrupt police with the attendant probability of charges? If he was put into jail – who would ever know? The police could take all of his money and then where would he be? After quickly considering his position he roared off in the direction of Goma.

Throughout the drive he was terrified of being stopped by the police who may have used their radios to put out road blocks. He reasoned that they would anticipate him making for Goma and so he decided to give it a miss but he was determined to see the gorillas. Before driving up into the mountains he went through five heart-stopping police check points but there were no problems. He reached Rutchuru the next day and spent the whole of it watching the gorillas. It was fascinating and he could have stayed longer but he was still worried about the possibility of a police hunt. He nervously approached the border crossing point into Uganda but the guards were totally absorbed in a game of draughts.

So, now I was free of the threat of imprisonment and rotting in a cell for years and I entered English-speaking East Africa into Uganda. Winston Churchill called it the "Jewel of Africa". To tell the truth, I think he was right, especially as the first area I entered was Kisoro and Kabale. It is an area of rolling hills with volcanoes towering high above them. Every inch of the land was cultivated. Each family has a three acre plot. On it they have their house, sheds and a water tank and then a patchwork of fields on which they grow cash crops and food for themselves as well as fruit trees, cows and goats. It was just a mass of agriculture and people on a beautiful landscape.

The road runs north by the side of Lakes Edward and Albert, only a dirt track with no traffic. The first game I saw was a herd of impala and Grant's gazelle, then a huge herd of buffalo. Fortunately they were not near the track, hippos at every crossing but they remained in the water at that time of the day, wart hog and baboons in the road alongside antelopes and zebra, a load of fresh elephant dung on the road. I stopped and looked down to my right and saw the herd grazing on some trees and bushes about 100 metres away. Out with my camera! Two large cows turned round, trumpeting and flaring their ears and looking extremely threatening. Guess what next. Lion, but not near the road, they were up on an ant hill lying in the sun. I came out of the park that evening feeling on top of the world – nothing like a free safari for a budget traveller. Just before reaching Kasese, between the road and Lake Edward, there is an old volcano crater full of water. It is about one kilometre from the road. I spotted it and drove down through the bush to the water's edge. Impala, Thompson and Grant's gazelle were all drinking. Flamingos and dozens of other birds wading and at least 50 hippos wallowing in the water. The scene blew me away. I cruised through them on my bike sending animals and birds scattering in all directions. Really, this was the Africa I had dreamed of.

Chapter VII

Jambo, Kenya

In Kampala Giles met up with many of the people that he had encountered along the way. He was introduced to Matt, an English-South African, and his partner, Ely, a wealthy American woman. They were travelling in a custom built Land Rover with all the gear for a hard safari. Matt and Giles hit it off immediately but Ely was more difficult to tolerate. Through a terrible African rainstorm they travelled in convoy, clearing customs at Busia and pressing on to Kisumu where Giles got his petrol tank fixed.

When they arrived Giles was only too pleased to take up the offer of the wealthy Ely, to pay for a good hotel which provided all the comforts and delicious food – luxuries that Giles experienced for the first time since leaving home!

…but, oh, dear – she really was American. That evening we decided that as the Masai-Mara National Park was so close by, the next day we should beetle off down there instead of heading straight for Nairobi. I was keen because it meant seeing animals and we could put the bike on the back of the Land Rover. After a huge breakfast (the food was free and I just gorged myself) we headed south.

I should tell you about Matt and Ely. Matt had struck a deal with her in Botswana: she would pay for all the fuel and necessary purchases en route, for a three month tour from Botswana to Zambia, Zaire, Uganda, Kenya, Tanzania – then Kenya to Ethiopia and a return to Botswana. So, Matt knew her but not as a travelling companion. The only reason he had not booted her out of the jeep was that he was enjoying the benefits of a free safari, apart from the wear and tear on his vehicle. So, I guess having me along relieved the tension building up between them.

The Masai Mara National Park lived up to Giles's expectations. The abundance of game was staggering and Giles recorded scores of species in his diary. The birdlife was equally extensive and Giles was in his element. He was hugely impressed by the massive fertile plain that stretched all the way into the

Serengeti in Tanzania. Whichever way he looked he could see the great plain-grazers and the stalking predators. After two days he had seen and photographed so much that he was quite pleased to satisfy his urge for speed again by racing up the road to Nairobi.

In Nairobi they stayed for three days with Ely's friends the Armstrongs; revelling in deep, steaming baths, vodka and tonics, French wines and superb food. Then it was off to Tanzania. Giles left his motorcycle at the Armstrong house and made up a threesome in the Land Rover – destination: the Ngorongoro Crater. Inside the crater sits Lake Magadi fed by a network of small rivers running on one side through a large marsh area. There is a huge concentration of game in a quite small area. After a day and a night there it was time to head back to Nairobi. From there Giles telephoned Sally Higgin, an old friend of the Thornton family and he was promptly invited to dinner. He loved the Higgin's house! Just outside Nairobi it is a beautiful spot with a large garden and meadows and a superb view out towards the Ngong Mountains.

Giles joined Matt and Ely again to visit the Northern Frontier Department (NFD). This area runs from north of Mount Kenya and up to the borders with Ethiopia and Sudan. It was a different side of Kenya – the lush greenery of the Serengeti was replaced by a rough, dry, boulder-strewn desert which Giles immediately loved. Those nights spent sleeping under the millions of twinkling bright stars and listening to the ever-changing night symphony of Africa's wildlife confirmed to Giles the 'rightness' of his decision to travel through Africa. When the journey was over he returned to Sally Higgin's house once more; it was there that he met the Dyers, a family that was to be instrumental in changing his life. It was Easter, 1991.

The following letter was written by Giles, to his parents in October 1991 from Nasir in Sudan:

Dear Mum and Dad,

So, now what happened to the last six months? It has flown by with such speed, in fact it's going faster and faster. Well, the main part of my time since Easter was spent at Borana Ranch, which belongs to the Dyer family and is run by Michael Dyer. It is situated on the northern side of Mount Kenya on the edge of the NFD, which is semi-desert.

Michael and his wife, Nicki, have two children and they live in a wonderful house on the ranch. It sits high on the escarpment with one side facing Mount Kenya and the other has a mind-blowing view over the Northern Savannah. The Dyer family is very close-knit. Michael's mother, Rose, is the landowner, which includes 20,000 acres of arable wheat growing land on the lower slopes of the mountain; 40,000 acres at Borana, which is bush and open plain and 500 acres at Ngare Ndare, which is irrigated and includes a vineyard, lucerne, bananas, lemons, oranges etc.

Then there is Rumuruti which consists of 40,000 acres of bush and this is where Rose's brother, Gilfred, lives. All of Rose's children work on the ranches and live within 30 kilometres of each other. This is very remarkable, particularly when one takes account of the fact that most families in Kenya seem to be ripped apart by family feuds. Tony Dyer, the ex-white hunter, now derives the greatest pleasure tending his vineyard and fiddling with his flying machine, not forgetting the yacht kit that he has assembled around the back of his house – there it sits 100 kilometres from the sea and all ready to go. I met Michael and Nicky Dyer at Sally Higgin's house at Lamuru outside Nairobi. I asked Michael whether I could work on the ranch. He was keen and said: "Whenever you're ready, just cruise on up." He drew a map for me but failed to tell me of the road conditions! A week later I set off on the bike to Borana. The map showed a turning off the tarmac near Timao. I managed the turning, but a storm was breaking overhead. The turning took me onto a mud track but it was not just mud. Black cotton soil is the name given to the type of material forming the surface of the track. When water is added to it, it becomes slurry and even small amounts of water turn the surface into a very insecure mixture. On the other hand this was a big storm and the slurry became a few inches thick. The bike stood little chance of staying upright and for the next two and a half hours I waged war with the track, clutch slipping, feet bouncing along the ground, trying to keep the machine upright. I fell countless times with the rain lashing down in torrents. I had to lift the bike up time and time again. I wondered how and when it would end. At last the road began to dry out. It had been a local storm, in fact when I reached Borana it was bone dry. There I was, soaked to the skin, covered in mud, arriving at Michael and Nicky's house which was absolutely dry. They understood right away because they had had some interesting drives themselves when using the same track.

Borana is a classic old colonial ranch. The family want to keep the wild animals, but also run a commercially viable flock of 6,000 Merino sheep and a herd of 3,000 beef cattle. In order to maintain the game, it is important not to overgraze the pastures, so the cattle are rotated around a vast area. It works extremely well, almost too well; the numbers of zebra and antelope such as eland and impala are so great that they have to be culled. My first job on arrival was to zero-in a •345 Mauser rifle and then go out and shoot some zebra. Michael's last words to me as I departed were: "One bullet – two zebra." "Yes, Boss." I replied as I went off in green trousers, Drysabone, sunglasses, sun cream, water bottle, binoculars, ammunition and rifle – what an adventure.

So began 15 days of a sport that I had never done before. I guess it was like deer stalking except that I didn't have to select an individual target. Through the binoculars I would choose a herd. Each herd consisted of 70 to 300 beasts. Then I'd walk into a position where I was downwind of the herd, skirting them very wide, usually in a half crouch position. When I was about 300 yards away, I'd fall onto my belly and crawl. The terrain is covered with knee-high grass and thorn trees (Whistling Thorn) about six feet high. I then crawled forward getting closer and closer. I had been told "One bullet – two carcasses" so I had to make sure. When I took my time – patience was rewarded. One day I was into a herd of 70 odd and I managed to get within 50 yards. I lined up the sights on a big male and wapped it. The whole herd remained still; completely confused as the animal fell where it had stood. I quickly turned the rifle to the left and shot another. Then the herd ran for a bit, but not far enough – another bang and they really started to run. They ran straight past the bushes which were screening me from their view. There was time to hit another before they disappeared across the ranch. I walked back to the camp area where the men lived and collected a truck and two men who were excellent skinners. I left them to skin the fallen zebra and went off to find another herd.

It was a great 15 days. I felt very good walking out in the heat and then stalking close with my heart beating in my ears with excitement almost every time. Yes, there was great satisfaction in the kill, especially when there are so many zebra and it is control culling that just has to be done. Of course, culling is illegal in Kenya because of the wildlife policy that is in force. Sadly, the skins cannot be tanned with the hair on and sold as rugs due to the 'No Trophies' rule. Thus, instead of achieving $200 for each hide, the skins have to be tanned with the hair off and then they are sold as horse leather. The tanning is done at Ngare Ndare, where Rose and Tony live.

The classic all-timer occurred one evening. After watching the sunset from a hill, I was driving home when I passed a cattle trough with a zebra drinking from it. As I drove on a plan began to come together. Michael and I decided that a •475 should be ample to do the job. The next day I built a hide 10 yards from the end of the trough and the following evening we entered the hide and waited. As dusk faded into darkness, the zebra arrived and lined themselves up 15 in a row with their heads down drinking. Michael lifted the •475 and aimed at the nearest zebra, just behind the head at the top of the neck – BANG! The noise shook me; six zebra fell at the trough and three more staggered 20 yards and collapsed. It was indeed a fine shot, but there was some luck involved as well. Perhaps a world record – who knows?

So, what else did I get up to at Borana? The family decided that it was a worthwhile commercial venture to attract tourists by building a lodge. They planned that a unique building, a high class, high price, distinguished and exclusive lodge with a maximum of 12 bedrooms would be erected. The lodge site had been chosen by the time that I arrived and construction planning was under way. Michael brought in a chap called Murray Levet, who had run Little Governors in the Masai Mara for five years. He is quite an arty type and has been responsible for various building schemes around Kenya. He would be responsible for the design and construction. He was a very humorous fellow and great fun to have around. He also had endless visitors staying with him in his cottage, so there was always a party going on there. The design of the lodge is simple; a main building with a high thatched roof, very open with a sitting room, dining room, large veranda, hall etc. Then there are to be separate small cottages connected by a pathway to the main building. Each cottage, like the main building, is to be built with walls of the stone found on the ranch and a high thatched roof supported by cedar poles. The cottages will have huge bedrooms and sitting rooms with a fireplace and veranda and also a large bathroom. The views from the cottages will be magnificent – looking down to the lake and river at the bottom of the valley buffalo, kudu, eland, waterbuck, impala, gazelle, warthog, duiker, hyena, bushbuck, giraffe and zebra will all be seen drinking and grazing there. The elephant, when I was there, tended to come for a few days and then move on. This was fortunate because they really do destroy the trees and bushes. The herd that stayed for a month left a path of destruction.

17. "The Haringey Council Gas Van"

18. With brother Ben and Roland Purcell, at Val d'Isère

19. Snow boarding perfected

20. Ready for the head count by the Sobat River, Sudan 1991

21. The UN delivery boats and their drivers on the Sobat River

22. Riek Machar in his office at Nasir, Sudan 1991

23. Michael and Nicky Dyer with their sons, Llwelyn and Jack, at Borana February 1992

24. The view over Kisima farm below Mount Kenya

25. Rose and Tony Dyer at home in Ngari Ndari, Laikipia

26. With local tribesmen in Katavi National Park, 1992

27. Tooth extraction croc-style after a devastating drought in Katavi, 1992

28. A picnic with Roland Purcell and friends at Katavi

29. Giles and Damian Bell scrambling up Mt Londigo to reach a paraglider launching sit[e]

At the time I left Borana, Murray had almost finished his cottage and was half-way through the construction of a guest cottage. I was involved in the work, collecting cedar poles from the forest, plastering the walls and as a general 'gofer'. Most of the time, however, I spent helping Michael with the sheep, cattle or the Angora goats (filthy smelling monsters). The cattle are run through a spray every week to kill the ticks. If this was not done they would soon die of ECF [East Coast Fever]. We vaccinated against foot and mouth disease and branded the young stock each month. Michael, being very keen on the health and condition of his herd, was an education to work with. The sheep were sheared while I was there. The shearing shed was filled with 12 shearers and 30-odd other men classifying, cleaning, weighing and baling the wool. It took 10 days to shear the herd of 6,000.

Of course, the true love of my stay at Borana was the bush. The animals and the scenery were all so wonderful. Getting to know, recognise and name the smaller, rarest and more timid game and birds was most satisfying. A drive out in the evening, looking for something special, was always rewarding. The cats were always good to see but my feelings towards them changed. I now have a healthy respect for them after an evening encounter, on my motorcycle on my way to Ngare Ndare to have dinner with Tony and Rose. I was travelling along a small bush track, winding down the escarpment towards their home. Dusk was falling and the track was steep, forcing all my body weight onto my arms. When I arrived at the bottom of the hill and came onto the Ngare Ndare plain, I stopped to rest my back by lying along the seat of the bike. After a minute or two I had the feeling that I was being watched. I sat up and there was a lion 10 yards away to my right. At first it looked like a lioness, but then I noticed its big paws compared to the rest of its body. It could be a young male, prior to growing its mane. I looked to my left – another young male, looking more sheepish and backing away into the bush some 20 yards away. So, here was this young male looking directly at me, ears pricked, in a crouching position with its tail flicking back and forth.

This was a show of great interest; a distinct display of the behaviour of a lion that is more than interested in eating another beast. For some reason it never crossed my mind to turn around and take another route to the Dyer's house. No. I was going straight there. I edged forward and that was just what the big cat liked. Lions, like all cats, become even more excited when their prey moves and shows signs of life. This lion was not in the least perturbed by the noise of the bike or even the blast of the horn. In fact it became even more interested. It moved towards me, belly on the ground and obviously as keen as mustard. For some reason I kept my cool, but I wanted to see what would happen. My mind registered that moving excited the cat and it was better to be still. So I stopped and looked at this killing machine before me, totally wild and free to kill as it pleased. I realised that the other lion could be somewhere nearby but a quick look around registered nothing. I was rather keen to keep an eye on the bigger lion that was now only six yards away. In order to continue my journey I had to proceed around a corner, which was exactly where it was crouching, but to move seemed to excite the beast. I had my helmet on and a leather jacket and gloves providing some protection, so I decided to move forward, slipping the clutch. As I reached the corner, the lion moved from its crouched position to cut me off. As I began to ease my way around the bend he was just two metres away beside me. I took a quick glance over my shoulder to see what was up – all clear! I roared on to Tony and Rose's with my heart racing and a weird feeling, which I am sure, is exactly how a mouse must feel when the tabby has stalked it and it has escaped by the skin of its teeth.

I was soon at the Dyer's house and told them what had happened. We concluded that these must be the same two lions that had eaten a camel the night before and some cattle three days before that, because they were in the same area. Tony said that we should get in the car and go after them with his •375 and see if we could find them. If there is a chance of shooting a killer lion you must take it. The chances were good that the lions had been walking along the road towards the camel corral. Rose got behind the wheel with Tony and I standing in the back of the Toyota Land Cruiser. When we reached the spot it was almost dark. There was no lion to be seen. We drove on along the road with only the side lights of the Toyota to help us – still no lion. After about one kilometre we turned around and headed back – a flash of a pale colour caught the corner of my eye and I called to Rose: "Stop. Reverse and swing the headlights to the left." Rose, being a completely bush-wise lady, had the car in place and the two lions beautifully illuminated in front of us. Tony aimed and fired killing one of the lions instantly. The second beast ran off. Rose switched off the engine and the lights and we waited. Tony said that with luck the other lion would return soon. It was now very dark, but we could see the carcass lying some 10 metres away. We waited and waited; an hour passed, my tummy rumbled and then Rose said that she could *see the movement of a shadow. On went the lights – sure enough there was the lion sniffing his fallen mate. Tony's rifle cracked again and the lion took off into the bush. Tony said, "OK. That's it. We'll come back tomorrow and see what's what.*

The next morning Michael came down to Ngare Ndare with his gun and dog. Tony was armed with his •375, Michael with his •475, his head tracker and his four dogs and me with a •345. We set off on foot following the trail of blood (there had been teeth and bone lying beside the dead lion when we had inspected it). We walked through the thick bush for about two kilometres and then the tracker stopped dead; the dogs became very sheepish and the tracker pointed out the lion lying down under a tree. Michael fired two bullets into it and approached to examine the body. It was another young male and its lower jaw had been shattered. We had the right beast. We loaded the lions onto the Land Rover and took them back to Ngare Ndare to be skinned.

Lion kills at Borana were fairly common with one or two cows being attacked every two to three weeks. Sometimes there would be a spate of kills and each time that happened, we would take a steel, welded mesh cage and set up a hide close to the remains of the kill in the hope that the lions would return. On most occasions nothing happened. The lions are very crafty. One occasion though, Michael's godson came with us and he shot a huge male lion with Michael taking out a second animal. It happened like this: late in the evening three males came into the old kill and settled down with much blood-curdling growling and the most awful crunching of bones and ripping of sinews. We watched them for a while to see if any more would appear. After about 20 minutes we could wait no longer for fear of being detected. We each aimed at a different lion and fired. Two went down and Michael shot one on the run. It took six men to lift the carcasses onto the Land Rover. The hides were tanned and then made into gun cases for people to admire later.

Leopards were reasonably abundant with sheep and goats being taken at regular intervals. The leopard is quite rare elsewhere in Kenya so we trapped them and then sent them off to be released into the game reserves. The trapping was done by one of Michael's trackers. He would pick up the trail of a leopard close to the site of the last kill and then follow the route taken by the cat until he reached a classic site where leopards would pass by and hunt. He would then set up his trap with the door open at one end and a lump of half-eaten goat inside. There is an efficient mechanism which closes the door once the animal is inside. Standing up close to a leopard, even if it is in a cage, is forbidding. It makes a truly blood-curdling sound deep down in its throat and then, if you move, it roars at you and you think that the cage will break open. You cannot help flinching and stepping back. Tony Dyer, the leopard specialist during his hunting days, steps up to the cage and does not show any sign of fear. He talks to the animal with his face only inches away from the bars.

Each of the Dyer brothers has his own aeroplane. As for Tony, or 'Biggles' as they call him; he is the most experienced and the greatest pilot of them all. He has a wonderful plane – a de Havilland Beaver, made in 1952. He is often carrying out contracts for the Kenyan Wildlife Society and also performs many other private tasks. While I was staying at Borana, he was flying every 10 days for the WWF [World Wildlife Fund]. They had fixed 50 transmitter collars to elephants around North Kenya. We would fly with a receiver and track their movements. It is amazing how far they moved – up to 50 kilometres in 10 days. It was excellent flying over the huge plain of Laikipia and then around the Mount Kenya range. The largest herd we saw in one place totalled 500 – a real spectacle! The problem is that all the elephants have moved south out of the NFD and onto the white man's ranches, because they know they are safe there. But the damage they do is horrendous and the area they have in which to roam is much smaller than the NFD. So poaching control, which sometimes involves killing Shifta[7], is a big problem.

(Giles's letter ends abruptly at this point suggesting that he had found a courier to carry it to a post office.)

During a visit to Tony and Rose's house in October 2006 I was taken to see the spot where the lion incident had taken place and the account given to me by Tony and Rose tallied exactly with that related by Giles. Tony had a number of interesting observations to make on Giles:

"He really was a remarkable lad. He became a wildlife specialist in his own right without any formal training – it was just his natural instinct coming to the fore. You know when he was working for Alan Root [the subject of a later chapter] he lived for long periods in the bush with those little pygmies – they

---

7   *Shifta: Groups of men, principally from Sudan, had for years, been crossing the Kenyan border. Particularly attractive to them was the plentiful ivory tusk and rhino horn which both commanded (and still do) high prices on the Arabian and Far Eastern black markets.*

could duck and weave through small holes in the bush whilst Giles, at his height, must have had a very uncomfortable time following them around the forest. I don't know how he managed to communicate with them but he must have done because he always got the job done. Giles had a great and very unusual rapport with Africans – a rapport that was much better than anyone else I know.

"You asked me if I could remember the first time I met him. Of course I can. I was at a formal luncheon party given by a cousin of mine at Borana. I was excited because an Italian writer (who is still in Kenya by the way) had taken a taxi all the way from Nairobi to meet me. Can you imagine that? All the way from Nairobi! A taxi for about 150 miles. Anyway I sat down with him and very soon afterwards this young man sat down on the other side of the table and said to me: "Is it true that you had the hots for my Auntie Dawn?"

"This was typical of Giles – not only the unconventional opener to the conversation but his appearance uninvited. You would be at a dinner jacket party and he would turn up dressed in his old Brazilian raincoat, torn of course but everybody would make him welcome because he could get away with it.

"You know there was an element in his character that simply did not allow whingeing. He had no conception of the word. I remember he arrived with us one day after a hell of a lot of cross-country motorcycling and he had just done a 2,000-feet descent off-road and about 100 miles of bush driving. I asked him if he had had any punctures and he simply said, "Of course." Mending a motorcycle tube puncture is no easy matter and he would have had to do it many, many times with all the sharp thorns and rocks he would have encountered. But there was not a single word of complaint. He once took a trip around Lake Natron which I thought I knew well but he found a river from the south which he couldn't cross – it was too deep. He took his bike to pieces and carried it across section by section and re-assembled it on the other side. On crossing he saw a crocodile where there were meant to be no crocs – so it was the first sighting and it did not deter him from his task.

"Giles's diaries were very good but you have to know the country and read between the lines to appreciate the enormity of some of his adventures and the acute discomfort he must have been experiencing. For example, when he was out shooting zebra at Borana he would be up well before dawn and with no regard for his own comfort he would crawl for hundreds of yards through the scrub and thorns to get very close (still pre-dawn). At that time there would be no wind and the zebra would be unaware of his presence unless there was a long-necked giraffe with the group which, of course, could see much further by using its height advantage. In those conditions he would be in a position where his first four to six shots would kill the same number of zebras before the rest of the herd knew what was going on. No-one else did it that well – he was very, very good and he prided himself on that.

"I have many friends in the SAS; they often train out here and I think Giles had many of the qualities of that regiment. Their ethos is to go out there and get the job done and then go home. They are not reckless."

A further little story reinforces the statement as to how well Giles got on with Africans. Whilst he was at Borana he met William Kupe, a member of the ranch security group. Kupe, a Masai, was skilled in the arts of tracking and stalking and he found in Giles an eager pupil who quickly mastered those arts. Here was a relative stranger to Africa who quickly began to recognise the many different spoors left by the passage of the wild animals. He could use the natural light from different angles to observe disturbed grass, leaves and pebbles to detect the line of travel. He was able to look through the scrub instead of at it and detect whatever may be lurking in the dappled shade. He was quick to spot fleeting movements and he was fast and silent in gaining cover for himself to observe the game. In return for these lessons Giles, a remarkably good shot, taught Kupe how to shoot and handle firearms safely. This 'tit-for-tat' tuition was to stand both parties in good stead. Kupe was eventually to become the head of Borana ranch security – a position he holds to this day.

Many years later, Brian Thornton and I took a walk around part of the Borana ranch with Kupe; it was obvious that he had held Giles in very high esteem as well as considering him "... my best friend...". He reminisced about their shooting days together and their adventures in tracking down big game just for the hell of it. Rather prophetically he described the occasion when they were on an anti-poaching patrol and they came across the maggot-ridden carcass of a hyena. Giles turned to Kupe and said, "When I die I do not want my body to end up like that. I want to be burned."

There is some interesting background to this in that some years ago Michael Dyer had taken a message at Borana ranch informing him that an eight-year-old Masai boy had been badly mauled by a buffalo. The village was some miles away and it was at the height of the rainy season which meant that the intervening ground would be a muddy morass – Michael did not think that he could get a vehicle to the village but he was determined to try. By dint of great skill he did make it only to find that the boy was close to death and he did not think that there was much chance of survival. He did not give much for his own chances of getting the vehicle with the injured boy and mother now on board back across the soggy ground so he summoned a tractor from the ranch to come and help haul his fragile cargo to solid ground. Eventually the boy made it to the hospital at Nanyuki. Some four or five years later there was a knock at Michael's door and he was confronted by a skinny Masai lad of about 13 years – it was the boy he had rescued and he said that he had come to work at Borana. That was the beginning of Kupe's career on the ranch.

But what about Borana. What is its history? In 1918, at the end of the First World War, Will Powys was demobilised from the East African Mounted Rifles after four years of distinguished service, which took him over much of German East Africa (which became Tanganyika and then Tanzania), and the eastern part of the Belgian Congo. He returned to his pre-war job of managing a ranch for the Cole family who were some of Kenya's earliest pioneers.

The British Government of the time was trying to encourage farmers to settle on and develop some of the wide, empty areas in the highlands of Kenya. The African population in much of the country was very sparse and the Government had created large, empty buffer areas between the various tribes to try to cut down on inter-tribal and inter-clan warfare. When Will Powys heard that plots of land were available to veterans, to be drawn from the hat, he immediately applied for his chance.

By great good fortune he drew the block situated around the Kisima spring to the north east of Timau. This fine spring was the best source of water for miles around and was to be a significant factor in his success in developing his new land which was open, treeless, windswept country teeming with wild animals.

At first he sent his nephew, Theodore, to camp on the land and manage it for him. Theodore was later to be murdered by tribal warriors while working on another Cole ranch in the Rumuruti area. Will Powys continued his work for Galbraith Cole and took most of his salary in the form of sheep. In a few years he had built up a fine foundation flock for himself.

Then, in 1927, he set off with his sheep, a horse and a mule, and a wagon pulled by oxen. It took him several weeks of trekking to cover the 100 miles of virtually trackless country from Gilgil to make his new home in Timau.

At long last he arrived. While crossing a ford in the river a mile below the Kisimi spring the wagon rolled over and his wooden Australian wool press was broken. That was soon mended and the Merino wool that it has tightly compacted into 400lb bales has twice, over the years, made top prices at the London or Bradford auctions. And, the old Merryweather ox wagon, built in Pietermaritzburg in South Africa, is still resting in honourable retirement in a shed at Kisimi. It last saw service in the film *Out of Africa*.

Soon after Will Powys's arrival on his new land there was a great storm and he lost 200 sheep in one night. The weather continued to be cold and misty. Kisimi is 8,000 feet above sea level and there is often frost at night. In desperation he searched for warmer land at a lower altitude. This was found on the Ngare Ndare River and he was able to buy the land where his daughter, Rose, now lives. Incidentally, Ngare Ndare means – River of Sheep – in the Masai language.

Many of his pioneer soldier-settler farmer neighbours were unable to make ends meet. Few of them had drawn land with any permanent water. They were soon disillusioned and bankrupt. These were the depression years of the 1930s. Will Powys continued to farm his sheep successfully and bought-out some of his neighbours. One of the purchases was the land around Borana Lodge. On the Kisima farm he built up fine studs of Black Galloway and Red Poll cattle. His Merino sheep flock, which had been started off by putting imported Merino rams to cross with local Masai ewes, eventually became pure-bred Merino. One visiting Australian sheep man said that he would like to see Kisima rams at the Royal Sydney Show. He said they would not win prizes but would attract most favourable attention.

The early Kenyan farmers had to learn the hard way. The sheep Will Powys had moved to Ngare Ndare started dying of blue-tongue. He saved the survivors by moving them back up to Kisima. Since then there has become available an effective vaccine for that disease. During the El Niño rains many wild animals died of blue-tongue.

Will heard one afternoon that there was a desirable piece of land nearby that had come up for sale. He promptly saddled up a mule and rode through the night to arrive early the next morning at a friend's farm on the far side of Nanyuki. During a quick breakfast he asked that friend if there was any conflict of interest with him trying to buy this land – for his friend also had land adjoining the piece for sale. Once he had been told that there was no conflict, he borrowed a fresh horse off his host and rode on another 30 miles to Nyeri, to get to the nearest telegraph office, where he arranged to borrow money to make the purchase. He rode about 70 miles in 24 hours – and he got the land.

Will Powys and his wife, Elizabeth, were a wonderful team. She too was a true pioneer and had also drawn a soldier-settler farm by virtue of her distinguished service at the Front in France as an ambulance driver and hospital administrator. She was gassed and suffered its effects for the rest of her life. During one shelling there was a direct hit on the trench in which she was sheltering. Two nurses were killed and the blast blew off her shoes. She then ran bare-foot half a mile for help.

Will and Elizabeth had three children: Rose, Charles and Gilfrid. Charles was killed in a gun accident in 1964. Gilfrid is head of the Kisima enterprise and lives on a ranch in Rumuruti. He has built up fine studs of Boran cattle and of Somali camels.

Elizabeth had a daughter by her first marriage, Delia Douglas, who married David Craig. They and their family, particularly their son, Ian, are the founders of the magnificent Lewa Wildlife Conservancy which has given the world a lead in private land conservation coupled with community development for the benefit of their neighbours. When Delia's father, Alec Douglas, handed the Lewa land over to his daughter and son-in-law he told them to make sure they left room for the wild animals.

These instructions were prophetic and started a new attitude towards wildlife by ranchers. Over much of the Laikipia District wildlife is protected and is flourishing. This protection can be costly because the ranchers and farmers lose considerable numbers of their domestic stock to lions, leopards and other carnivores. But on the other side of the equation the landowners are enjoying ever-increasing rewards by opening up their land to visitors. In the long term the Laikipia District will be as important to the wildlife of Kenya as are the largest of the National Parks. It is a complete ecological unit. There is a wonderful diversity of flora and fauna.

Rose and Tony Dyer have four sons: Michael, Francis, Martin and Charles. Martin and Charles run the crops and livestock at Kisima. Francis has now bought Manda Bay and he and Bimbi live there and manage it alongside their partners. Michael and his wife, Nicky, manage the Borana Ranch. Michael is active with several directorships in local group ranches and the Laikipia Wildlife Forum which represents the interests of the many and diverse landowners in this district. Nicky manages a tannery and leather workshop employing local disabled people. She also contracts a lot of decorative beadwork to local women's groups.

Throughout the world – cattle ranching – which is the principal activity on Borana – has suffered a decline. In 1990 Michael and Nicky decided that they had to diversify into some new activity, hence the creation of Borana Lodge.

The Lodge has an idyllic setting. It is just 17 miles north of the Equator. At an altitude of 6,000 feet above sea level, it enjoys freedom from the malaria mosquito but is not too high to cause any physical discomfort. The nights are cool and there are fires in the rooms every night of the year. The clear view of the occasional snow and permanent small glaciers on Mount Kenya is a wonderful contrast to the huge panorama of mountains and desert to the north.[8]

It is small wonder that Giles was so quickly fascinated by the Powys and Dyer families with their roots steeped in the history of Kenya. Perhaps in some way the two families also recognised the pioneering spirit which was quiescent in Giles for they took him in and befriended him almost as a family member.

The contents of Giles's letter show how his love of the country was growing as he learned more and more. Even so, the fact that the letter was written in Sudan contains the hint that the itchy foot syndrome had returned to him after six months or so on the Borana ranch. So, why was Giles Thornton in Sudan and how had he got there?

---

8   *This brief history is from the Borana website (www.borana.co.ke) with the kind permission of Tony Dyer.*

Chapter VIII

With The United Nations In Sudan

Giles was living a full and rewarding life at Borana but such was his nature, that after seven or eight months in Kenya, he wanted to see even more of Africa. Through a friend he was offered four or five months of combine-harvesting work but a chance meeting led him to turn the work down.

Giles went to Nairobi to see Sally Higgin who happened to be hosting a party that evening. Amongst the guests were some men who worked for the United Nations (UN) in Sudan. One of those men, Alistair Scott-Villars, was interested in employing Giles and arranged an interview for him with the Directors of Operation Lifeline Sudan – a feeding and medical project. At the interview Giles stretched the truth about his boating experience and was given the job of Boating Logistics officer and told to be at Wilson Airport the next morning. The offer of US$2,500 as starting pay held great appeal!

Giles flew from Wilson to Lokichokio[9], a frontier town on the Kenyan/Sudanese border which lies just to the south of the Kenyan administered Elemi Triangle. The site was the major launching point for the Southern Sudan operation of both the UN and the International Committee of the Red Cross (ICRC). Here Giles was given a briefing on the complex situation in Sudan and a potted history of the war that was raging in that tragic country. The conflict was resulting in abject poverty and starvation on the one hand and, on the other, a huge influx of refugees (many of them injured by bombs and mines) into the bordering countries of Kenya, Uganda, CAR and Ethiopia.

The war had broken out because of the dissatisfaction of the Southern Sudanese with the activities of the dominant Northern Sudanese who, administering from

---

9   Lokichokio: Once a sleepy village occupied by families of the Turkana tribe. At the time of Giles's visit the village had blossomed into a township housing administrative elements of the UN and the ICRC. It had a major airstrip and a hospital (used mainly for treating the war-injured refugees from the Sudan conflict)..

afar, were neglecting the south. Aggression was also fuelled by the fact that the population in the north was mainly Muslim whilst that in the south was predominantly Christian. The two dominating tribes in the south (the Dinka and the Nuer) had been feuding since time began but an uneasy truce was made and the Sudanese People's Liberation Army (SPLA) was formed under command of Colonel Gerang who had gained control of the major towns in the south. However, before Giles's appearance on the scene, there had been a rift between Colonel Gerang and some of the sub-commanders of the SPLA which resulted in the force splitting into tribal factions. The Nuer group, under Commander Riak, was based in and around Nasir while Colonel Gerang's Dinka tribesmen were in Kapaeta. The wet season was fully under way and about 80% of Southern Sudan was under water. This kept the Northern Army troops in their barracks but it did not prevent the Russian Antonov aircraft of the Northern Air Force from carrying out routine high-level bombing missions on known SPLA camps.

Giles had only one night in Lokichokio before being shipped in a Twin Otter light aircraft northbound for Nasir. From the air he witnessed yet another drastic change to the African scenery. In every direction stretched the almost sinister, green swamps divided in a haphazard manner by watercourses flowing into the White Nile. Huge rain clouds to the east periodically blocking the rays of the sun created a strange eerie pattern of light and dark on the murky waters below. The ochre coloured dwellings and warehouses of Nasir came into view and soon he was able to pick out the airstrip. After a perfect landing in a strong cross-wind Giles disembarked to find that the airstrip was actually made of bricks just laid onto the earth. He was quickly swallowed up by a host of people and inundated with introductions and questions. It was a somewhat bemused young man who was shown to his tent to be told that it was called the 'Pleasure Dome'. The name created immediate fantasies in his fertile mind!

Nasir was designed and built by the British using Egyptian labour. The warehouses are alongside the River Sobat and Nasir, in its heyday, was a major port. The River Sobat rises in the Ethiopian Highlands and flows into the White Nile and Nasir is the capital town of the Sobat Basin province. The surrounding area is flat and the town becomes an island during the rainy season. The British left when Sudan became independent and the town was occupied by the Northern

Muslims. The SPLA recaptured the ground and then it was re-taken by the North again. This to and fro reversal happened on several occasions and, of course, the resultant bombing took its toll on the structures. Most buildings were shells at the time of Giles's stay. The old District Commissioner's house escaped some of the bombs and, having half of the roof still intact, it became the headquarters, radio room and kitchen for the UN operations. The project staff was housed in tents adjacent to the house and along the river.

The Pleasure Dome was one of the tents that overlooked the river. Three people slept in it but it also had an area large enough to be used for whatever evening entertainment developed. Pitched only inches above the level of the river, it was necessary to surround the Dome with sandbags. Giles's accommodation was a grubby, unused corner of the tent where there was a mattress and a suspended mosquito net. It was here that people congregated in the evenings. Both ends of the tent would be opened during the day and the sides rolled up in an attempt to encourage a cooling breeze. This was Giles's home and he was at ease with it – he always enjoyed sitting there with a beer and a cigarette contemplating the current work and his own future.

There were many expatriate workers at Nasir – 'the swamps of hell' as they called it. Only six worked for the UN: The Camp Commander, an Australian called Ian Lethbridge, who was principally with UNICEF; the Boats Logistics Officer, Giles Thornton; and the four people – Charlie, Dave, Simon and Dale, who were part of the World Food Programme. Alongside was a number of non-governmental organisations which included the French organisation Soledad, which contributed two nutritional nurses and the International Rescue Committee which supported operations with a doctor, two nurses and a hygienist. All the catering, cleaning and other domestic provisions were in the hands of a Kenyan company (formerly the Kenyan Oilfield Services) which was formed to fulfil the needs of Chevron[10]. Most of those workers were Kenyans. The SPLA had a civilian wing called the Sudanese Refugee Rehabilitation Authority which

---

10 *Chevron: Prior to the war starting, the oil company, Chevron, had carried out a large scale seismic survey of Southern Sudan and had identified the likelihood of large subterranean oil deposits. Twenty five wells had been drilled and a pipeline to Port Sudan (on the Red Sea coast) had been planned. In part this discovery contributed to the war and Chevron was forced to evacuate after spending huge amounts of money.*

was supposed to act as a quasi-police liaison group between the SPLA and the refugee citizens of Sudan.

Giles's operational fleet consisted of a 30-foot, seven-tonne capacity boat on loan from the SPLA nicknamed BGB (big green boat) which had to be turned over to the SPLA, complete with fuel, whenever they required it. He had three large inflatables of two-tonne capacity powered by 50 hp Evinrude engines; four small inflatables of one-tonne capacity with 25 hp engines; three wooden skiffs with one-tonne capacity and 25 hp engines and two aluminium speedboats with 25 hp engines used by himself and for transporting nurses. The 14 men who provided crews for the boats were a mixed bag both in terms of experience, ability and reliability – only four of them spoke any form of English. Giles was also delighted to discover a few wooden slats that would make usable water skis.

The camp at Nasir owed its origins to the plight of the Sudanese refugees. When the war had started eight years earlier, very large numbers of refugees fled to Ethiopia and in particular to the town of Gambela nestling in the low foothills of the Ethiopian Highlands. At that time the government of Ethiopia was sympathetic to the plight of the Southern Sudanese and had no real objection to the 600,000 or 700,000 people settling there. In early 1991, however, the government was overthrown in a coup and the new rulers had no liking for the situation. When the Northern Sudanese asked the new Ethiopian regime to throw out the refugees – they agreed. First they bombed and strafed the camps at Gambela and then the army moved in killing and looting. The unfortunates were then herded back onto the road and rivers to Sudan. The first UN assessment team, led by Alistair Scott-Villars, found thousands and thousands of people trudging along the River Sobat towards Nasir. They were wet and hungry, coming under attack from local inhabitants (of their own nationality) and their morale was rock-bottom. They wanted only to return to their former homelands but Commander Riek Machar, sitting in Nasir with his own hungry troops had a better, if selfish, idea. He sent his troops to round up all of the refugees and shepherd them to Nasir. He had astutely realised that the more starving and homeless people that he could gather in one concentration – the greater were his chances of persuading the UN that this was the place for them to base themselves. His stratagem worked beautifully!

Giles, although advised not to dwell too deeply on the fate of the refugees, obviously felt for them as passages from a letter home show:

Whatever you want to call these people: refugees, returnees or displaced persons. These were the innocent Sudanese who were feeling the rough end of war. Here we had thousands of people all without food or shelter and carrying just the meagre belongings with which they had walked out of Ethiopia.

There were seven big camps and two smaller ones. The largest was at Nordang where a whole race of people called the Oudak was encamped. This was all that was left of a tribe that used to number 50,000 souls – now they were down to 20,000. The Nuer, the tribe of the Sobat Basin, despised the Oudak and regarded them as dogs and they had plundered them ever since they escaped from Ethiopia and now the SPLA was using them as a political pawn at Nasir.

The other displaced tribes such as the Dinka, Torpot, Quaranga and Mandadant, to name but a few, were camped next to villages so that the SRRA was able to have the village chief on hand.

Then there were the orphans, 30,000 children without a mum, dad or relative. These were the really vulnerable souls and, of course, the most useful pawns in the hands of the SPLA. They were a great recruiting bank and were used to keep up the numbers of the armed forces.

There were also small pockets of Ethiopian refugees who had fled the new regime that had kicked out the Sudanese. They had their own camp and were by far the most demanding and aggressive. They expected the world to help them and to be returned to Ethiopia without delay.

The camps consisted of a mass of small grass huts. There were few trees in Southern Sudan, just a few growing on higher ground round the swamp. But with the huge influx of people, wood was needed to cook so every tree for miles around had been chopped down. The Arab troops from the north had sown anti-personnel mines around every tree – 'Boom!' – there was another leg amputee. There were at least two mine casualties every week.

Sanitation was non-existent. People walked off into the swamp dodging thousands of other people's turds, did their own and returned to camp. Fortunately the river was there and drinking water could be obtained upstream of the bathers.

Each camp had an intensive feeding centre, where the skeletal cases were looked after. They were mainly children who had been brought to the camp early enough and had been spotted by a doctor or nurse and then carried to the centre with the mother. Flies, flies, flies, there were flies everywhere in unbelievable numbers, doing very well for themselves amongst all the dirt and crowded desperate people. One often saw little children just covered in flies around the mouth, eyes, nostrils and ears.

Food was brought to the camps every two days and distributed accordingly. They did well but the children kept coming for it. One or two camps received too much because the UN was under the impression that the numbers were greater. When this happened the sorghum or wheat was promptly distilled into "waragi" a very powerful booze. Five of the camps had "waragi" stills on full bore production! I felt the numbers were being greatly exaggerated but the UN could not question the figures given by the SPLA and quantities of food found its way into the barracks for feeding the troops.

If we started kicking up a fuss by saying that the numbers of people were not as great as we were told, or that we knew that the army was scoffing huge amounts of food – we were told by the UN to shut up. If you became a bit too cocky then you would be sacked, as happened to Jerome. Some villages did better than others; all probably arranged with the SPLA, so that they could grab the excess with ease and without the UN being aware of it. But how weird it was that when we tried to raise the issue we were just told to be quiet and do our jobs. OK, OK, just keep the boats running and count the dollars at the end of the month!

The children I mentioned earlier, who were all in one camp, were in a hell of a state when I first arrived in Nasir. The vast majority were thin and pathetic and yet they were receiving the greatest amounts of food per head by far, more than any other camp. It was so obvious where the food was going – straight into the barracks next door. The UN did eventually become angry about this but the children did not get any better. Then the ICRC stepped in. They put two Swiss aid workers into the camp. They slept there and kept an eye on the children 24 hours a day and the SPLA was no longer able to plunder the food. The children then did start to put on weight. Despite the ICRC's best efforts many of the children continued to be led away to become recruits in the army.

Giles was responsible for the maintenance of the boats and ensuring that they were ready to meet the programme of movements. These ranged from taking large quantities of food to the various camps and transporting the doctors and nurses around their different outposts. He found that he had to exercise his right to sack those members of his boat-driving team during his early days.

He decided to carry out a 'policing' operation to check that his drivers were delivering food to the right destinations. Each driver had a weigh-bill outlining his boatload and this had to be signed by the consignee but it was a system that was easily manipulated. Chugging gently downriver in the wake of the BGB he spotted it moored in the reeds close to the army barracks. He pulled in and found the driver, Samuel, unloading five sacks which were destined for a camp further downstream. Samuel produced a note written by a captain in the SPLA instructing him to drop off the sacks at this location. Samuel was despatched back to the mooring station and from there Giles took him to the office of the Camp Commander, Ian Lethbridge, and then to the SRRA from which point Samuel was taken to jail. Giles asked the official if he might have a meeting with Commander Riek Machar in order to introduce himself and to meet his wife, who was a friend from Nairobi[11]. The official agreed and later that evening Ian and Giles cruised up to the heavily defended SPLA base at Ketbeck.

Emma greeted Giles warmly and he enjoyed meeting her again:

Then came the formal introductions to the Commanders who all spoke immaculate English having been educated in England at Universities such as Bradford, Leeds and Newcastle. This was followed by all the usual first meeting bullshit and then, when tea was served, I explained exactly what I had seen Samuel doing. I handed Riek the note and asked him what he wanted me to do about it. Riek read the note and began a deep African laugh and then, looking up at me, he told me to leave it to him. That was the end of the matter.

So Giles had shown that his easy-going nature could be tempered with a touch of steel when required but he was still obliged to fire two more boat drivers for dishonesty and one for having a bad work attitude before he welded them into a hard working, happy and relatively honest crew. After all they had the best jobs in Nasir. They received extra food; they were paid with salt, soap and other

---

11 *The wife of Commander Riek Machar Degideron was Emma McCune, a Yorkshire girl who had been working for the UN when she met and fell in love with Riek. They were married in a church at Nasir in July 1991. Emma was also a friend of Sally Higgin and Giles had indeed met her in Nairobi. The marriage meant, however, that she was no longer employable by the UN in Sudan. The story of Emma's marriage and her subsequent tragic (and suspicious) death is told in* Emma's War: Love, Betrayal and Death in the Sudan *by Deborah Scroggins.*

goodies such as cooking oil, milk powder and sugar. Also, being on the river they were able to conduct a little personal trade in giving people lifts, fishing and selling the produce and not having to spend all of their time in the often oppressive confines of the Nasir base.

Giles's observations on the flotsam and jetsam of people attracted to aid work are very interesting:

The aid workers, of NGOs, came in two forms. The first were the kind that were there to "save the world", to save lives and to ride their guilt trips. The second were the aid mercenaries who needed the money but also liked the idea of being in the wilderness of no-go land. The UN workers are on fat salaries and most, but by no means all, are mercenaries. The guilt-trippers work for small NGOs like IRC and German and French small aid organisations with names that I forget. These good people work for tiny salaries; just enough for them to buy some toothpaste and soap when they return to Kenya for a bit of R&R. So, I fell into the mercenary category.

When I first got there I started meeting the other aid workers. The Camp commander was on R&R and it fell to a French chap, called Jerome, who was definitely a mercenary working for WFP, a part of UN, to show me around and introduce me. I first met another WFP chap, Simon, a New Zealander and a traveller who had been in the aid game for two years. I got the feeling that he had become too deeply involved. He was always rushing about and he looked terrible – he contracted bilharzia and left after about three weeks but he returned in November with a much more mercenary point of view. Then there was Charlie Villars (also WFP). I recognised the name and face instantly – yes – we were at school at Wellesley House together. He was a year younger than me but we had a big laugh about meeting up 16 years later in Southern Sudan. There was Dale who had been in the WFP for two years and was a workaholic. He really loved the job and was nicknamed the "Ninja Chicken".

Dave was an ageing hippy who had been with UN for five years. He was not climbing any promotion ladders and was not worried about it. He cruised around doing the minimum of work and was totally besotted with one of the nurses. Dave was, for me, a great calming influence. "Take a chill pill, man." These chaps looked after food distribution and were called the "Lizards" – after the monitor lizard.

Ian Lethbridge of UNICEF was the Camp Commandant. He was responsible for big money and he liked that. He was a career man and signed on to the UN for five years. Ian was very cool and performed his task well. He did not mind too much if some things were not quite above board. He enjoyed his fat cheque at the end of the month and the two weeks R&R every two months. He was a good guitarist and country folk singer, he would start wailing and strumming almost every night.

The nurses were all sorts. There were the up-tight, sour-faced bitches and there were the cruisers, but all of them worked like I have never seen before. The toughest by far was Gilly, whom I had met in Kenya. She lived next door to Sally Higgin in Limuru. This chick – she worked like I don't know what. She was first up and went for a 2 km run up the airstrip and back. Then she was first off in her boat and God help me if it wasn't gassed up and ready to run when she wanted it. Off she would go to the far reaches of the Sobat Basin to check on her Sudanese trainee nurses who were working in the camps. Then back at base in the evening she would be strumming her guitar with Ian and Dave would accompany them on his harmonica. One could always get a glass of wine when going visiting before dinner – it was great.

There was Jeannie, who, I'm afraid was a bit up-tight – in fact totally and utterly up-tight. She worked so hard and became so emotionally involved that she couldn't understand why someone like me was not on the same wavelength. Anyway, good old Jeannie was busy saving lives all day and would come back from her camp, which was three kilometres away just to have a pee. That did not go down well during the petrol crisis days. Fortunately she disappeared off to the USA for the whole of November which was like a big rest for all of us. She returned in December, however, an even more demanding, silly American.

The two French nurses, Isabel and Solidad worked together as nutritionists, weighing the children and measuring heights. Pumping extra food into the ones whose height to weight ratio was totally wrong. They were fun and enjoyed a good party, which was sometimes thrown in the Pleasure Dome. They never hassled me nor I them. They were paid 'zero points' and felt pissed off watching the 'Lizards' doing very little for good money.

John Carsello was the head of the doctor and nurse scene. When I first met the guy, I knew something was far from right. He had very poor co-ordination and was definitely a bit odd. He was an American, an ex-Vietnam medic. Later, after he left in November, never to return, I found out he had some sort of disease that buggered up the nervous system. He was also a raving queer with his tent bum-chum, Wayne.

Wayne was an Australian and a jerk, a deviant and a poof. He was supposed to be in charge of the sanitation in all the camps, but alas he was too busy poking his nose into other people's business. The Sudanese despised him. My drivers wound him up mercilessly. The SRRA gave him a very hard time and eventually, in November, the SPLA made him persona non grata and he left with his tail between his legs. There was one thing that Wayne could do well – water ski.

And, of course, there was 'Pieces', a retired Isle of Man fisherman and his wife. Tom and Sheila had flown out to Africa at their own expense and went to the UN in Nairobi to ask if they could be flown to Nasir, so that they could donate thousands of lines, hooks and fishing nets and teach the locals how to use them. A great charitable thing to do and I admired them both, but he could be such a bore when he wanted the music turned down.

For some time Giles had been enjoying water skiing using the wooden slats he had found in the storeroom. This activity had a real bonus. It was always difficult to gauge how many refugees there were around the camps – it was suspected that there were often far less than the community leaders were claiming – in this way they got extra food to supplement their cash incomes. It was noticeable that whenever there was a skiing session the camps virtually emptied as everyone flocked to the river sides to watch the antics of the crazy whites. This gave the UN watchers a good opportunity to do a body count which was most useful.

The work with the UN was a rude awakening for Giles. In his opinion many of the employees were simply there to grab some easy money. There was no real sense of duty. He was appalled at the vast amount of wasted food that would have eased many lives had it been delivered to the right place at the right time. On one notable occasion he took over the radio when an aircraft was preparing to drop supplies of rice and made the simple statement: "Don't drop the rice! We don't need it and these buggers are just turning it into alcohol and getting pissed."

Giles returned to Kenya in the New Year of 1992 and from there he organised a safari for his parents and brother, Ben. This concluded with a family visit to the coast where they stayed near Sally Higgin's house. Giles did intend to return to Sudan at some point before continuing his journey down to South Africa but before doing that, he wanted to make another lone safari and see yet more of the country he was beginning to love.

Chapter IX

Tanzania

For the first six months of 1992 Giles stayed at and around the Borana Ranch but he did not forget that his original intention had been to travel to South Africa. This was in his mind when he undertook a lonely safari south to Tanzania. In the following letter to his parents, he graphically described his journey.

At last I left Kenya at the beginning of June. I said all my goodbyes to the Dyers and Sally Higgin and all the other people who had become such great friends. I gathered up my belongings, which seemed to be spread all over the country in different people's homes, and loaded them onto my motorbike.

I did not go far on my first day out. I crossed the border at Namanga and moved south through Tanzanian Masai country. After a quick five hour drive during which I passed Kilimanjaro, I arrived at Arusha where I was able to stay with Damien, Justin and Ruchenda Bell, friends who I had met in Kenya. They run a company which provides luxury, tented safaris in the Serengeti, Tarangiri and Ngorongoro. I spent a few days there helping out in the workshop and getting information on travel conditions and possible routes from the brothers. My plan was to ride down into the Great Rift Valley for a week and then return to Arusha – after that I would ride down to Dar es Salaam to meet up with Richard Bonham on 26 June. I set off for Lake Natron and the volcanoes of Gelai, Shombole and Ol Doinyo Lengai. This is in the heart of the Masai lands, right down at the bottom of the Rift Valley, a very harsh and exciting area in which to travel. Arusha sits at 4,500 feet above sea level and during the journey to Lake Natron, I dropped down to 1,500 feet and found the soda lake covered in flamingos. I used a track that Damien had told me about. It was no longer used by four-wheeled vehicles but a bike could get through. I bumbled along over rocks and stones, along the trail that was no more than a cattle path, down onto the valley bottom. There I could see the volcano, Kitumbaine rising high in front of me – behind it Mount Meru rose to an even greater height (12,000 feet).

The track was all volcanic ash and it made for some tricky riding. I passed Masai manyattas (collections of houses and cattle corrals). There was game everywhere. The land was very dry and the track led straight to Kitumbaine and then turned around the side of the volcano. It had not been used by vehicles for over three years. Since that time the heavy rains have caused a huge amount of erosion and there were many big washouts to negotiate. This required a lot of hard work and concentration. It took three hours before I was able to head away from Kitumbaine. Soon I saw Ol Doinyo Lengai, the volcano I planned to climb, for the first time. The track to the volcano passed over a vast plain and I stopped to take it all in. There were wildebeest, eland, Grants and Thompson's gazelle and giraffe amongst the small clumps of trees. The grass was longer here but still very dry. I could see herds of Masai cattle with dust pluming up behind them. It was late afternoon and the sun was getting lower giving me good visibility. Imagine the scene: a huge plain, 30 miles wide and 100 miles long. To the west the Ngorongoro Highlands rising up to 8,000 feet, to the north Ol Doinyo Lengai, a perfect steep-coned volcano; to the north-east an enormous topless volcano, Gelai, rising to 7,000 feet, to the east Kitumbaine, another vast topless volcano like Gelai, 40 miles across the base and reaching up to 7,500 feet, to the south a line of smaller volcanic peaks with Empaki, the highest, at one end and Mount Meru at the other. Sadly, Kilimanjaro is too far away and is obscured by Kitumbaine. So, this was a truly majestic place.

I carried on along the track towards Lengai through a few Masai manyattas and herds of cattle being tended by young lads. I looked for a campsite in the late afternoon because I wanted to walk in the beautiful evening light. I turned off the track and headed for a small group of flat-topped acacia trees directly facing Ol Doinyo Lengai. My plan was to climb it the following evening and night under a full moon as the heat would have been too much for a daytime climb. I stopped and walked over to one of the water springs and sat on a sort of volcanic blowhole just as the game began to arrive for their evening drink. It was late but it was the night before the full moon so it was in the sky before the sun set – it was enormous. All the game came! What was so marvellous was a jackal had a den just below where I was sitting and the mother came out with her cubs to play. They make the most eerie sounds. I was hoping that a cat might come along and maybe make a kill but all I got was an old hyena skulking around and making the gazelle nervous. There was a stiff breeze blowing and it took a while to find a safe place to light a fire. I found a dry dusty patch of earth and cooked the meat I had brought with me. I put up my mosquito net just in case the little buggers were about with malaria in their proboscies! While I ate my meat I heard sounds of bird flight and looked up to see great 'V' formations of flamingos over head – they seemed to be heading straight for Lake Natron. Flight after flight crossed the sky – long after I lay down to sleep the birds kept coming.

I woke early and after a brew of tea I roared off across the plain, passing Lengai on my left and headed north to the lake. There were many Masai settlements and I soon found out why. There is a large river coming out of a gorge in the cliffs which form this side of the Rift Valley. It is good pure water from the Ngorongoro Highlands, hence its name in Masai, Ngare Siro (sweet water). I stopped, bathed and filled my water bottles and then, leaving my motorcycle with a Masai elder who was sitting outside his mud hut, I walked upriver. As the canyon became deeper there was a series of waterfalls, palm trees, ferns and thick lush bush everywhere. Baboons scattered as I scrambled up one side of the first waterfall. There were deep pools of clear water and a lovely cool temperature (it had been 40°C on the plain). The trees were figs and palms reaching up for the light. The river became quiet and then I saw the spring where water was welling up through rocks and reeds. I could see the stains on the rocks where the high water of the wet season had left its mark. I walked back down the river, stopping to swim in one of the pools below the waterfall. I read Damien's notes on how to reach the base of Lengai and I realised that there was no way that I could get there on my bike.

Leaving the bike behind was not a real problem. I reckoned that it would be a five hour walk to the base of the volcano and then a four hour steep scramble to the crater. I packed a small rucksack with five litres of water, an extra shirt and my 'Drysabone' and left the bike with the Masai, who now told me that he was the chief and not to worry about the bike because the fee would not be too big! He pointed me in the right direction and told me to follow the car tracks half-way to Lengai and then there would be just imprints in the dust to guide me. I set off walking at 4.30 p.m., and I should have been at the end of the track by 9.30 p.m. that evening. Walking straight towards the mountain, I passed the last few Masai bomas (huts) – at every boma the men came out to greet me and ask if I was going to the mountain. They seemed to think it was a long way, but, not bothered by this fact, I was going on alone. The dusty gravel was hell to walk on. The evening light was, as always, beautiful. I passed a vast herd of cattle with just one small Masai boy looking after it. I stopped and turned to see how far I had come – I was amazed. I had climbed many feet vertically as well as making good horizontal progress – the Masai seemed miles away.

I was puffing now, sweating too, but I felt good. The grass was now very long and up to my waist with bushes and scrub getting thicker. I was well above the area where the Masai grazed their cattle. In fact nothing seemed to graze at that elevation. Huge gullies, 50 to a hundred feet deep appeared, running down the side of the mountain. The sides of these were nothing but white ash, and water erodes that stuff like a knife through butter. The track ended and I was facing a 45° incline that towered above me in the dark. I had a peanut butter sandwich, took a swig of water and slept. The full moon bathed me with light as I woke a couple of hours later. I picked up my bag and started to climb again. There was plenty of light and I was able to use the shrubs to help me to pull myself up the incline that was now about 50° and covered with the fine, white ash. The views in the moonlight were incredible. I was tempted to stop for more sleep but it was getting very cold. I put on my spare shirt and the jacket and reasoned that as Lengai was an active volcano, it must be warmer inside the crater. The last hour was a scramble over smooth, hard rock. I began to see a red glow on the immediate skyline above me. That would be from the bubbling lava inside the crater. Then, without any warning, because my head was looking down, I came over the rim and found myself peering into the crater. It was cold on the rim but warm air was rising from the depths. Inside it seemed solid for about 40 feet below me but there were six sub-cones and one major one rising about 15 feet above the others. Three of the cones were hurling molten lava onto the floor of the main crater; the largest one, in the centre, was the most active.

It was now 4.00 a.m., and I still had to wait another two hours for sunrise. It was so cold that I slipped inside the rim of the crater to take advantage of the warm rising air. The active cones were about 40 metres away and blowing their lava away from me. The eruptions were taking place about every four or five minutes and it was very much like a fireworks display. Even with the full moon the red-hot ash glowed in the night sky. After about an hour of watching this beautiful, natural phenomenon, I began to doze. Dawn, when it arrived, was grey and unpromising. There were too many clouds to be able to see the sun on the distant horizon but the daylight views of the Rift Valley which lay all around me were amazing. I walked right around the crater rim just enjoying looking out over the Masai lands and into the Serengeti, into Kenya and across Lake Natron which seemed to be completely pink with flamingos and the colour of the soda algae that covered it. Then I was forced to remember that I had to face the incineratingly hot walk back to the river and my bike. It would take a good four hours. The descent of the volcano took only one and half hours of tumbling down the loose gravel and ash. Then I reached the track and turned in the direction towards the Masai elder's village and my bike.

After the Ol Doinyo Lengai experience, I returned to Arusha to stay with the Bell brothers, Damian, Justin and their sister Ruchenda for a couple of days before, on 24 June, setting off to meet Richard Bonham in Dar es Salaam. My plan was to pop in and visit a friend whom I had met in Kenya and who lived in Tanzania in the Usambara Mountains which was about halfway to Dar es Salaam. He had built a house on the edge of a 500-metre high cliff and he was a fanatical hang glider pilot. He had lived there for five years, flying every time there was a suitable wind. Serious up-draughts occurred right in front of his house. His instructions on how to find his house could not have been simpler: "Go to Loshoto town and ask." So that's exactly what I planned to do. The road to Loshoto was a motorcyclist's dream; tarmac surface with tight corners and hairpin bends. The 40 kilometres journey took no time at all. Loshoto is a market town for all the people farming in the Usambara Mountains and at the first place I asked about the flying contraption and the man called Carter. The chap knew immediately who I was looking for and gave me directions up a tiny dirt pathway just wide enough for an ox and cart. The track ended in someone's farmyard and the family gathered around as though they were expecting me. I mentioned Carter's name and they pointed to a pathway leading up the hill behind the farm. I put the bike inside one of the mud houses, flung the saddlebags over my shoulder and trudged up the hill with the kids carrying my other bag and toolkit.

Up and up we went and around the shoulder of the hill and then on to the top of a ridge with a thatched roof hut perched on the top. We walked along the ridge to a rocky outcrop jutting out over the cliff. On this platform, Carter had built a single room house out of rock and stones. It appeared to look out across the world. Carter was not at home but his housekeeper, George, a Tanzanian coast cruiser, who had been with Carter for four years, was there. He was very pleased to have a visitor – in fact he was chuffed to bits. The cloud was swirling along the tops of the cliffs but when it cleared I was able to look out over Masai land – an endless savannah as far as the horizon. Behind there were shambas (subsistence farms) all over the hills. The forests were being diminished year by year as the people hacked them down. It was a very spectacular position. The clouds cleared off completely and I just sat there looking at the view. George brought out some raw meat and began calling out and whistling. Soon a bird of prey arrived, circling, swooping down and then landing on George's gloved arm. It was a Marshall Eagle. A local chap had given it to Carter as a chick. Now fully grown, with a huge plume of white with black patches down its chest, it stood an impressive three feet high. This was a massive bird – he ate quickly, tearing at the meat between his talons. Then he was gone as quickly as he had arrived. George said that there was also an Augre Buzzard and a falcon that had been reared from birth. Carter flies with his birds. They take him to the big thermal up-draughts which lift him to the heights where the vultures cruise searching for food below. He has shot many hours of film of his birds and also of the wild ones that he joins in thermal circling – truly amazing films.

George had taught himself how to parascend under a canopy shaped like a wing, just as one sees in the Alps, but without skis. One day, after watching Carter and his friends flying under canopies and hang-gliders for months, George was on his own. He took a canopy up to the lift-off point, laid it out as he had seen it done before and then ran forward. He was up and away. He was very frightened, but kept his cool and descended until he reached the bottom – a four-minute flight. Immediately, he wanted to do it again. Now he is an amazing flyer. He has been at it for two years and he goes up for as long as he likes. The only thing that brings George down to earth is the cold. He just becomes frozen after a couple of hours up there. The next morning I walked along the cliff top, watching the many raptors and vultures launching themselves off the rocky ledges below me. I returned to find George crawling out of his hut. I had breakfast and said goodbye. The boys were already waiting to carry my bags to the bike. I went off down the amazing road to Mombo and then onto the main drag to Dar es Salaam. I had a map showing me where to find Bonham – I was going to help him with the last minute shopping for safari equipment.

Dar es Salaam is not a beautiful city. It has that hot, humid and sweaty feeling like Mombasa, but the dirt and filth are everywhere. Clearly there had not been a street cleaner about the place for 20 years or more. In the very centre of the town, where the shops are (which sell very little) the tarmac had disintegrated and subsided below the mud and sand years ago. Thus it is both dust and sand blowing about all over the place, into the shops and cars. The sewage is leaking and forms huge mud pies and pools of evil-smelling effluent right in the centre of town. So I will leave you to imagine the state of the outskirts. The whole place is very backward. It's as though everything to do with development in Tanzania came to a halt 20 years ago and has been slipping rearwards ever since. I was pleased that I did not have to find a cheap hotel in such a place. All I had to do was to follow the map and ask directions in order to find the house. I left the grime of the town and went on to the northern coast road. The place I was looking for belonged to Bim and Lizzy Theobald. Bim is the head man of Lhonro in Tanzania while Lizzy runs the bookings, transfers and supplies for Richard Bonham Tanzania (a safari company). I drove up to the house and jumped off my bike. The three of them came out to greet me. I was black and brown with the mud and dust of the journey so I was escorted straight into the bathroom and left to it. Bim and Lizzy make a very English couple, living in Dar es Salaam, but having many friends from Kenya, Europe and South Africa who come to stay and, therefore, they have never got to know many other local expatriates. They were incredibly generous and kind-hearted and Bim, being very much a businessman, loves having completely unbusinesslike people like me to stay. So, I was made to feel very welcome. The next day I was put to work. I was sent on my motorcycle, rushing around the town, buying parts for engines, boats, radios and food. The streets of Dar es Salaam, being more like ploughed fields, suited the bike very well and I got the bits and pieces in record time.

Bonham's lorry set out for the Selous at 5.00 a.m. and all the men travelled in a Land Cruiser pick-up. The distance from Dar es Salaam to the Selous is only about 175 kilometres but once into the park there is a further 100 kilometres to drive to Richard's camp site. However, the road out of the town is old tarmac with six inch deep potholes spread across the entire width. The broken tarmac lasted for 100 kilometres with us weaving all over the road to avoid the worst holes in first and second gear. The final 75 kilometres to the park gate is sand and dust which was much easier to drive on, but still slow going. Thus it took 12 hours to reach the gate. First we travelled through forest broken up by the occasional open glade where *antelope and buck grazed. I noticed endless hippo trails cutting across the track, their highway from the river to the night time grazing. There was no way that we were going to reach Richard's camp site before nightfall so we pulled off the track and drove a good mile to a glade and camped under a large acacia tree. The lads made a fire and put down the bedrolls without a single order from Richard. We ate ugale (maize porridge cake) and some beans. Then we just rolled up in our bags and listened to the night. Some hippos were snorting in the distance; a lion grunted a long way off and the hyenas whooped loudly – quite close. Yes, it was great to be in real bush country! It was the classic African scene of dense vegetation and clearings. I was woken by a pair of ground hornbills calling to each other, although they must have been 500 metres apart, their booming call carried easily across the camp site. The sound of the ground hornbill is probably my favourite call of any bird or mammal in Africa. It always makes me feel good to be alive and it is almost always the sound of the early morning. We rolled up our bags, drank some tea, packed up and moved on. This time all the men rode in the lorry except for Lucas, the foreman, Richard and me – we went on ahead at a faster pace.*

Our first stop was at Metambwe, the headquarters of the Northern Selous administration and the game warden base, to say hello to the warden and check in. The warden was not there, he was in Dar es Salaam but he would return – sometime! We went to the store to dig out some of Richard's camping equipment, which he keeps at Metambwe during the closed season. There were chairs, tables, tents, outboard motors, boats, etc. They were all in place just as he had left them six months earlier. The lorry would go along later to collect the stuff. We then stopped by one of the rather grotty lodges to pick up Richard's other vehicle which is used to transfer the clients from the airstrip to the camp. After that we set off for the camp site. We caught up with the lorry which had just had a half-shaft replaced. Moingy, the driver told us that he had carried a spare half-shaft for six years and now, at last, it had paid off.

The next 20 kilometres from the airstrip involved just bashing through the bush. Every year, when the camp is reopened, the track has to be cleared of the branches and bushes which have grown over it. So we bashed on, crossing some dry riverbeds and over some large open areas which were full of impala, wildebeest, kongoni and zebra. Then, as we crested a ridge, I had my first view of the Rufiji River. It was much, much larger than I had been expecting. There are large sandbanks stretching out into the middle and trees growing tall, thick and green along the banks. Even at a distance of five kilometres I was able to see large families of hippos in their respective deep pools. We drove down to the river and into the riverine forest which was cool and pleasant after being in the direct sun. As we entered a clearing, shaded by the trees, there was the river in front of us, nearly one kilometre wide at this point. It was an expanse of brown water with great sand bars and islands with tree trunks that had been washed down in the floods to lodge on the sand. There were hippos everywhere in the water and on the sand – crocodiles. What a spectacle there was before me. I just had to sit down and gaze at the scene. Some waterbuck were walking out across the sand bar to drink and there was endless bird life flying past – especially fish eagles with their call that so closely resembled a seagull. The hippos were constantly snorting and hooting to each other, their big gaping yawns showing off the lethal 10 inch long incisors. The crocodiles just basked in the sun, waiting, waiting for an opportunity.

The Selous is a wilderness. It is a Game Reserve and not a National Park. There are many different rules about walking and hunting (if you have a license). You can travel by boat and camp anywhere. Most of the Selous is divided into hunting blocks with the exception of a strip of country on the north side of the Rufiji River which is reserved for photographic safaris. It is the largest Game Reserve in Africa, being the size of Ireland and it is mostly covered by forestation with sand rivers running through them. There are some large open spaces, some swamp and some plains with riverine forest always running alongside the main rivers.

Richard Bonham's safaris in the Selous are truly what I believe safaris should be like: nothing to do with vehicles and certainly out of contact with any other people. The clients fly in from Dar es Salaam and from then on the only car they see is the one in which they take the one and a half hour trip from the airstrip to the main camp site. That is going to change this season because Richard has obtained permission to cut a small airstrip on one of the high ridges near the river. The clients will then walk from the aircraft down to a boat which will then take them to the camp site. From the time they arrive, the safaris will consist of short three hour walks in the cool of the morning to fly camps on sand bars, shaded by the large trees on the banks of the Rufiji. The tents, food, drink etc., is all brought to the fly camp by boat. Then an evening walk around that particular area follows. The clients sleep under mosquito nets or small tents if they prefer that. This pattern builds up to a six-day (or however many *days they want) walk with 20 to 30 porters carrying the food, booze, luggage, tents etc. The clients and Richard walk ahead of the porters looking at game and surprising themselves by how close they can approach the animals when they move through the bush quietly. Richard carries a gun just in case an old buffalo does a charge out of the bush or an ageing, single hippo, caught out of the river in the daytime, decides to charge (which he invariably will do). The alternative is a large circular route ending with a walk right back to the camp. This is the pattern to which the Selous is ideally suited: walking and boating.*

We had 12 days before the first clients were due to arrive. It was ample time for the campsite to be cleared. There was work to be done servicing the boats and engines; doing some fishing and taking the walks the clients would take to see what changes had taken place in the closed season. During this work, Richard became aware that his men craved meat – some of them had not eaten meat since the season closed! So, we went off on a buffalo hunt and Richard managed to bag a young bull. Back at the camp the young men beamed with pleasure as the skinned and butchered carcass was taken from the truck. The morale in the camp was transformed and there was a lot of laughter and singing as the meat was cooked and devoured. On one of our boating trips we came across a dead and rotting hippo on which the crocodiles were feasting. Richard cut the engine and we drifted towards it. The crocs were biting off enormous chunks of the body under the water – then they would surface and open their great gaping jaws, take a huge swallow and dive again for more. The boat passed alongside the dead hippo and grounded on the sand. That had not been the plan! There was nothing for it but to get out of the boat. In water up to our knees, Richard pulling and me pushing, we tried to get the boat free. Richard gave a shout and was into the boat before me. He had trodden on the tail of one of the crocs! We had to get out again and haul the boat back into the main channel and we did that at great speed.

We returned to the camp where we found visitors. A group of rangers were in camp with the stand-in Warden. Ninga, the real headman and a friend of Richard's, was still in Dar es Salaam. The stand-in was a shifty looking character and did not look like the friendly kind. Richard had not met him before. They talked for a while, then, pointing at me, the stand-in said: "Who is this? Has he got a work permit? Has he paid a park entry fee?" He clearly wanted money and was looking for a bribe.

Richard does not bribe anyone, but the last thing he wanted was to have any problems brewing at the start of the safari season. He explained that I was his cousin and just helping out for a few days. He told the official that I would be leaving before the first clients arrived. He eventually left after a few beers and a kilo of buffalo meat had been devoured. Richard explained that he would have to stand by his statement and that I really would have to leave.

That evening we had a further crocodile incident. We heard excessive splashing and a commotion from the river and we shone the light onto the water. There were literally hundreds of red eyes twinkling away at us. Crocodiles were swirling around, ripping flesh and opening their massive jaws as they swallowed. They had found another dead hippo. What was amazing was the number of the beasts following the carcass. As we shone the spotlight across the river, the eyes reflected the light back and it seemed as if we were looking down on a town at night from a hill or an aeroplane. There were hundreds of tiny lights. The men decided that they would never swim again! I have to say that from then on I had a distinctly odd feeling whenever I was washing at the river. The water was so murky that you couldn't see a thing. When I dived in to get wet and soap up and then dived in again to rinse off, I can tell you I was out in seconds. Crocodiles I do not like! I hate them! They are so evil looking. So like a dragon – a prehistoric animal that has adapted and evolved over millions of years into a perfect killing machine. They can even live up to 100 years and grow to be between 16 and 20 feet long, weighing in at two tonnes. I have no qualms at shooting those beasts.

The next day we went walking in the forest and out onto the flood plain that was now covered in bush about six feet high. The bush was thick but the buffalo and elephants had trodden a maze of paths through it. Richard wanted to have an adrenalin rush – or so I supposed. He said he would never bring his clients into this area and proceeded to walk on, loading his rifle as he went. In this type of bush you can only see up and down the trodden path and a couple of feet to either side. When you come to a corner or junction you look carefully before proceeding. In fact it is a very tricky situation. My heart was pumping when we encountered the first buffalo. There was a crash and a snort about five metres away – we froze – the animal had our wind. Then there was a burst of commotion as the buffalo charged through the dense bush, crashing onward blindly. It crossed our path about five metres ahead of us, leaping over and not even glancing at us (thank God). What a noise. Bonham turned to me and grinned – we continued.

There was very fresh elephant dung on our path. My hackles went up (well they would have done if I had any) when I saw the big padded footprints. It looked as though the elephants were moving to our right, browsing on the foliage so unsuited to its main predator – man. However, Bonham was there with his white tribesman. We knelt down and stayed still for a long time, trying to listen for their sounds to get a clue as to their whereabouts. Then we continued northwards, stopping every 10 metres to listen. We heard some wood snap and a tummy gurgling; a sound that only one animal makes. They were somewhere dead ahead of us but we could not see them and the wind direction was not in our favour. We could easily find ourselves in a real muddle. Discretion was definitely the better part of valour and we retreated, taking another path so that we skirted around them. Suddenly we found ourselves beside a sand river; a nice change from the claustrophobic pathways. The elephants were grazing beside the dry river bed. We sat and watched the family of five young mums with calves, some teenagers and the much larger matriarch. They were browsing away, totally unaware of us. After half an hour we moved off back to the camp negotiating our way past a herd of buffalo on the way.

We had been lucky to see the elephants – they are very shy and as a result of the heavy poaching activities in the late 1970s and 1980s they disappeared if they saw or got the scent of man. The rhino had been almost completely eliminated from the Selous during those years. Although researchers and game wardens reported having seen rhino dung and spoor they had not set eyes on the animal for a long time.

After 12 days in this paradise, I was really beginning to have the most wonderful feeling of peace and good vibes. I did not want to leave, but I had to and so I boarded the aircraft that brought in the first clients of the season. We were in Dar es Salaam in 35 minutes and Lizzy picked me up and took me back to the Theobald house beside the sea. We did some water-skiing that afternoon but the next day I had to get on my bike and head north to Arusha to meet the Bell brothers.

*30. In the Congo Rainforest
with the Mbuti pygmies, his hunters,
October 1992*

31. Kitembo equipped to go hunting in the rainforest

32. Giles and The Rev. Père Leon Mondri at Opienge

33. The Water Chevrotain

34. The Aquatic Genet with prey

35. The young Owl that was raised on mice

36. In bed with the Pygmy Antelope

37. Alan Root enjoying a meal with the Kingfisher

38. Showing off Josephine

39. Napoleon and Josephin

40. "The man who would be King" with Maasai friends

41. With Sally Dudmesh in the Chyulus

42. With the "Save the Rhino" fundraising expedition on the summit of Kilimanjaro, December 1994
Clockwise from top left: James Hersov, Giles, Will Stanhope, Johnny Roberts, – ,
Tom Kenyon-Slaney, – , Eliseria (Tony Fizjohn's No. 2 at Mkomazi), Christina Franco,
Kees Hoft (with camera), William Todd Jones (in costume), – , David Stirling

43. Inés
Sastre

Chapter X

Malaria in Mahale

Giles arrived at Arusha feeling cold and strangely tired. After a hot bath and a whiskey he went off to bed thinking that he had got a chill. He slept well but in the morning he was groggy and very cold. Mid-morning and he decided to go to bed but even fully clothed and covered by a duvet and blankets he could not get away from the shivering cold. Appraising the situation Damien and Ruchenda took him to Dr Mohammed for blood, urine and stool samples from which the doctor diagnosed dysentery. Back at the house his condition rapidly deteriorated. Ruchenda nursed him by making him drink a lot of water and swabbing him down with cool, damp cloths. He descended into deeper fever and they took him back to the doctor who, after a further blood test, diagnosed malaria and said that he would take him into the local hospital. Ruchenda refused to accept this and told Giles that he would probably catch something far worse than he already had if went into the State Hospital. It took five days of nursing before the fever broke leaving Giles weak and emaciated. There is a good chance that the ministrations of Ruchenda and Damien saved his life.

In Arusha, Giles was introduced to an interesting man with whom he struck an instant rapport. Roland Purcell is an Irishman who had moved to Kenya some 10 years prior to meeting Giles. He had begun his life there as an auctioneer for Sothebys, working in Nairobi selling antiques, cattle, cars etc. He soon realised that life in Africa took place outside the capital city. In an old Suzuki Jeep he made many lone safaris into the wilds. During his travels through Zaire, Rwanda and Western Tanzania he became fascinated with the primates and in particular he loved the chimpanzees and gorillas. It would have been about five years after he arrived in Kenya that he decided to set up a camp in Tanzania in a Chimpanzee National Park close to the Mahale Mountains which swept down to the eastern shores of the magnificent Lake Tanganyika.

The issues in achieving this plan were daunting to say the least. The first problem was getting to the isolated region. From Kigoma, close to the border with Burundi, he took the ancient German-built steamer, which plies its trade over the full length of Lake Tanganyika. He persuaded the skipper to make an unscheduled stop at Mahale where he and his provisions were dropped off into canoes to go ashore. This seemingly simple manoeuvre actually took two hours in darkness. After this experience Purcell had his own boat built and he hired a driver. After that he was able to make the 14-hour journey from Kigoma to Mahale on his own terms. Three years later he had to review the situation as he was not getting a viable number of visitors. He concluded that the unreliability of air travel between Dar es Salaam and Kigoma and the subsequent 14-hour boat trip were the reasons. So, the enterprising Roland Purcell built an airstrip just outside the park boundary, learned to fly and bought himself a six-seater Cessna 206 aeroplane. He could then advertise his safaris on the basis that clients could fly to Nairobi, from there to Bujumbura in Burundi to be collected by Roland in person to fly into Mahale. The operation was a great success. Being one of the few persons in that part of Africa with a viable aircraft allowed Purcell to earn extra income by flying people and cargo around the place. The only snag was that aviation fuel (Avgas) was in short supply and in Burundi it was very expensive. He needed to stockpile fuel at strategic points. That was the situation when he met Giles in Arusha and asked him if he was interested in a few months work "….driving my car around the bush." Giles accepted eagerly.

The first task that he was given was to transport six, 2,000 litre drums of Avgas from Arusha to Kigoma using Purcell's 4X4 Toyota Land Cruiser. The distance was 2,000 kilometres and was expected to take three days and on that basis a meeting on the airstrip at Kigoma was arranged. As Purcell took off with his provisions for the Mahale Mountains, Giles filled the drums and prepared to leave early the next morning. He left at first light along the Tanzanian 'highway', which more resembled a track over the Scottish Highlands. It was hot and dusty but Giles pressed on as fast as he could. After driving for 14 hours he tucked his Toyota into some bushes, had a snack and a warm beer and went to sleep. By the afternoon of the next day he realised that his journey was only going to take two days so he took some time out to relax.

He reached Kigoma three hours before his rendezvous with Roland which gave him time to look around the town. Kigoma is the end of the line for the railway from Dar es Salaam and it houses the jetty where the Lake Tanganyika steamer docks. It is a wealthy town but this is not displayed obviously as the trade is almost all black market. Gold from Zaire, gemstones from Zambia all find their way to Kigoma and onto the secret market; the local millionaires shipping their ill-gotten gains out of the country and away from any half-hearted investigations that the Tanzanian government might make. Giles drove out to the airstrip in time to hear the familiar whine of the Cessna's engines. Roland's face was wreathed in smiles when he saw that Giles and his precious cargo had arrived on schedule. Soon they were on their way into town to put the Avgas into storage, have some tea and buy a few provisions.

They returned to the aircraft loaded down with a drum of Avgas, some vegetables and beer to take the short flight to Roland's airstrip. From there it was a mere 45-minute boat trip to the beach side camp site. They arrived as the sun was setting to be welcomed by the vista of a fire and hurricane lamps twinkling in the tents. Giles then took a refreshing swim in the second largest fresh water lake in the world, Lake Tanganyika. Generally Roland would pick up his clients from Bujumbura in Burundi – they would stay for three nights and two days then he would fly them back and pick up the next group. This was the start to some of the most relaxing times that Giles had yet experienced in Africa. He even managed not to be rude to the American clients! He did not have much empathy with our transatlantic cousins as an extract from a letter demonstrates:

...there is a flying boat in East Africa, a Catalina built in 1934 and used during the Second World War for hunting submarines. A Frenchman, Pierre and his wife, Antoinette, bought the machine a few years ago with the idea of doing trans-African trips and East African safaris. The company is called 'Catalina Flying Boat Safaris'. The boat is positively beautiful and when she lands in the water she looks quite at home. She manoeuvres in the lake and comes up to the beach where she drops anchor. The doors open and out pour ghastly Americans, 20 of them at a time – a truly horrendous sight – nightmares are created from such visions!

The Catalina goes to marvellous places but the only people who seem to have the money and time to go on such trips seem to be elderly Americans. So, while I enjoyed the sight of such a beautiful bird landing, I would then run off into the forest until nightfall.

The Mahale National Park was set up about 20 years ago in order to provide the resident chimpanzee families with a safer habitat. A team of Japanese researchers have been studying one family for over 25 years. There is one camp which houses the Park Headquarters and the ranger's sleeping quarters; another for the Japanese researchers and then, to the south, is Roland's domain. This is set on a white sand beach with the thick forest rising behind it. Ramesey, the cook, supervises the meals and his cookhouse tent is set at the back of the beach. The client's tents are pitched along the edge of the beach. The boats are tied up in a corner and the main campaign tent – or dining shelter – is a little way back from the shore. The lake is clear providing a clean horizon – there is no land in sight. The water is excellent for diving – a habitat for multi-coloured fish of all shapes and sizes. The backup of thick, virgin forest is a haven for birds, butterflies, apes, bushbuck, forest hog and small cats. If there is a paradise on earth than this must surely be close to being the spot and Giles's favourite time for walking in the forest was in the late afternoon when the chimpanzees and other species were at their most active.

It took him about two weeks to fully recover from the effects of the malaria and noting this, Roland outlined a plan. He wanted to carry out a reconnaissance of the Katavi National Park which was 40 minutes flying time inland from Mahale. He wanted to land there and then take a good look around by car with Giles as the driver. He wanted to meet the warden and discuss making an airstrip. They flew back to Kigoma in the Cessna where Giles prepared the jeep and put a barrel of diesel fuel, food and beer in the back before he departed to Katavi.

The journey to Katavi was uneventful except that it was Giles's first experience of driving through tsetse fly country. These nasty little gnats are very irritating disease-carriers and get through every crevice into the cars and have a quite painful bite. He reached the village Sitalike ahead of schedule where he met up with Emallie the head warden of the park. He was surprised and pleased when Emallie told him that there was already an overgrown airstrip quite close to the headquarters. He supplied Giles with some of his rangers armed with pangas and spades and within three hours the strip was clear.

That night he camped by the side of Lake Katavi and it was an ornithologist's dream. The seasonal swamp was home to every imaginable bird: fish eagles, yellow-billed storks, open-billed storks, spoonbills, herons, goliaths, egrets, bitterns, ibis, jacanas, vultures, cranes, moorhens and many species of geese and ducks. There were literally hundreds of hippos and Cape buffalo. Giles made his radio call to Roland and settled in to enjoy the wildlife. To avoid the curious hippos he would toss his mattress onto the roof of the Toyota and sleep there!

At 11.30 a.m., Roland's aircraft appeared. He had brought his girl friend, Zoë, with him and they had barely time to greet each other before the villagers ran in from the other end of the strip accompanied by Emallie and some of his rangers. Emallie was pleased and impressed to hear about Roland's plans and gave him all the assistance he wanted by providing information prior to the reconnaissance by car. That night was spent at the same camp site.

The flight next day in the Cessna showed what great potential there was in the Katavi Park:

We rose at dawn, after a very noisy night provided by the hippos. We had tea and took off... we had the doors off so that I could lean out and take photographs. However, the slip stream was very strong so it was quite difficult... we flew over Lake Katavi and the swamp where we had camped. I looked down on thousands of hippos wallowing. From the air they looked like maggots on a festering corpse... flights of all kinds of birds rose up into the air below us and 200-300 strong herds of buffalo scattered as the noise of the Cessna scared them.

We flew over a huge expanse of open ground covered with seven-feet-high grass. Roland banked the plane and we headed straight for a group of elephants gorging themselves on the grass... we banked to the right passing even more elephants and then we saw a large black shape ahead of us; we soon realised that it was a massive herd of buffalo. It is no exaggeration to say that there must have been 2,000 or 3,000 head. We flew low alongside the herd and my camera was on auto-drive. We went on to Lake Chada following the river that flowed out of the great swamp... it was full of crocodiles – these were the beasts that caught my eye – I was awestruck by them... Lake Chada was slightly drier than Katavi so the hippos were more confined but they still looked like maggots from the air. In fact it was like some ancient primeval or prehistoric scene: wallowing masses of herbivore flesh with groups of evil satanic carnivorous reptiles waiting in the sun. It was such a strong image that it is still with me today... over the forest and we saw still more elephants... when we landed and I stepped out, I felt very wind-blown and also as if I had been to the cinema – like a type of shell shock but a feeling I was very happy with.

Roland decided that Lake Chada was going to be the place for his camp in the Katavi National Park and work soon went ahead with the project. Years later, and by then the wife of Roland Purcell, Zoë was to make some fond recollections about Giles:

"Giles, apart from being a wild and wonderful friend, was with us on some key safaris, not least when we started opening up Katavi National Park in western Tanzania and founded Chada Camp, a fantastic safari camp in a million acres of bush that nobody ever visited.

"I can still see him standing in his ragged trousers on top of our beaten-up Land Rover, surrounded by the wilderness and masses of animals. He was pointing us in the right direction as we landed our little bush plane there for the first time. He'd brought the car in; 800 kilometres across Tanzania so that we could explore on the ground. On that safari we had to wash in a river while the other person stood above you with a panga poised, it was so full of crocodiles. He utterly thrived on the adventure the African bush laid out for him – the dust, the risk, the roughness and the physicality.

"He hated it when I tried to make things more comfortable on safari. Sometimes, much to his disgust, I'd bring along a few blankets, or, the ultimate sin, extra food – any time spent at base trying to organise a safari properly was time wasted to Giles, and having more than a carrot and a piece of old biltong that he'd produce from his sock just spoiled things. What he loved more than anything was what came to be known as a "proot safari" where you basically went into the bush with nothing, and just tried to get as mucky and hungry and generally messed up as possible. Ultimately a safari with Giles was a total liberation.

"I loved Giles as a friend and co-conspirator in a time in East Africa which, in a way, defined us all. It was extreme, irresponsible, free, fun and wild. We made a terrible fuss of him when he died. In a way, he came to symbolise the passing of that amazing last gasp of youth, and he became a sort of icon to a small bunch of us, which, in some ways, would have utterly appalled him."

Giles was still planning on completing his journey to South Africa whenever he finished working with Roland. However, unknown to him, in Kenya, the fates were conspiring to delay his departure once more. The beginning of a letter to Brian and Verity, written in January 1993 explains this:

Dear Mum and Dad,

When I was still in Tanzania, working with Roland and driving round the Serengeti with tourists bouncing about in the back, a Mr. Alan Root, met Michael Dyer and Andy Roberts at Wilson Airport in Nairobi. Alan Root got onto the subject of Zaire and his need to find someone to work with animals and live in the forest. They both put my name forward. "But, where is he?" Root asked. They hadn't a clue, but at that moment who should come round the corner but Roland. He had just flown in with some clients from the Serengeti. Of course he knew my whereabouts and gave Alan the radio frequency on which we talked every evening. That evening Alan called me up on the radio and explained the job over the airways. I accepted immediately, "What a place to go! When do we start?" "In 12 days time. Be in Nairobi for a briefing."

So much for my plan to leave Kenya and head off to South Africa. Instead I found myself moving north from Tanzania to Nairobi.

Chapter XI

In The Rain Forest For Alan Root

Alan Root, to whom Giles was about to be introduced, was already a legend in Africa. He had moved from London to Kenya with his parents when he was very young and had worked as a trapper, a guide and a light aircraft pilot before settling on a career filming wildlife. In the mid-1970s he had brought the first hot air balloons into Kenya after he had recognized the fact that light aircraft were too fast for good filming and helicopters were too noisy. He taught himself how to fly the balloons and, with his first wife, Joan, had soon produced some stunning films. Sometimes, to the disapproval of purists, he used tame animals in his films but his argument that this allowed him to capture animal behaviour in the greatest of detail is indisputable. Despite his occasional use of tame animals, much of Alan Root's work was carried out under dangerous conditions: he had suffered severe leg injuries during an underwater attack by a hippo; had been bitten by a leopard and a gorilla and been stricken by malaria and river blindness. He had also lost his right hand index finger due to it being bitten whilst he was handling a puff-adder.

Giles headed north on his motorcycle and made his rendezvous with Alan Root for breakfast in Nairobi during late September of 1992. Root accepted him almost on the spot and years later, when asked why he had taken on an inexperienced man like Giles, he replied:

"It may sound a little pompous but I was looking for another, younger Alan Root. I did not need experience – all the Mbuti pygmies had all the experience I needed to locate and trap the animals – they had done it for years but, of course, they were hunting for the cooking pot. I had been in and out of the area for about seven years and I was very tired. I'd had malaria and river blindness and all sorts of other bush diseases and apart from all my other commitments – I was, as I said, just very tired. Giles was immediately likeable – his humour was infectious. But what a man! When I first met him we arranged to meet again on a particular day but I had to cancel it for some reason and when we met I told him that I was delaying for four days. He said, "It's going to be hot and very wet down where we're going isn't it?" I replied that it certainly would be and he responded by saying: "In that case I'm going off somewhere hot and dry for a couple of days." Damn me if he didn't go off to Lake Stephanie – that's a hell of a journey – one which you'd normally spend a few days preparing for as it's God knows how many miles away. But he just chugged off on his bike – just like that.

"I know something about the hazards of solo motorcycling. I remember when I was travelling alone on my bike and I crashed into the bottom of a dry river bed. The machine fell on top of me and I was trapped and helpless. Fortunately there were no hot parts of the engine close to my skin but I just did not have the physical strength to lift the machine. I was well and truly stuck. I remembered that I had passed a chap on the track about 10 minutes before the crash, so I waited helplessly and hopefully. He eventually did reach me and he was blind drunk! He said, "Hey, Mzungu, why are you lying there?"

"I'm trapped under my bike. Please help me."

"Why you trapped under there?"

"And so it went on with me getting more and more frustrated but he eventually got the message and gave me a hand. If he had not come along there's no way of telling how long I'd have been there.

"Another time I was in a similar predicament but I was upright. The bike had overbalanced and again I didn't have the strength to right it. This time I was in water and in the pannier bags was all the film footage that I had spent a very long time getting. Up the river bank came three women who had obviously never seen a white man before. They were just pointing and giggling and it took me a long time to persuade one of them (the biggest) to come and lend me her muscles."

At the second meeting and refreshed from his lonely sojourn in the sun at Lake Stephanie, Giles learned that the plan was for him to travel with Root to Epulu (Zaire) and be briefed on the rare species that were required for filming. The pair were flown by Charlie Trout whose plane was carrying spare parts to repair Root's aircraft. Root had crashed at Epulu three months earlier. He had landed in long, wet grass which had snagged a wing tip and slewed the plane around damaging both the wing tip and tail edge. The crashed aircraft was still blocking the Epulu airstrip so they made their landfall at Mambasa, a Protestant Mission about an hour-and-a-half's drive from Epulu. Giles found the airborne journey to Mambasa fascinating – the flight plan took them across Lake Victoria and Kampala and then on over the Ruwanzori Mountains and Lake Albert. It was his first view of the massive Zairian rain forest from the air and the sheer vastness of the horizon to horizon carpet of trees criss-crossed by rivers was staggering and he began to get a notion of the scale of the work he was about to undertake.

They were met at Mambasa by Leo, an American employed by Root, and without ceremony they quickly unloaded their cargo and set off for Epulu in Leo's Land Rover. Along the drive Giles remembered his earlier motorcycle ride through Zaire; the screaming children and staring people; the chickens, pigs and goats all over the road. Nothing much had changed. There were still lorries broken down along the verges with various engine parts spread out as the hapless drivers tried to figure out how to reassemble them. They pulled in to Epulu at nightfall to find that Leo had organised food and beds. The travellers were tired and after a few beers and tall stories they went to bed. Giles was the first up in the morning and went to explore his new base. There were a number of pens housing various bird species and the Epulu River was only a few metres from their concrete, tin-roofed house which was dry and clean. Giles reflected that this was a perfect situation – what more could he ask for?

Root introduced him to the livestock and explained what had to be done with each of the species. All the birds were very tame and could be hand-fed. One of the priorities was to find a male Hornbill as a mate for the female in one of the pens. Then Giles's staff arrived and he spent a little time getting to know them. Two girls: Vomie, the cook and Ailsa, the cleaner were joined by Roger and Michelle, the pair who would be responsible for cleaning the pens and feeding the stock. Kango was delegated as Giles's personal manservant whilst Seko would be the night watchman. Tsabane, a Mbuti pygmy, would collect forest fruit and termite nests for the birds to eat and finally there was Bamanane who collected locusts for the birds. Giles thought that they were a fine looking crew who would serve him well in Zaire.

Then it was time to go to the airstrip and take a look at Root's little Cessna 185. The three months had taken their toll and it was a sad sight. It had turned green with algae and looked to all intents and purposes as though it had been there for years. Charlie Trout set about the two-day task of repairing the sorry little plane, taking off the damaged parts and replacing them with the second-hand bits that had been purchased in Nairobi. Giles helped for the first day but then he was taken on a mini-tour by Root to meet other local expatriates and various officials. Carl and Rosie Ruff were a Swiss-Dutch couple responsible for running an Okapi capture operation funded by a wealthy American. Teresa and John Hart, who had been running a project in Epulu for 20 years, were not there at the time but Giles met their assistants, Ken and Erica, who were to become great friends. The two other whites at the Okapi station were Steve, from Seattle (a zoo-keeper) and Karen, a Swedish veterinary trainee. Epulu is a small town that sits in the centre of the vast Ituri Reserve. The township is entirely surrounded by thousands of kilometres of rain forest.

The next day Root's still green aircraft was pronounced ready for the flight to Nairobi. Charlie Trout was to fly his own aircraft back to Nairobi and Leo was to drive to Rutchuru to meet up with Root's cameraman who was coming in to film the gorillas. Root handed a fistful of dollars to Giles to tide him through until December and then climbed into his plane. Everyone held their breath as he charged up the runway and became airborne. Giles saw another side of Alan Root – after it had been sitting on the runway for three months he would have expected Root to handle the craft gingerly. No such thing! He banked steeply and buzzed the spectators before hauling back on the stick to clear the trees. Leo and Charlie departed for Mambasa which would then leave Leo facing a four-day drive to Rutchuru after dropping Charlie at his aircraft. All of a sudden Giles felt extremely lonely so he decided to start up his motorcycle and take a little tour as he thought things through. His basic task was to trap certain rare or at least very elusive species of animals, put them in pens and then get them used to being handled by humans. He reviewed the daunting list:

*   Palm-nut Vulture
*   Yellow-backed Duiker (baby)
*   Water Chevrotain (baby)

* Pygmy Antelope (baby)
* Flying Squirrel
* Giant Otter Shrew
* Aquatic Genet
* Gaboon Viper
* Rhino Viper
* Anything else that Giles might deem to be of interest

With the exception of the two vipers the animals listed have a common factor – they are all extremely shy, well-camouflaged and very, very difficult to trap. Giles had a quite daunting challenge.

So, with this impressive and difficult target list, Giles set about his planning. He confidently assumed that he would be successful and hired some local men to construct pens for each of the animals on his list. He enlisted the aid of Claude, a Zaireois recommended by Ken and Erica, to help him to find suitable Mbuti pygmies from the local tribes to assist with the trapping. Giles set about getting to know the animals that were already under his care. The Palm-nut Vulture was stand-offish and would require some work before he would accept hand feeding. The Black Casqued Hornbill was tame and Giles named her 'Fiona'; the Vulture was 'Affie'; the duck, 'Matilda', was incredibly fat and happily entered the house from time to time looking for scraps.

Vomie was given two sacks; one of rice and one of beans and told that these would constitute lunch and dinner for the foreseeable future. The house looked out over the River Epulu. There were lots of Monitor Lizards and a few crocodiles to keep Giles alert as he made his morning and evening ablutions. The intense forest sounds and the music of the water cascading over the rocks acted as efficient lullabies that quickly put the listener into a deep sleep at night. The evening deluges of rain usually presaged a pleasant night temperature. The mornings invariably brought the most beautiful sunrises which never failed to give Giles great delight.

Giles began to learn a little about the Mbuti Pygmies. They are a most unusual race and can be quite frustrating to work with. They tend not to take anything in life very seriously – the only things that really matter to them are honey, meat, beer, marijuana and the wind, but more of this later. These five items are so important to them that the rest of life goes by in a blur. They laugh and giggle at everything. They are completely content within their own communities and enjoy their tightly held traditions. If a plan is made to hunt the following day it means nothing if they decide at the moment of departure that it is better to stay home that day or have a honey hunt instead. There are basically three classes of Mbuti Pygmy. Some have established themselves close to the roads where they live in mud huts and work in the fields, grind grain and collect wood for the villagers. Others live about one kilometre into the forest – they will cut trees, plant and harvest crops and are generally more independent than the road dwellers. They will penetrate deeper into the forest on hunting trips. Lastly there are the Mbuti pygmies with whom Giles was to work mostly. They live five to 20 kilometres into the forest. Some will have their own *shambas* growing crops for their own consumption but many are more nomadic moving through a circuit of village sites where everything is fashioned from whatever materials the forest provides. They carry their essentials (cooking pots, *pangas* and knives) with them as they move around. They can vacate a village site at great speed once they decide to move.

The latter are the most traditionally minded Pygmies whose only contact with the outside world is through the likes of Giles. Mostly they will be entirely naked and will not bother even to visit the exterior. The tallest are about four -and-a-half feet in height and they do much of their hunting with nets. Each net is about five feet high and can be as much as 30 yards long. They will string out the nets and then drive the game towards them. These were the forest folk with whom Giles developed a great affinity and they taught him a lot about animal ways and helped him to develop his own tracking skills. Giles was to find that there were many drawbacks to using the Mbuti. They were addicted to their marijuana but this was nowhere near as debilitating as the effects of a good *pombe* session[12]. Marijuana has uses other than as a personal narcotic with the Mbuti. They tend to smoke it using pipes – passing the pipe around the circle as

---

12 *Pombe: A highly alcoholic concoction brewed from distilled grain which is popular throughout Africa but the small stature of the Mbuti makes them particularly prone to rapid drunkenness with prolonged hangovers.*

they sit – even the small children are included in this pastime. If they are using dogs to hunt then before they start they will blow their smoke into the dog's nostrils which makes the animal calm and relaxed. Another problem with the Mbuti was that they had little understanding of Giles's need to capture animals alive. Surely they were provided by *Mungu* (God) for food.

Giles and Claude toured many of the Mbuti villages with Root's list of requirements. There was considerable excitement at the fact that there seemed to be easy money on offer but Giles made it quite clear that only the species that he sought, (young and in good condition), would be paid for. He was encouraged by how many of the villages appeared to know of nesting spots for the kingfishers and hornbills and he quickly located 20 sites where he spent many hours watching and building hides from which the cameraman could work. Only four of the sites were active at the time but this should be sufficient provided that Root arrived in time. The kingfishers which Root wanted to film were unusual birds in that they hollowed out termite nests which hung from the trees and built their own nests inside. The male bird would then seal in the female with mud leaving just a small hole through which he could pass food and she could clear out the debris from herself and her chicks. The female stays inside the nest for three to four months during which time she moults all her feathers, lays the eggs and rears the chicks. The male has to feed her throughout and when the chicks are hungry he has a mammoth work load.

So, Giles had two active kingfisher and two active hornbill nests when he spoke to Alan Root on his scheduled evening radio call. He asked Root when he would be coming to film the nests and was told that it would not be for three weeks as he was still busy with the gorillas in the Verungas. Giles pointed out that the birds would soon be flying the nests but Root simply said that he would have to take his chances. Consequently none of the nests were filmed despite the careful work that had gone into building the hides for the cameramen. The last kingfisher flew the coop the day before Root arrived. Giles then threw himself into a massive campaign with the Mbuti as he tried to persuade them to upgrade their efforts to capture the other animals on his list. Occasionally they would try to fool him like the time when they produced a 20-centimetre-high Pygmy Antelope telling him that it was a 'baby' – the long horns and large testicles gave the lie to this and Giles was able to demonstrate that he was not an ignorant foreigner who would easily part with his dollars. One of Giles's letters home shows that he was beginning to feel a little isolated and despondent:

The first weeks had passed without finding any of the animals despite a great deal of walking in the forest checking nets. I became a bit sceptical and my mind was turning negative. What am I doing here? Can I really live here and do this? Am I mad? Life is too short to stay here like this; I prefer the open savannahs – not this mind-warping forest. It was a kind of shock. I reckon now that I must have been going through a cold-turkey stage, with no social life. It did, however, last for a few days and I was beginning to feel that the job was not for me. Then I began to see more clearly the experience which I was gaining in this tropical rain forest and I told myself that it was a simple challenge to see whether I could stick it out until Christmas.

Then, one evening when I was supping a beer at Ken and Erica's place, Abebu, one of the Pygmies, came running in saying that he had caught a baby 'Lendo'. Now none of us knew what a 'Lendo' was. So I hoped it was something important and went off with Abebu to have a look. It was a duiker, but large, about 24 centimetres high with baby milk teeth. It was not on my shopping list but I took it all the same.

Here was my first animal, which I had to look after and I racked my brain to decide what I had to do. I stuck it in a box, covered it and put it in a quiet place for a few hours. I spoke to Root on the radio and asked for advice and whether he wanted me to keep it. 'Lendo' is a bay duiker and grows to be about two feet tall. We decided to keep him and rear him in order to provide me with practice for when the important duikers, which we wanted, came along. I chose 'Ivan' as the name because the Pygmy name of 'Lendo' resembled 'Lendl', the tennis player. Also his colouring was similar to that of a Russian winter hat. Ivan Lendo took to the milk bottle very quickly and did not mind being pampered. However, I do remember his first two nights as being very active – he is nocturnal. He crashed around the house trying to find a way out. Root had informed me that any new animal had to be kept in the house for maximum human contact so all the beautiful pens I had made were not required. Never mind. From then on the house began to fill up.

The days in Epulu became a more routine affair. Giles would give Ivan his morning feed and then rush off to the Pygmy camps with fresh fish and crabs to use as bait for the traps which they had set for the Aquatic Genet and the

Otter Shrew – he would walk with a different group every day to ensure that the traps were being properly baited and that the Pygmies were not eating the food themselves. The traps would be moved every five or six days. Back to the house to feed Ivan at 11.00 a.m., and then perhaps a dog hunt which had to be short in order to get back to give Ivan his second meal in the late afternoon. Each night included a period of handling and talking to the various animals.

They had to be given maximum human attention, talking, stroking, feeding by hand, letting them crawl all over you, lick you, bite you – what a beautiful job it would have been for a real animal lover! Me? I'm afraid that I regarded all these animals through the eyes of a farmer: "OK. Get more food into them – OK. Better give this chap another five minutes petting – OK. Who's next for a bit of attention?"

The next animal to arrive at the house was a wife for Rambo, the bush baby, who bounced around the place in the evenings and was a great entertainer. She had to be kept in a cage otherwise she would have taken off back to the forest. Rambo was let into the cage each evening to help her eat her food of mealy worms, locusts, grasshoppers and moths after which he would be let out for some high speed cruising around the house before scampering off through the tailor-made little door to his pen. Giles was very attracted to the little Bush Babies – they are sweet little beasts, extremely agile and can leap three to four metres with great accuracy despite being only about 10 centimetres tall.

Over the next few weeks the animals continued to arrive: two varieties of flying squirrels were caged and fed on avocados and bananas. A potto came along! This is a remarkable little animal probably related to the South American sloth. It has big nocturnal eyes and hugely strong hands and arms and is only about six inches long. He took up residence in the aviary. Woodland kingfisher chicks were brought in adding to the daily burden for Giles – they had to be fed six times a day with tiny pieces of crab meat, fish and insects. They became very tame and were soon flying around and landing their metallic blue bodies on his head and shoulders. Simon, the white-bellied duiker came to stay and became tame very quickly.

Giles was constantly being offered snakes but he took only the very large ones. The snake pit began to fill up with gaboon vipers, five feet long, as thick as a man's thigh with heads that were as broad as a hand. The smaller rhino vipers had incredible colour markings, were about three feet long and as thick as Giles's arm. The snake pit was accounting now for at least five mice every day. Water snakes were kept in a pool and Giles was surprised how quickly they adapted to being handled by man and stopped biting with their sharp little teeth.

Alan Root visited Epulu in November and some good footage was taken of the palm-nut vulture feeding before they set off to find a location from which to film the wild flying squirrels. Giles's Pygmies took them to a good site where there was a hollow tree. One of the Pygmies hit the tree a few times and sure enough a squirrel came out of a hole, climbed higher into the tree and launched itself into a glide path that took it about 50 metres into another tree whereupon it repeated the process. Sadly when they returned with the cameras the next day – the squirrel had vacated the hollow tree so Alan had to return to Kenya without footage.

Giles's house was by now a veritable menagerie. Two chevrotains had joined the zoo. These shy, nocturnal creatures are members of the antelope family – they grow to only about six inches in maturity and love water. They will invariably feed along the river banks and have many of the mannerisms of a pig. They have a snort-like call, trotters and they root in the ground with their powerful little snouts. The usual method of escape from predators is to jump into the river and either swim away or walk along the bottom. One of the pair was very young, still on milk and Giles had every hope of being able to tame it.

It was not uncommon to see Giles with an owl on his shoulder cooing in ecstasy as he scratched its head. It had arrived as a chick and been hand fed on pieces of mouse. Giant squirrels were bounding around the place and Giles had taken to keeping the largest of the gaboon vipers in his house even though he thought it to be the most evil looking of all his charges. Gerald Durell would have been envious indeed of the surroundings at Epulu! As Giles took stock, he realised that he had done rather well: he now needed to catch two more types of duiker, the elusive aquatic genet and a giant otter shrew. The latter is an interesting species. It is a member of the otter family that is only about six inches long and it lives on crabs, small fish and insect larvae. Spending most of its time in small forest streams it had eluded all the traps that had been set for it so far.

Giles thought that he understood the rarity of the aquatic genet when he tried to describe it to the Pygmies. The animal had never before been seen alive by any zoologist. The Pygmies, even after looking at pictures of the animal, declared that they did not know it. It was not until Giles talked about the fact that it lived in and around rivers and ate fish that they seemed to understand what he was talking about and they excitedly proclaimed this to be the 'Apokekeke'. They were offered a reward of $100 for the successful trapping of a very young one. One fine afternoon Giles was beside himself with excitement when a Pygmy ran into the camp shouting "Apokekeke – I have caught one!" Giles's heart was pounding as he made the half-hour cycle ride followed by an hour-long walk to the trap. His disappointment was severe as he surveyed the large chestnut body of a marsh mongoose peering at him in indignation from the confines of the trap. His disappointment, however, was not as great as that of the Pygmies when they discovered that there was to be no reward! Giles explained the differences with the aid of some pictures and at that moment he found out that 'Apokekeke' was the Pygmy name given to several animals of the mongoose family. He was beginning to believe that the aquatic genet did not exist.

Giles had an innate sense of honour initially instilled in him by the values of a close and loving family and furthered by the philosophies of Gordonstoun School; this sense developed to an even higher degree through the warmness he felt for Africa and its varied peoples. One of his principles was "a fair day's work for a fair day's pay". Corruption was anathema to him even though it was a way of life in some parts of Africa. He had grown fond of Epulu and its inhabitants in a quite short space of time and he often reflected on the uncertain future of the township. Sometimes his feelings spilled over into his diaries in an uncompromising fashion:

So, this is Zaire. Not a country known for its economic prosperity, stability, high standard of living or value for human life. In fact it is so fucking backward that it is quite pathetic. President Mobutu, who has many titles and self-given names, such as "The Cockerel who leaves no hen uncovered", causes much of the problem. He runs the country as if it were his own private company, creaming off a very large percentage of all active businesses and 100% of State owned companies. He never invests any of these taxes for the benefit of the country. Thus Zaire is accelerating in reverse and the speed is increasing each year that goes by. Rot and decay are everywhere. The towns, villages, roads and ports are all a shambles and the country is virtually bankrupt. A very sad state of affairs. The only ray of hope lies in the elected Prime Minister and Mobutu's archenemy. Zaire is now in the grip of monthly looting of all shops and the private houses of expatriates or Zaireois. Mobutu's army is not paid. Thus at the end of each month the soldiers go on looting sprees, followed up by the rest of the dispossessed people. After the first four looting sessions the shops closed down and no longer exist. There are secret vendors working from their homes, but shops – no way. All the shabby Greek, Indian and Lebanese traders have gone. So what will the army go for next? All the expatriates have left Kinshasa and Kisangani. There are missionaries out in the middle of nowhere and there is Epulu with its white population doing research and similar projects. How long will it be before the golden egg in the forest is grabbed and scrambled? I will be leaving in a month's time. I wonder if I will be here to see, at first hand, the fall of Epulu. Hopefully I will just hear about it on the radio one day when I am skiing in France.

There were also more local problems for Giles to contend with:

I have a problem with one of my employees, a Pygmy called Tshabane. His only job involves collecting leaves from a certain tree every evening ready for my squirrels to eat. He also collects forest fruits for the duikers. However, Tshabane, like every Pygmy, has a deep and unrepentant love of 'pombe', a 90% alcohol concoction made from maize. When they drink the stuff, they consume at least a litre each and behave like two-year-old children for at least 12 hours. They become totally incapable of doing anything. His communication has gone, his co-ordination is deeply disturbed and he can only walk when assisted. Anyway, I do not know why I have not sacked him. Probably because he only goes on a binge once a month and it is better to have a boozer you know than one you don't.

Throwing a party is high on the agenda in the Pygmy way of life. When the moon is gaining in size and into its final swelling to the full – that signifies 10 days of parties. There are celebrations for newborn babies, marriage, hunting successes, new houses and almost anything that you can think of. It is just a good excuse to get out the drums, dance, shout, sing, scream and drink *pombe*. The really big ceremonies are for the discovery of a new source of honey, for death and for circumcision.

The Pygmies do not fear much in life but, there is one dread that is so deep that they react most strongly to it – wind – wind that makes the big trees fall over, causes branches to break off and crash to the ground. Just before the big rain storms hit, wind comes roaring into the forest, the strength is dependent on the size of the storm. Most winds in Zaire are ferocious and though those prior to the rainstorms last only five to 10 minutes – they are very, very powerful. Then the winds drop and the rain begins – in a tropical storm rainfall is measured in many inches per storm. The Pygmies live in a world of trees. The products of the trees support their life. They provide building materials, fuel for the fires and fruits and succour for the animals they eat. The trees surround them in the most literal sense but – the trees can also bring death as Giles was to witness:

The hazards are great. One of the first things they do when arriving at a new campsite is to cut down all the trees that are within threatening distance. They never walk in the forest or on the road when there is a storm coming. Around Epulu the rain arrives every evening between 4.00 and 6.00 p.m., and the Pygmies make sure that they are at home or at another camp before storm time. When I first heard about this fear of the wind, I thought it all rather comical, like 'Asterix' and 'Obelix' thinking the sky was going to fall on their heads. Come December, it all became too real.

One morning I set off on my bike for a roadside village called Saliety, about 20 kilometres from Epulu. On my arrival there was not a Pygmy to be seen. I found a villager, looking very glum and I asked him where all the Mbuti were. He explained that there had been a 'disaster of great proportion'. He explained that a tree had fallen right on top of a Pygmy camp killing several of them and causing other horrific injuries. I hurried off along a footpath, about a two kilometre walk to the camp. I passed many Pygmies with white body paint on their faces and they hardly greeted me. I don't think they were pleased to see a white man coming to such a scene of devastation.

The camp was unrecognisable. An enormous tree had come down and its top branches had embedded themselves into the heart of the living quarters. There was much weeping and wailing going on. I recognised the chief from another camp and went over to talk to him. He told me that seven had died and then he showed me the injured. I wish that he had not. There was a broken arm with the bone protruding above the elbow; a chap with his cranium split open but he seemed to be alive; a broken shoulder blade; a broken pelvis and leg and others in a real mess. The camp had been full of people sheltering from the storm. I explained that I could get a car and we could take all these people to the hospital.

I was thinking of the Mission Hospital at Yakunde, some three hours away. Everyone refused. They would not go into the white man's world of medicine. I concluded that it was me that they did not trust, as I was new to the scene. I ran back to my bike and roared back to Epulu where I went to John Hart's place. I explained what the scene was at Saliety and off he went in his car to help. I later found out that he managed to get some of them to Epulu, but local Pygmies and relatives promptly whisked them off to their camps where local remedies and techniques were administered. I never inquired about the outcome, but sadly I have not seen their faces again. On the other hand they could have been taken deep into the forest to camps of which I was not aware.

Whatever the feelings of the Mbuti were about Giles's appearance at the scene of the tragedy – they were not antagonistic as they demonstrated a few days later:

Yesterday the Pygmies took me to an impressive spectacle. It was truly one of my favourite experiences of the forest so far. We walked for about three and a half hours from the road near Bandisende, which is 30 kilometres east of Epulu. We walked south towards the Ituru River. We eventually came to a clearing where elephants had churned up the earth. There was fresh dung, tusk marks and footpad prints. We moved off into a thicket and settled down one row of trees away from the clearing.

Over the next two and a half hours we watched colobus, red-tailed and mangabey monkeys coming down to the ground and eating the soil by the handful. I asked my companions why but only got a shrug of the shoulders. I can only assume that they were after the mineral deposits but the soil was red clay and there was no taste of salt. Then, just as we were about to leave, two elephants came into the clearing. They had arrived in complete silence, we had not heard a sound and even the Pygmies had not been aware of their approach.

They were young, with small, dead straight tusks about a foot long. We concluded that they were males. These two lads began lifting the clay to their mouths in their trunks, happily scoffing whatever it was that nature provided and, thankfully, completely oblivious of our presence. I looked for a climbable tree in case of attack but there were none. There was no escape. The elephants plodded around smelling the ground and tasting the earth from time to time. They stayed for about half an hour and then moved off. We smiled and whispered to each other, my heart was still racing and we backed off towards the path. Then the Pygmies broke into rapid chatter and enthusiasm. They asked me for a gun and bullets. Oh dear! They really wanted that ivory. Then they all began to laugh at my expression and trotted off up the path. It made me think that there might be a villager offering large sums of money for ivory. I still wonder about it but I kept my mouth shut. As I walked back, I kept replaying the scene of the monkeys and the elephants in my mind. I realised how fortunate I had been to witness such a spectacle.

What a day yesterday was! A fantastic, marvellous, extremely lucky thing happened. YES! I caught Osbornictis, the elusive aquatic genet! I have caught the first ever live one and now the only one in captivity in the world. I am now the 'All knowledgeable Osbornictis professor". A feeling of the greatest elation is upon me!

This is the story: the day before yesterday, I was walking in the forest with my trappers to inspect the freshly moved traps. I have always checked the traps whenever they are moved. On the way to the area where they were, we passed a very dark Mbao forest. The canopy was so dense that very little light fell on the forest floor. There was a small sand and shingle stream running through the trees and I remarked to my chaps that I had a very positive feeling about this stream.

Anyway, we went on to the larger river where it was more open and sunlit and we checked the traps. I decided that we should pick up two of them and go back to the small stream in the dark forest that seemed as if you were in a great cathedral with the lights turned off. We found some suspect footprints and set one trap and then walked on to site the second trap near a deep pool. I then returned to the bike and drove off to Epulu. The next morning I returned to the village with fresh fish for the traps and found big smiles on everyone's faces. "Apokekeke" they cried. I quietened everyone down and then went into the hut where the trap had been taken. I lifted up one edge of the sack that was covering the trap expecting to see yet another mongoose peering at me. But no! There were the big nocturnal eyes, white face markings, big whiskers, a chestnut coloured body and a black bushy tail. "Oh my goodness, we have Osbornictis!" The one animal that Root had really wanted me to catch. "We've got the bugger!" I wrapped up the trap in sacks and set off for Epulu. I put him into his new home and waited until nightfall before feeding him.

104

I placed a big washing bowl of water with four fish in it in front of him. By 8.00 p.m., he had scoffed the lot. He seemed very relaxed, not too timid and certainly not stressed out. Telling Root the news on the radio that night was excellent. He whooped and whooped – he could hardly believe it. What a break through in trapping history that is. Now we have to film him doing his stuff under water. The tamer we can make him the better.

Today Root said he wants more, so I guess we put more traps out in that area. Maybe we can catch a mate for our chap. I have not yet dared to pick him up, hoping that he will begin to feel at home and settle down. Then I'll have to grab the 'critter' and check out the underside department to make sure of the sex. But wow! Who cares – we've got one. Yippee!

I have deduced that Osbornictis is a female, so she is now called Dorothy or Dot. She is very calm and watches me put the fish in the bowl every evening. She does not seem the least bit worried if I stay and watch her eating. She positions herself by the edge of the bowl peering into the water and watching the fish swim around. Then she lunges with her head, which goes under the water, and she grabs the fish with her needle-sharp teeth. What a silent and agile lady she is. She never makes a sound apart from the splash of the water as she grabs the fish.

After this very successful introduction into trapping and taming Giles took a long break during which he visited Europe before returning to Tanzania to combine work with exploration. In August 1993 he returned to Alan Root's employ again to begin yet another hunt for an elusive endangered species.

Chapter XII

Napoleon And Josephine: The Congolese Peafowl

On 7th August, 1993, Alan Root and Giles departed Wilson Airport and flew to Goma in Zaire. Giles's thoughts were drawn back to his collision with the pedestrian three years earlier. As soon as they disembarked they were surrounded by the usual razzmatazz of human vultures demanding urgent attention to 'serious problems'. Alan calmly took care of the necessary cash distribution and sent the various 'officials' back to their squalid offices.

The plan was to buy two motorcycles, take them to the Maiko National Park and put Alan's project into action. He wanted to locate, trap and then film the Congo Peacock which had not been seen since 1950 – he knew that it would not be easy to find the bird. The Congo Peacock (*Afropavo congensis*) was not known to science until it was discovered in 1936 in central Congo. It was a sensational discovery; not just because of its probable Asiatic affinities, but also that such a striking bird had eluded ornithologists for such a long time. Subsequent expeditions failed to find it. The species is said to show an historic link between both peafowl and guinea fowl. Rumour had it that the peacock was likely to be in the area of Loya.

The plan had to be altered almost immediately. Goma had been reduced to a virtual ghost town as a result of the incessant looting by the soldiers. Alan's friends all seemed to be off on holidays or business and so they had to go to Epulu and rent a couple of machines from the WWF. Then the decision was made that Giles would ride one of the bikes to Opienge, hire some local workers to repair the existing airstrip and Alan would fly in with the second bike and all the necessary stores before they both then continued the journey to Loya.

The journey to Opienge was difficult but Giles travelled light and made it to his first night stop at Km232 without incident. Here he met the local missionary, Jean Pierre Albert, who filled him with rice and beans whilst he delighted in recounting the difficulties of the next leg of the journey to Opienge. Giles spent an uncomfortable night on the four-feet-long bamboo bed in the Mission. After receiving instructions from Jean Pierre to look up the 76-year-old priest, Père Leon Mondri, in Opienge, he set off at first light:

The path Jean Pierre described sounded like a nightmare of mud – it was! It was overgrown with trees and thick bush, fallen trees, river crossings and bridges consisting of tree trunks. As I turned off onto the track I was soon into undergrowth that clung to me and the bike. There was a lot of mud and some outrageous bridges. Some were 15 to 20 feet across with just a single log. Good balance was required. The worst thing was the bamboo which shut out all the daylight. Where it had rotted it fell across the path and I had to drag the bike, lying on its side beneath the fallen bamboo. I had to pull it under the fallen trees. Some stretches, which were in good shape, let me drive in second gear, smiling, for at least 30 seconds, before having to dismount and haul the bike under or over some other obstacle. The worst thing was the ants that lived in, or were crossing, the barriers at the time – they delivered a nasty bite and left me itching all over.

I watched the kilometres click up on the tachometer and I was pleased. The bridges were most entertaining. Some had two or three tree trunks across so I was able walk on one while balancing the bike on another. Then there were those with single trunks, where I decided to go for it and ride across whilst being thankful that I have long legs. One bridge foxed me completely. It was constructed of narrow branches of small diameter and it hung down in a curve. There was no way I could wheel the bike over it. I unloaded it and carried everything across the water and I was about to dismantle the bike itself when three chaps pushing bicycles appeared. They literally carried my machine across. I paid them in soap and salt and they were very happy. It seemed that they collected soap, salt and other merchandise from the trucks which pass through Km232 on their way to Kisangani. They then loaded up their bicycles and pushed them all the way back to Opienge (110 Kilometres). The weight of those bikes is immense! I was chuffed – I was over half way there. But I was getting too cocky.

BANG! A searing pain struck my left foot and the bike slewed to the left, pulled by an unseen force as I fell into the undergrowth. The action was quick and violent even though I had been travelling slowly. My foot throbbed but I could move my toes and there was no immediate sign of blood. God it was painful. I got off and lifted the bike. The gear change lever was bent double. The accident seemed to have been caused by a log hidden in the undergrowth at just the right height to trap my foot between the lever and the log. By the mercy of God the log had been sufficiently rotted to break under the impact otherwise I would have had a shattered foot. My footwear was just a pair of Bata 'tackies' which gave no protection. I managed to bend the gear lever back into some semblance of its former shape cursing as I did so and the pain did begin to ease a little.

On arrival at Opienge, Giles made his way to the large church and was about to ask for Père Mondri, when he noticed the smiling, white-haired, short figure of the priest appear at his bedroom window. The 75-year-old pastor, who had spent his last 43 years ministering to his flock in Opienge, greeted Giles warmly with a bottle of 'Primus' beer (which was certainly enjoyed). As he passed the beer over, Père Leon Mondri used the sum total of his English to say, "How do you do? I love you." That evening was spent chatting at the Mission half in French and half in Swahili. Throughout the day people came and went just to stare at the tall, long-haired visitor. Père Leon Mondri told Giles about the nearby airstrip and arranged for a guide to take him there on the following morning.

Opienge was a large town which stretched for about eight kilometres. The Protestant Mission was on the far side of town and Giles stopped to introduce himself to the jolly, black-faced Pastor. The airstrip was easily long enough for Alan Root's Cessna and Giles hired men to clean it up. By late afternoon he was tired and returned to the Mission.

The scene at the Catholic Mission was not quite so hectic now; there were only about 50 people there, most of whom were children. I sat down and was given a glass of a harsh liqueur; the local brew of distilled palm wine. Leon called it 'cognac', downed his glass and drew on a most vicious smelling cigarette. Then he never stopped talking for between four and five hours; he paid no attention to my obvious fatigue and I was too polite to tell him that I was hungry, smelly and tired. By the time the huge introduction and explanation of the relations and such of every person in the room and a tour of the photographs that lined the walls was through, it was 8.00 p.m. We had endless Beethoven, which was really marvellous to hear, 'The Emperor' was followed by the 'Violin Concerto in D Minor' played so loudly that conversation was impossible. Leon smoked ceaselessly and his glass was always emptied quickly. At last, at 10.00 p.m., food arrived and Leon ordered 80 percent of the people out of the room. Those remaining, all of whom were children, sat at the huge table. They all stay at the Mission and help Leon in return for food and shelter. I was ravenous having not eaten since the night before and having worked all day trying to stay with my bike. I was also rather light-headed after all the 'cognac' and I definitely needed something inside me. The meal was monkey, rice and beans. After dinner I headed straight for my room, showered and crawled into an old hospital steel bed. It was comfy and I slept.

Giles made his daily radio call to Alan Root to tell him that the airstrip was ready. Root said that he would be there in two days. Giles received a visit from the National Park Guide, Alexis, who was very relaxed and pleasant as he examined the various permits to hunt and trap the peacock. Not only was Alexis happy with the paperwork – he was also eager to help in the hunt. He assisted Giles as he made enquiries amongst the locals about the possible whereabouts of the peacock. The general opinion was that it would take two to three days to walk to the area where they may be found.

The arrival of Alan's aircraft was greeted with great excitement – it was only the second touchdown at Opienge in three years. The townsfolk turned out in their hundreds, jabbering excitedly as the Cessna came into view and overflew for the pilot's initial check. Alan had brought the second bike and also the provisions for their trip into the rain forest. He had contracted the services of Kitembo, who spoke English and all the local dialects to assist with the local administration. Leon's hospitality that day was tremendous: a huge lunch with more of the highly potent palm cognac and the provision of beds that had already been made up. Alan Root later recalled with great pleasure the happy days at Opienge:

"I remember when we took Père Leon for a flight in my Cessna. The back seats had been stripped out so that I could carry more cargo so it meant that he had to kneel down to look out of the window. I remarked that it must have been very uncomfortable. "Not a bit of it," he replied, "I've spent half my life on my knees!" Leon would give one of his orphan kids a single shotgun shell each day and send him out to shoot meat for the evening meal. It would invariably be a monkey and there were many nights when Giles and I would share an old jerrican of palm wine and monkey stew with Leon and the kids. Giles displayed his sense of humour one day in a manner that I thought might give us problems. Père Leon came out of his church one Sunday morning and there was Giles hanging from a huge metal crucifix outside the building – Leon thought this was absolutely hilarious – you couldn't take offence at Giles no matter how bizarre his actions might occasionally be. You know throughout the time that I knew him if I was ever feeling a bit down or tired I'd say that I was "going get my jump leads from Giles" – I'd go and visit him and I would soon be cheered up by his infectious good humour and his outlook on life. I remember asking him once how often he visited his parents and he simply said: 'Not as often as I should but they have lots of other sons and they won't miss me.'"

Alan and Kitembo would be on the ground for two weeks during which time Alan hoped to see the peacocks or at least make sure that Giles was in the right place with the right people and a suitable budget. At Leon's house they decided that the Maiko National Park was probably the best bet. Just outside the park there is a village called Balobe where Alexis would be able to introduce them to some hunters[13]. Despite a riotous night of feasting, drinking and singing everyone was up and ready to move at dawn. Kitembo rounded up the porters and checked their loads of supplies before setting off on the 60-kilometre walk. Giles took Alexis as his pillion passenger and Alan mounted the second bike as they pointed themselves at the heart of Zaire. The track was similar to the one Giles had used on his journey to Opienge and they took time out to film some of the more hairy log bridge river crossings. At the stop for a sardine lunch Alan reviewed the history of the Congo Peacock:

"In the 1930s a renowned ornithologist was travelling through the rain forests of Zaire looking for new species and he spotted a distinctive and peculiar feather in the cap of one of the native bearers. He asked what it was from but the wearer could not give a name to the species. He asked if he could have the feather and when he returned home he tried to match it to a bird using all of the known reference books. He could find nothing like it. Some 10 years later he was visiting an institution in Belgium and he spotted two stuffed birds covered in dust on

---

13 *In reality these 'hunters' would be poachers who were let into the park by the game wardens for a 'fee' to be paid in meat. This state of affairs is not surprising as at the time of Thornton and Root's visit the wardens had not been paid for 10 months.*

the top of a filing cabinet. He asked what they were and was told that it was just a couple of old peafowl that belonged to an old man. He asked to see them and sure enough his feather matched the plumage of one of the stuffed birds. Thus the Congo peafowl was entered into the reference books but sightings of it were extremely rare and at the time that Giles went to work, the last recorded bird was trapped by a Portuguese hunter called de Medina in 1950. They wondered if it was possible to find some of the native hunters that de Medina had used all those years ago."

At Belobe, Alexis introduced one of his friends, Monsieur Etienne, who greeted them with open arms (and the ubiquitous cognac). Alan explained the reason for their safari and the search for the Paon Congolaise and asked for help in finding some of the older hunters. Fascile was introduced – he had trapped with de Medina and said that he knew where to find the birds. He was given the task of recruiting six younger men who would do all the energetic work under his directions. Fascile described his plans for trapping; he said that at both dusk and dawn the birds would call to each other as they roosted in the trees. This would make them easy to locate. It would then be a simple matter of placing nets around the trees and flushing the birds into them at first light. Alan favoured using the techniques of well-placed snares as employed by de Medina and eventually they settled on using a combination of methods.

We gathered all six hunters and the porters from Opienge into a group, gave them all a cup of firewater and then had a good chat about salaries, bonuses and presents. Early the following morning the sky was grey and the cloud was down to tree height. This was perfect weather for a long trek – a lovely cool temperature. We all set off, the hunters striding ahead with five dogs at their heels. They were small hunting dogs which never barked because it had been beaten out of them over the years. For the first seven kilometres we followed the old Belgian road that I had used on my trip from Km232 to Loya. Once it had been a full width road but now it is reduced to a very narrow footpath – how quickly the forest takes back its own. At Loya there was a Ranger post beside the river. Here the Rangers lounge and rot. Unpaid for 10 months, their heads were pickled by palm wine and their livers hit by malaria and cirrhosis. What a mess! Anyway they rowed us across the river in two canoes and returned to their huts exhausted after their day's work.

Here, at last, we entered the pure virgin, unadulterated rain forest. Our group began to stretch out as we wove our way through the forest following the path. The dogs put up some guinea fowl and we all stopped and looked, thinking that maybe they were peacocks, but the characteristic alarm call of the guinea fowl put an end to our optimism. Six hunters, four porters, Alexis, Kitembo, Alan, five dogs and myself; we were a fine band of professionals I can assure you. We walked and walked, stopping briefly to drink at small streams in which the water flowed super cool and refreshing. As we marched along under the canopy it was cool and not at all oppressive. The sun is shut out by the roof of foliage, only breaking through in rays of bright light streaming down to the earth where the various plants eagerly reach up to them. However, it is necessary to weave and duck, grip and stagger, hop and scratch your way along. It is a serious workout, particularly for Alan and me, who are both over six feet tall and we must duck all of the time. Thus during this long flog of walking through the forest we became very hot and sweaty and the small streams were wonderful stopping places in which to drink and splash. At 2.00 p.m., Fascile stopped the column and explained that we would not make it to the planned campsite in time to erect shelters. He said it would take about five hours for the porters to make their 'barazaa' [temporary rainproof shelters] *from sticks and leaves. So, we decided to stop right there by the stream — we had walked for eight hours and we were all tired — especially the porters.*

Alan and I put up one tent while Kitembo and Alexis fixed another. The hunters and porters began cutting branches and forest vines which are long, very pliable and can be used just like rope. Others were collecting broad leaves with which to thatch the roof. Within three hours the barazaa was complete and the men went off for a quick but fruitless hunt. So, it was beans and rice again and an early night for Alan and me. The hunters chattered long into the night, obviously excited to be included in such an escapade in the National Park and, what is more, quite legally. The prospect of big money on the capture of the Paon, including the bonus of eating meat in large quantities was clearly a great motivation.

I woke to the sounds of movement outside. There was a grey light coming through the canvas of the tent. Alan slumbered on while I opened the zip and peered out at the trunks of the surrounding trees. As I staggered out I was greeted by cries of 'lamouka!' from the hunters — it means 'you have woken'. I replied with 'Jambo' and off I went to the stream for a wash and freshen up. On my return, breakfast was well under way. It consisted of beans left over from the night before which were to be eaten with manioc flour porridge. This flour is the basic diet of the forest dwellers and consists of ground, sun-dried manioc. When you want to eat it, you pour it into boiling water, stirring and mixing it continually, adding more of the flour until it thickens. What emerges is completely tasteless glue. It makes 'ugale' which is porridge made from maize flour, seem positively delicious. This sticky compound goes by the name of 'foo-foo'. Alan called it 'Pattex' after the East African glue that is used for sticking everything and is found everywhere in even the smallest village shop. When Alan announced that his breakfast was 'Pattex' there was a roar of laughter from the hunters because they knew just what he was talking about even though he was using English. We broke camp by 7.00 a.m, and began walking up towards the hilly areas.

We were heading into the Jungua Hills, an area Fascile and the hunters had told us was full of peacocks. Everyone was definitely optimistic and there was a happy and good feeling all round. After a couple of hours we arrived at the Jungua River which drains the surrounding hills and is about 10 metres wide. We followed the course of the river for another two hours until we came to an old poaching camp which Fascile obviously knew about though he wouldn't admit it. It seemed that nobody had slept there for about two years and it was in a bad state of repair. We cleared the area and made a large enough space for the barazaa and three tents. Barazaa construction was carried out with more care this time because the men were going to be sleeping here for at least the next week – or – until we had caught something in the shape of a peacock.

That evening the hunters brought in a blue duiker which we had for supper. We had not heard the sound of a peacock call but that was not surprising due to the close proximity of the River Jungua and the roar of the water passing over the rocks. It was clear that we should have to cut paths to the tops of the hills where we could position ourselves for morning and evening listening sessions.

We hunted with nets all the next day and found the feather of a peacock. There was absolutely no doubt due to the iridescent hue and the black stripe along the length. This gave us a great boost but in the nets we caught only blue duikers, which were great for the pot. That evening, Olembo, one of the hunters and I cut a path to the top of the hill behind the camp. I sat on a log and listened to the evening chorus of turraccos, hornbills, cuckoos and other canopy birds all singing their dusk music but – no peacocks. Olembo and I returned to the camp where Alan was jumping with excitement – he had been out walking with Mapore (Fascile's son and one of the hunters) and he had heard the heavy beat of wings at ground level. They had rushed over to the place and seen a large bird 15 feet off the ground in an evening roost position. There was very little light and when he shone his torch on the creature he immediately saw the classic black and white speckles of the forest guinea fowl. Alan's adrenalin was flowing; they really thought they were close to catching a peacock.

That night we feasted on duiker and it poured with rain. It rained and it rained, turning the soil around our clearing into a river of mud as the water took off down the slight gradient and sped off on its long trip to the Atlantic Ocean some thousand odd miles away. It rained for three or four hours and then drizzled for the rest of the night. Fortunately I had dug a trench around my tent and had put layers of leaves underneath, so the floor covering was several inches off the ground. The rain water ran off the flysheet into the trench and I slept very well.

Because the rain had soaked everything and would rot the nets, the next morning we decided that we would set snares. The nets are made from the natural fibres of one of the forest trees and if they become wet they rot and break. To begin with we went to the area where we had found the peacock feather and set long lines of snares through the forest. The snares were set in a barrier of sticks and leaves with small holes for access; the barriers were about 100 metres in length and in each line there were about 20 snares. After finding the feather we were confident that there had to be a peacock in that neck of the woods.

After checking all the snares the next day and resetting the ones that had been sprung by various forest wildlife, we set off again to net another area. I walked down towards a small stream and saw a herd of bush pig wallowing in the mud. I counted eight adults and a large number of piglets. Their coarse orange hair shined brightly in the wet. Gabon, one of the hunters, got excited and sneaked down towards the pigs – the sound of the water masked the noise of his approach – he hurled his spear and missed. In his frustration he threw a lump of wood at them and whooped at the top of his lungs. The effect was immediate and very fast. The pigs ran in all directions. I saw a big sow with tusks sprouting out of the sides of her mouth coming my way and I was 10 feet up a tree very, very quickly. She was squealing with anger as she

44. Taking a wild dog pup from the den

45. The wild dog pups in their compound at Mkomazi

46. Tony Fitzjon at Mkomazi

47. Checking the wild dog pups in their compound at Mkoma:

48. Giles with three captured pups at Mkomazi

49. Crossing the Rufiji River in Tanzania with Emma Campbell

50. Opening oysters for Guy's stag party with brothers Ben, Guy, Jo and Sam, 1996

51. With Michael and Nicky Dyer in Old Constantinopl

52. The view across the Bosporus towards Constantinople

53. Discussing the route to Palmyra in Syria, 1996

54. Crossing the Negev desert near Aquaba

55. In the dust of the Denakil Depression in Eritrea

56. View over the Blue Nile Gorge in Ethiopia

57. On his way into Namibia. "Well you know what Giles did!"

58. At the Blue Nile Falls, Bahir, Ethiopia

sped past me. All the hunters were now chasing the piglets towards the nets. Alan was shouting to the effect that he wanted one of the piglets taken alive and he kept repeating the order. His exhortations fell on deaf ears. The hunting-killing frenzy was on! The taste of the fat of the suckling pigs was in the mouths of the hunters. This is when the African is totally out of control. He is engrossed in the hunt and it is virtually impossible to stop him unless you hit him hard or have a bucket of water handy. Mother pig ran straight into the nets and her weight broke the fibres easily but the piglets were not so lucky. They were squealing and bouncing against the nets and then the hunters were amongst them with their spear and pangas – raining blows on the animals and laughing as if they were crazy. Alan kept shouting that he wanted one alive but his voice went unheeded. In the end we had four piglets weighing in at about 10 kilograms.

The hunters were jubilant and we returned to camp for a feast. The suckling piglet made excellent eating. We ate one whole one between all of us and the others were hung over the fires to smoke and to be eaten over the next few days. The evening check of the snares revealed nothing and I now felt that we had disturbed the area whilst setting the snares and that it could be a few days before any peacocks returned. Alan, Kitembo and Alexis now had only a few more days left before they had to go back home. Alan was going to America for a film festival; Kitembo had work to do for the WWF and Alexis just did not like the forest.

The routine of early morning and evening tramping up to the top of the hills and checking the snares produced nothing tangible and so they decided to put out as many traps as they could. The hunters were getting decidedly morose and so Giles had a long talk with them. He slowly managed to draw out of them the reason for their low spirits. They were certain that the reason for not sighting the peacock was due to the haste with which they had left Belobe. The village elders had not had the time to organize a ceremony to bless the hunt. They were all looking very agitated now and Giles proposed that when Alan Root, Kitembo and Alexis left the camp the next day, they should take a guide with them. The guide could then organize a ceremony back at Belobe. He could then return to Jungua with the blessed rice and beans. The solution met with approval.

Returning to camp on the next night after another fruitless day, Giles was surprised to find Alan in an ecstatic mood. He was jumping up and down and slapping his thighs in great jubilation. He announced that he had seen a peacock and he was very, very happy. He had experienced a 'Double-O'. Giles, who was tired and just wanted a cigarette, was not too impressed by Alan's Ornithological Orgasm but he listened anyway. The peacock had been seen at a range of 20 metres and had been strolling in the vicinity of six of the established snares. This boded well for the future and the hunters perked up a little though they still insisted that the blessing ceremony was necessary.

Alan, Kitembo and Alexis, with Bernard as their guide, left just after dawn the next day and Giles was his own master again. The hunters fed very well and Giles introduced them to his jungle version of guinea fowl casserole which was greatly enjoyed. These were good and relaxing days. When Alan had been in the camp there had been a tendency for him and Giles to seek out their own company, eat separately and just talk in English. Now Giles was alone with his little band of hunters and he resorted to communal eating and long discussions into the night. He was totally at home in the smoke-filled barazaa huddled under the swinging bundles of meat.

Every morning they split into two groups to check the snares – Giles alternated between travelling with Gabon and Mapore in one direction and with Olembo and Mombe in the other; Fascile would be left behind to prepare breakfast. Still no peacock and the hunters were convinced that the reason was the missing ceremony. Bernard was due back the next day and that very morning Mapore returned to camp with some orange feathers which had an emerald green fringe. They came from a peahen and had been deposited around one of the snares. They were getting closer. That evening Giles walked with Mombe to check a snare line when Mombe stopped suddenly and pointed. There was a big peacock, electric blue with a large white crest and black primary feathers. Beside him was a peahen with a red-brown breast, emerald green back and a brown crest. They scurried away at speed and Mombe said that he had seen two small fluffy chicks also.

Giles was quite moved to have seen the peacock cruising along with his wife and kids. Their return to the camp coincided with that of Bernard who carried a letter from Alan that stated that he had paid cash for the village elders to hold the party which they euphemistically called the 'blessing ceremony'. Apart from that – all was well and he had departed on his motorcycle for Opienge.

At the next check of the snares there was a surprise. A porcupine had been caught but it was not an ordinary porcupine. Giles recognised it at once as a species that Alan was keen to capture and film. It had a long tail with a ball of spines at the end[14] and he explained to Mapore that they needed to take it back alive and build a pen for it. As they walked back to the camp with the latest addition in the basket, Giles began to think that their luck was about to change and he had the strangest feeling that by the end of the day he would be a peacock richer. He and Mapore had begun to build the pen for the porcupine when they heard a strange call drifting through the forest. It was a long way away but it persisted; a sing-song tune floating eerily into the camp. It was not a birdsong that Giles had heard before. The next time the call came it was closer and recognisable as a human. A very happy human! Mapore broke into a wide grin – Giles followed suit – they knew they had a peacock. The singing grew louder and it became clear that it was Mombe calling Mapore. As Olembo, Mombe and Gabon walked into camp with their grass basket there were handshakes and hugs all round. It was a special moment but a pen had to be constructed quickly. They worked at a fast, determined pace. The forest offered all the building materials close to hand and within two hours there was a three by three metres pen for the peacock and a somewhat smaller one for the porcupine. The peacock house was two metres high with a waterproof roof and a roosting branch. Alan Root later mentioned one of his great concerns: "The birds had to have raised platforms and roosts as I had a terrible fear of the siafu ants eating them. These ants are ferocious – they will eat a small living animal – there have been cases of them eating human babies. They move in their millions."

Giles got his first good luck at Paon Congolaise and what a magnificent bird it was. It was the size of a large turkey but with wonderful colours. On the mainly black back-plumage, there were fringes of emerald green; then electric blue on his primary wing feathers, the tail and breast. His face was a mottled red with a magnificent head-dress of white and black plumage. He was a very angry bird and stormed around his new house looking for a way out. He ignored Giles's peace

---

14 This was probably the African Brush-tailed Porcupine. These can grow up to 3 feet long and weigh as much as 8 pounds. The meat of these animals is very popular and is consumed in great quantities so Giles was lucky to have been able to rescue it.

offering of a bowl of water, forest seeds and bulbs. Giles decided that he would try again later as he knew that when a bird has been captured the priority is to get it eating and drinking as soon as possible to ward off the effects of shock.

Giles began to have problems with his little team. They had just earned US$30. They had never been so rich and they wanted to get back to Belobe to begin their spending spree. Giles pointed out that if they stayed on in the forest and caught the peahen and even some chicks then they would have at least twice the amount of money when they returned to Belobe. The hunters agreed to stay on for a further five days and then they would collect all the traps and return home. Giles had to be content with this concession.

The snare-checking routine went on but with no further luck. In between patrols into the forest the hunters constructed large baskets in which to carry the peacock and the porcupine. They would be transported in their containers suspended from a pole carried by two men. Giles told the men that he wanted to take two days to make the journey back to Belobe because he needed to give the animals a smooth ride. It was also necessary to let the peacock rest for a couple of hours in the afternoon before giving it the evening meal. The men were a little disgruntled at taking so long to make the trek but they had little choice as they would not receive their money until the animals arrived in Opienge.

The first thing to be done on their return was to construct spacious pens for the peacock and porcupine and organise a food supply. The hunters were far from happy. They wanted their money. The journey would take two days with Giles going ahead on his bike to organise the building of yet another set of pens at Opienge. During the respite in Belobe, Giles found out that a peahen had been captured and was being cared for by Leon at Opienge.

The peacock was released into his new aviary just outside Giles's bedroom window. The bird was eating well and looked fat and healthy – all he needed was a mate to keep him company. Giles was feeding him half-a-dozen times each day and at night he roosted happily high up in the branch provided for him. The hunters were paid and agreed that within 10 days or so they would be back in the forest hunting for a mate for the peacock. Giles spoke to Leo at Epulu on Leon Mondri's radio and made arrangements to get a message to Alan Root (still in the USA) that a peacock had been successfully trapped.

Leon Mondri was on hand to help Giles with the naming of the peacock and the porcupine. As Zaire was basically a Francophone nation it was decided that an aristocratic French or Belgian name would be appropriate for the bird – hence the peacock became 'Napoleon'. The porcupine became 'Jezebel'. They were now Giles's main preoccupation. The date was 20th September and he knew that Alan Root would be arriving on 5th October and he was determined to find a 'Josephine' for 'Napoleon' before that date. There was, however, another problem – Giles was coming down with some sort of stomach bug that was painful and debilitating – he remembered, in his diaries, a four-day period of stomach cramps and fever during which he manfully carried out his duties of care with the animals. When the bug cleared up he decided to get over to Belobe to see what progress Bernard and the other hunters had made.

With Alexis he made the journey quite quickly. As the track had been used a lot over the last few weeks, most of the undergrowth had been cut back, mud holes had been filled and some of the log bridges had been stabilised. Giles was angry with what he found:

Bernard was swanning down the main street when I arrived and he looked sheepish. I drove into Etienne's compound and called a meeting. Everyone seemed happy that I had returned. I asked them why they were not back in the forest but I got no reply – they just looked at the ground. As we talked I began to realise that they were no longer hungry for money. Well, so be it! I was pissed off to say the least, because they had taken a whole load of nylon cord and it was not being used in the forest. I asked Bernard to return the nylon and this got his back up. Nylon is a very valuable commodity out there – it can be used for so many things and it is pretty well rot-proof. But, I demanded its return and Bernard slunk off in a sulky shuffle. I noticed that a young Kagana was waving at me from the door – he was beckoning me to leave the house away from the other men. There seemed to be no harm in this so I went along.

He was wide-eyed and hopping around. He begged me to give him some nylon because he was sure that he and his brothers could catch a peacock. I looked at him and reckoned that he couldn't be more that 17 years old. He pointed to his brothers, who were gathered some yards away. One was about 12 and the others possibly 15 and 16 years old. What was I to do? They seemed so keen but were they just after the nylon in the pretence that they were going peacock hunting? Bernard returned with the mound of nylon cord that we had used to capture Napoleon in Jungua. He had changed his mind and was now keen to go back into the forest. I could not know for sure if he was genuine. Anyway, I compromised. I split the cord between Bernard's group and the young chaps whose leader was called Maporee.

It was midday and time to head back to Opienge to check on 'Napoleon'. We made good time through the forest, weaving and bucking over the ridiculous bridges. One of the rivers had risen up over the logs so the balancing act had become even more difficult – it was very slippery and there were no handholds... we arrived at Chez Leon Mondri and found, waiting with him and his crèche of children, an old man with a basket. Immediately I realised that he had a peacock! Yes, it was female, but it was oh so weak! Its eyes were open, but it couldn't even hold its head up. The man was from a small village called Wandi which was eight days travel away. He had caught the peahen in the forest three days away from Wandi. He had given the bird neither food nor water and it had been bouncing around in the basket for five days. I was surprised that the bird was still alive and I found it difficult to contain my anger.

I quickly transferred the bird into a small pen in my bedroom. I mixed up some warm water and glucose powder and spooned the mixture up the beak. The bird did drink and I was encouraged. After six spoonfuls I examined the legs and wings. One leg was damaged but not broken or dislocated. There was loss of skin and bruising from the snare. It was too weak to stand. I left it for half an hour and went back to tell the chap that I didn't think it would survive. He understood and trekked off into town. I felt sorry for him because he had walked for so many days through the forest.

I returned to the bird and fed her some palm grubs. It was semi-force feeding – I had to open her beak and pop in the grubs so I decided to leave her until the next day. I checked on her during the night and she was dead – had I killed her? Should I have fed her more? Did I feed her too much? Oh Shit! What should I do?

(There is a rumour that Giles, who hated waste, ate the peahen for his supper.)

The trapper returned the next morning and I told him how he should look after a bird once he had caught it. I sent him off back to the forest with some salt and soap as a token of goodwill. Poor chap, he had caught two peacocks and both had died. If he had been able to keep them alive he would have been wealthy in his own terms.

The days went by and I was going a bit potty living in such a place. The endless people and the perpetual noise were getting to me. I had to return to the forest quickly but – how could I? – I had the animals to look after. My only escape was my morning jaunts to the outlying villages where I would ask the local hunters if they were keen to go to work for a US$100 reward. Some said that the peacocks were a two-day walk away and that they couldn't go because they needed to work on their crops. Others were keen and I handed over nylon cord and wished them luck. I had no idea if they would actually go or use the nylon to make various repairs to their houses, furniture and clothing. Time went slowly by and then Alan was back in Nairobi. He was due to come to Zaire in five days with an additional three days required to reach Opienge.

Père Leon's madhouse was exhausting but I slipped into a sort of routine. I adjusted and blocked out any thoughts of contempt for the people who were running rings around him and profiting nicely in so many ways. Every evening we had long chats about life in Opienge. He was fully aware of the actions of the people around him and their making money from the food, salt, sugar and other things he provided. He explained that he was there alone; he enjoyed their company and therefore he had to run a madhouse. Thus he is endlessly surrounded by children, adults, cats and dogs. He loves it and his life has been like this for 43 years. He did not feel lonely. He belonged there and this was how he lived. However, he was no fool. He knew exactly what was going on. He would shrug and chuckle – that would break into a cough and then a full lung-retching horror followed by a walk to the door where something ghastly would be spat out.

Alan flew in. He came in the smaller Cessna 180, much more of a bush plane than his Cessna 210 which is really an executive city-hopper. He came with cheese, wine and other goodies including rolling tobacco, which I had run out of the week before. It was good to see Alan again. A white man at last, who spoke English and laughed at all the ridiculous things I had to say. Père Leon was also very happy. He was so pleased to have the company of white, rational people. We were the first men who had stayed, gone away and then returned in his entire 40 years at Opienge. Alan brought goodies for Leon, who was ecstatic about the cheese, wine, salami, olives and nuts. In his usual generous fashion, he cut off chunks of cheese and salami and handed them round his flock, who were gathered all around. It was good to see him do this – so unselfish – so caring. A Man of God.

I talked to Alan and told him of the capture of 'Napoleon', the death of the peahens and all the other facts about our rather bizarre project. He was keen that I should stay put for another two and a half weeks and then close the project at the end of the month. My visa for Zaire would run out on 5 November, so he had to have me out of the place by then. Alan was very, very pleased to see Napoleon in such fine health but he stressed the need for a female.

The next day 'Napoleon' and 'Jezebel' were carried to Alan's aeroplane and off they went to Epulu. Now I had two and a half weeks to get the buggers off their arses and catch another peahen. At that point I must have had 10 different hunting groups out in the forest – someone had to be successful. On the other hand – if I left Opienge for too long, there was always the possibility of a peahen arriving without me being there. What then – yet another dead bird? However, I had to take that chance and go to check how the hunting parties were doing.

Alexis and Giles reached the hunter's camp in two days to find that there had been no more sightings. The hunters, however, admitted that they were spending a lot of time hunting for meat to sell to the gold camps. Giles wished them luck and set off back, with Alexis, to the village where they had spent the previous night. Early the next morning they headed back to Opienge at a relaxed pace to be greeted by one of Leon's men. He had a message from Belobe to say that a peahen had been caught. It was reportedly healthy and was eating and drinking. It was in a basket big enough for it to stand and walk around. Giles knew that he had to get to Belobe to take charge of the bird's care. The thrill of the capture made the arduous ride along the track seem like fun. A huge crowd was waiting for him but to the forefront was Maporee. Giles noted angrily that Fascile, Bernard, Olembo and the rest of the original group had not returned to the forest as they had promised so he curtly demanded that the rest of the nylon be returned.

Maporee and his young brothers took Giles into their house and sure enough, there in a huge basket, was a beautiful peahen. Maporee offered her some grasshoppers and she greedily ate them from his hand. At first glance she seemed to be very healthy and it was important to get her to Opienge as soon as possible. To Giles's surprise the brothers offered to carry the bird through the night to avoid the noisy and frightening attention of the locals whilst Giles went back to Opienge to clean Napoleon's old pen. Maporee and his brothers arrived with their precious cargo safe and sound.

When Alan Root arrived three days later he was euphoric. After a day or two spent filming some local waterfalls they flew back to Epulu to introduce 'Napoleon' to his new mate. It took her a few days to settle down but eventually she did. Alan Root had another successful film and 'Napoleon' had his 'Josephine'. Giles's reputation as a 'man of the forest' was boosted but he was only too happy to make his farewells and return to Kenya on 3rd November, 1993.

Chapter XIII

Retreat To Laikipia And Borana

The effect on Giles of three months living in the rain forest was negligible. His health, despite the attack of an undiagnosed bush fever, was good. He now had money in his pocket and needed a little fun and relaxation. It was inevitable that he should head back to Laikipia and Borana. Giles was always offered a bed in a cottage at Borana, but, inevitably, he elected to sleep on a raised platform outside the cottage – he wanted the stars above and the breeze around him. But before looking at Giles's activities over the next few months it is time to hear a female perspective of the young man. Some time ago Giles had been paying court to Sally Dudmesh, a strikingly pretty woman who had her own business in Nairobi. Late in 2006 she offered some interesting memories:

"'Tag and Release' would be a very fitting title for a book. I use this in the context of animal conservation – you capture the animal, touch it and put your mark on it but then you have to release it back into the wild. Giles was a free spirit with a huge love of life. He had a beautiful face and smile and a dynamic loving energy. He was a very tactile man and all his hugs were warm, close and long even after we broke up. I think a good example of this was at his funeral; everyone was hugging each other – even those who would not normally do that. There was huge warmth generated by the affection Giles had inspired in everyone.

"At one point Michael and Nicky banned him from the house at Borana. They simply got fed up of his noise and the fact that he would roar up to the house, shouting loudly and at full throttle on his motorbike and drive straight onto the veranda trailing mud and oil with him. He was a master of grunge (but his personal hygiene was good though he never washed his hair). Anyway Giles was banished to what he called 'Dead Rat Mansion' a somewhat dilapidated shack some distance from the main house. All this was in the days when he was beginning to court me and like an animal courtship display he would climb up onto the roof and dance and sing (this is when he was drunk of course). But all this was part of his natural playfulness. After all – there had been no tragedies in his life to calm him down or make him contemplative.

"There was a lot of vanity in him – he was certainly vain about his image and his scruffiness could be carefully calculated at times. Giles never just went into a house – he made an entrance. I remember at a polo club prize-giving ceremony when he made just such an entrance by parachuting in and landing just behind the MC who was giving out the prizes. If that's not stealing someone's thunder then what is? He could be incredibly mean also which was often embarrassing as it would never occur to him to buy a bottle of wine or something if he was invited to a party. But, having said that, he was generous to the extreme with his love and affection. He did love a party but his behaviour could be quite outrageous. For example he would suddenly decide to walk along the top of the table to chat to someone despite the fact that people were eating and drinking but he was so nimble and agile that he never knocked over a glass or trod on a plate. You would think that people would object to this but I suppose it is a measure of their love for him that everyone made him welcome, truly enjoyed his company and kept on inviting him to their homes.

"Giles lived life on the edge. He did not expect to grow old and said as much. In my time with him he didn't talk much about the future but then contemplation usually comes to people as they get a little older than he was then. We took a trip together once up into the NFD. We used my little truck which was not in the best of condition and eventually, out in the wilderness we were confronted by a group of bandits armed with AK47 assault rifles. I thought we were in trouble but Giles just took it in his stride and soon had them laughing at his antics and we left totally unscathed by the incident.

"When Giles split with me I asked him "Why?" He told me that he felt that he was in danger of really falling in love with me. I pointed out that surely that was in the natural scheme of things: people met – fell in love and that was that. But Giles argued that he couldn't accept the binding nature of such a love. At his funeral I imagined his spirit flying like a bird as the feathers that had been put into the pyre floated away on the wind."

Giles loved both free-fall parachuting and paragliding and it is difficult to determine which of these two sports held the most appeal for him. Both have their dangerous elements and both require significant cash outlay for the basic equipment. With paragliding there is no need for any other party to be involved; take-off is achieved by finding a suitable escarpment and using the wind for initial lift. Parachuting requires an aeroplane so the cost of a pilot and fuel has to be found – both activities are limited by wind conditions. The free-fall aspect of skydiving would have excited Giles. As a natural gymnast he would have found the acrobatics made possible in a fall from high altitude very thrilling. He would have experimented with the endless gymnastic possibilities. He would first have got himself into a stable position as he left the aircraft by extending both arms and legs into an 'X' shape and arching his back – adopting the aerodynamic shape of one of the curved feathers which he so loved. If he snapped his body into the 'attention' position he would have moved into a head down posture and plummeted straight towards terra firma. Throw out the arms and legs and stability returns. Bend the arms and legs at elbows and knees, draw them into the body a little and faster, but stable descent is achieved. Straighten the legs out and spread them a little at the same time as pushing the arms back to resemble a delta-wing aircraft and the head dips slightly and a noticeable traverse across the terrain begins. Cup one hand and begin a slow turn – every movement of the limbs and body has an immediate effect. Somersaults have never been easier! Don't get carried away – watch that altimeter! At 18,000 feet the skydiver will have horizons but at about 2,000 feet those horizons suddenly vanish and the ground seems quite close. It's about time to pull that ripcord and seconds later the jumper is swinging gently under his canopy and now has the time to look around, see where the birds are soaring and steer across to try to grab a thermal. Modern parachutes are so responsive that great accuracy is possible. There was a bit of the show-off in Giles (as there is in most skydivers).

It was not always expensive for Giles to get an aircraft and he would often be able to cadge a lift to a suitable parachuting altitude. It was during one of these occasions that Sally Dudmesh's comments on his vanity is demonstrated. He was flying across Laikipia in a light aircraft planning to jump into Borana when he spotted activity on the plains below. He asked his pilot to circle the area and he was able to see that a film crew seemed to be busy down there. He told the pilot that he was "...heading down to see what was going on..." With that he left the aircraft. On landing very close to the site he saw that it was indeed a film shoot and his eye was immediately caught by an extremely striking lady on horseback who was the centre of attention!

The story may be apocryphal! It was told to the family by a number of people. The lady in question was Inés Sastre. Inés, Spanish by birth and multilingual, was then 20 years old and on her way to becoming a noted model and film actress. In an interview in 2006 she remembered the incident in a totally different way:

"We were filming in Laikipia and I had been delayed in getting to the shoot because of aircraft cancellations and other transport problems so when I finally got there I was dirty and dusty and grumpy and very tired. I didn't notice much at first and then this man sitting on a horse spoke. I didn't, at first, think that he was talking to me but then he spoke again and I just looked at him. He tried again – this time I realised he was talking to me as he said, "Hello, I'm Giles Thornton." I still didn't answer so he tried again in French with a not so good accent, "Je m'appelle Giles". He said it about three times I think before I answered him I wasn't being deliberately rude – I was tired and confused and feeling deafened and dopey from the noise of the little aircraft. When I looked at him properly the first thing that registered was his beautiful smile. He just sat on the horse, very good looking, very confident and very relaxed and looked at me. I also saw a lady who turned out to be called Sally and a child who I assumed were his wife and child. It turned out not to be the case and after the shoot we talked for quite a long time.

"We became very good friends and I did a lot of shoots in Kenya and Giles and I made a number of small safaris on foot when we would spend the nights under the stars which was a first time for me. I guess we were two young people in love. Occasionally when we were walking and Giles was in one of his silent introspective moods and I would be chattering away in Latina fashion he would turn round and tell me to shut up and enjoy the peace and beauty of the bush. We would talk at night by a campfire sometimes and I remember him telling me that there was so much natural beauty and peace in the bush that possessions became meaningless. Once we talked about the millennium year which seemed so far away in those days and I remember asking him what he thought he would be doing in the year 2,000 and he replied that he didn't think he would be around then.

"Giles was so very good for me. I was a young woman and I had no real confidence. Life demanded certain decisions. There was the attraction of a well-paid modelling career stretching in front of me but there was also the matter of my unfinished education. I was confused. If I pursued the modelling then it would be difficult to resume my education after a long break. If I pursued my education then I might get bypassed in the modelling business. It was Giles who gave me the confidence to continue my education and he made me realise that I could do anything that I set my mind to. He showed me a new vision of the world – how much bigger it was than my first conception of it and that anything was possible.

"We went to Chamonix and Paris together after Giles had made a brief trip back to England and those were wonderful times. I bought him his first paraglider in Chamonix and it was nice to see his enjoyment in using it. Over that time Giles was involved in many things with the Dyers, Gilfrid Powys and his camels, Roland Purcell and with David Stirling who was organising funds for the "Save the Rhino" campaign. He had so much energy. I owe him so much – I believe that it was my time with Giles that gave me the drive and ability to secure the contract with Lancôme[15]. Although we were no longer partners the pain of Giles's death and the experience of his funeral, in a strange way, helped me in my acting career as a later film I made hinged on a bereavement and my feelings were very real."

Before making the trip to England, Paris and Chamonix, to which Inés Sastre referred, Giles spent almost a month culling zebra at the Borana ranch as a fax to his parents on 21st January 1994 shows:

I'm fit and well and about to go to Borana for culling zebra and giraffe. A bloody business in an odd, bloodthirsty kind of way. Now I will be returning to England for the last week of February or the first week of March. I'll be there for just a few days and then going off to Chamonix for a month with many stops at other places as well,

---

15 *Inés Sastre achieved real and lasting fame when she became "The Face of Lancôme" the huge Paris-based cosmetic company.*

but it will be Chamonix first stop. I hope Ben or Guy or some of the other boys will be going to the Alps around March or April so that we can meet.

Please note that I will be writing a cheque for my air ticket some time around mid-February. Thanks for sending the new carnet and insurance documents. Now please can you send me some kind of bank statement, because I may be buying a parachute if the funds are available? I'm off to Borana on Monday 24 January.

A fax to Brian and Verity Thornton on 6th July 1994 shows how Giles spent the next few months:

I have been up in the north of Kenya literally since I arrived back here. I went straight to Borana and found Michael and Nicky about to leave for Italy on holiday. They asked me to manage the ranch while they were away. I then worked for Michael's uncle, Gilfrid Powys. He was about to go up to the north of Kenya to buy camels and wanted some help when walking the beasts back again. I am writing this little adventure now and will send it to you when completed. I have been doing a great deal of paragliding up in the Samburu lands and consequently have become a 'God', being anointed with cow's milk and blood and given much homage. 'The Man who would be King!' it really is a strange feeling when people truly think you are a 'Mungo' (God).

I hope to be going to Tanzania on 12 July, probably for about four months. I hope to be working half of the time with Roland Purcell and half with Richard Bonham. In the meantime I have my hands completely full, because Inés arrived yesterday and wants to cruise around for a few weeks. Thus life goes on and is just so good.

Chapter XIV

Tanzania And Kilimanjaro

Giles returned to Tanzania to work for Richard Bonham. This letter, written
on 10th September 1994, describes his feelings for Africa:

Dear Mum and Dad,

*It seems a very long time since I wrote, faxed or made any sort of contact with
you. How inexcusable and lazy. I guess I have been roaring around a great deal
and have not made enough time to write. Please believe me, however long the times
may be between when you hear from me, I do think of you often and wonder how
the summer months have been passing down in Gloucestershire. It's hard to picture
actually as I have never been to the house in the summer months. Also it's hard to
imagine no tennis or swimming. All the same it is a beautiful spot with plenty of
shooting practice with all those bunnies!*

*I have been in Tanzania since early July working for Roland, running his camp
and doing a spot of exploring. There were very few clients this season due to cancellations
after the Western World saw the machete wielding Bantu men in Rwanda on their
televisions. The camp happens to be about 1,000 kilometres away from Rwanda,
but there are some strange people who believe everything they see on those horrible
television machines.*

*Nevertheless I could not be happier. There are long periods of two to three weeks
when there are no clients, which means that I can take long walks of three and four
days into the bush, returning to camp in order to resupply and then walking off again
absorbing this amazing stretch of country. It has such dense populations of game,
which are so varied it is like a theme park, without the plastic or the people.*

*The past four months have been a huge experience of ancient Africa. There is a
whole National Park of 2,550 sq kms all to oneself. There are no other tour operators,
no people, just wildlife in such ridiculously large numbers. There are buffalo in herds
of 2,000 head. Hippos squeezed together in pools, 300–400 in each pool. Crocodiles*

mixed in with the hippos and the crocodiles excavating deep holes in which to sleep or shelter from the sun as the dry season is now beginning to take its toll. There are elephants in family groups of 30 to 40 each, all with young, which is great to see. It is a sign that over the years the numbers will gradually increase after the massacres of the 1980s. Across the plains are scattered zebra, topi, hartebeest and reed buck with eland, roan antelope, sable antelope and giraffe coming out of the forest to water. Out in the swamps with the hippos and the crocs is an abundance of bird life. Herons, open-billed storks, yellow bill, saddle bill, crowned cranes, Egyptian and spurwing geese, hamerkop, egrets and every kind of bird of prey. The dominant feeder of the fish is the pelican, which really love the catfish. The fish eagles dive-bomb the pelicans hoping to scare them away before they eat all the fish. There is a large pride of 16 lions consisting of two black-maned males, eight large breeding lionesses and 16 young cubs from two mothers (this is only here at the camp!). Hyenas are plentiful. I saw 12 one morning finishing off the remains of a buffalo. The leopard is very difficult to see. So far this year I have seen only four different individuals. Thus, taking account of the fact that one is very lucky to see any at all, there must be a large number of them around. Also there is an abundance of suitable food for them. Impala, bushbuck, bush pig, warthog and vervet monkey are all good prey for the leopard.

The only difficulty in the National Park, not being a Game Reserve, as is the Selous, is that we are not allowed to shoot anything to eat. The result is that we have to drive for two hours to a small village to buy a goat or two. We also eat a great deal of maize meal and beans, but still you can live on that.

There are three chaps with me here in the camp. They keep everything in order and look after the clients when they arrive. We are expecting two more safaris, the last one timed for the first week of October, then we pack everything up and shove it all in a store at the park headquarters, which is a two hour drive from here. After that we fly back to Kenya and all I shall want to do then is get back into the sky on my paraglider and soar higher and higher with the eagles. I am afraid I have become totally addicted to the sport and the simplicity of it all. It provides me with such a high and enormous feeling of elation. I'm just up amongst the clouds with the simple aid of a hill, to get the initial lift and I start thermalling up and join the vultures and the other birds of prey. There are few hills here at Katavi and it is deeply forested so the paraglider stayed in Kenya. I am now looking forward to my return there and soaring again.

Last week Roland came by and stayed in the camp for a week, as he had no clients either here or at Mahali, his other camp beside Lake Tanganyika. We went for a big eight-day walk, carrying our supplies and taking water from streams and springs, which we had noted, when planning our routes from the air before starting out.

Our destination was to be a huge waterfall on the Rungwa River. The place was complete paradise. The Rungwa River cascades 1,000 feet over an escarpment of granite rock down into a gorge of clay and sand. In the pool at the foot of the waterfall is 100 sq metres of crystal clear water. In the pool is a herd of about 50 hippos and five monster crocodiles. There are fish in ridiculous numbers, which nibble you when you swim just off the sand bar at one end of the pool. Palm trees, fig trees and baobab surround the pool. If you climb up the waterfall a small way and look down into the clear water you can see hippo and crocodile very clearly with their whole bodies submerged. Also huge three-foot long catfish come to the surface and then disappear into the depths.

The river runs out over some stones and on into another hippo pool. The cliff side of the gorge is of clay at this point with thousands and thousands of carmine bee eaters nesting in holes in the cliff. These birds are so incredibly coloured in red with bluish-green that, with so many in one place it takes your breath away. The river bed is now golden sand. It is quite deep at the bends and only inches deep when it flows between the corners. We saw waterbuck, bush buck, lesser kudu and buffalo. There were footprints of lion, hyena, elephant and giraffe, but we saw none. Overhanging acacia trees provide perfect perches for the fish eagles overlooking the deeper pools. This place really amazed me; the crystal clear water falling over that black, black granite into the huge pool was just like a set for a movie. The pool is surrounded on one side by granite rock and on the other by a steep bank of trees. Then there was the sandy beach shaded by the acacias for us to sleep under. On the far side the river flows down the gorge. Behind the beach you can climb up out of the gorge and follow the hippo trail through the forest of miombo, baobab, acacia and bush. At the top there is an open plateau some 100 metres long and 50 metres wide of grass. From there you can see for about 100 kms into Lake Rukwa and over to the Rukwa escarpment and then way back towards Chada from where we had walked. To find such a place, quiet, unspoilt and all to oneself is quite out of this world. We wanted to stay for many days, but due to lack of food or any fishing hooks (big mistake) we set off back to Chada after only two nights and two days exploring this paradise.

In so many ways I wish I had come to Africa in the 30s and 40s when the white man had not really yet made such a mess of it all. By letting loose so many misguided folk, who are now committed to a drive of total destruction, the loss of the original Africa is assured. Also the massive increase in the birth rate has caused a population explosion amongst the blacks. There is no space for them all in the areas where food can be grown and the pressure on the land is now on, big time. Rwanda provides a simple case in point, with huge numbers of people in a tiny area and they keep on breeding. Then something has to give – a fuse blows – "Kill" – "Kill!" the machete rules OK! Rwanda used to have an amazing amount of wildlife in the 30s with three National Parks. Now with independence, missionaries, hospitals, medicine and "development" there is not one National Park left. All the wild animals have gone thanks to the 'progress' of man. Gosh! Don't I sound like a real old colonial bore? Africa is still a wonderful place, but you really have to search in order to find places like this and when you do: keep it to yourself.

I now have a strong feeling that I will be heading north at the beginning of next year. I want to go up through Ethiopia, Northern Sudan and Egypt. Then on to Israel, Jordan, Syria, Turkey and into Europe. I know I have said this many times, but it really is a very strong urge this time. The motorbike is in need of a revamp so that I can go onward to new things.

The difficulty is; I have become so very comfortable here. I am in a place in the world that I truly love, with all its surroundings. I have very good friends and the place is excellently suited to paragliding. But I do want to move on however hard it may be. A great deal is dependant on a meeting I have arranged in November with two friends, Johnny and Dave, who are planning to ride their bikes from England to Indonesia, Java, Sumatra and on to Australia; all in favour of the rhino.* I want to find out how serious they are about it. This will then decide how soon I must return to England and prepare for the journey. I would like to do it anyway, but whether they really want to go will be the decider on how much time my trip from Kenya to England must take.

Now, Father, you are probably fully aware of the status of my bank balance, if any, and I know that the wage I earned here in Tanzania will not cover the expenses *of the next year ahead. So I think I'm probably in a wee bit of a pickle. I very much want to skydive at the Kenya coast this Christmas for about two weeks, also to live, also to prepare the bike, also to have funds available for the return battle through those Arab countries. They will not be filled with wildlife, but vastly empty, with pockets of dense population of wailing Muslims. I seek your advice in finding out whether I should raid my piggy-bank. Not a great deal of cash will be required. As you know, it is possible to live cheaply in undeveloped countries, through which I want to travel. However, sports like jumping out of the door of an aeroplane are more expensive. What do you think? Can I, or can I not raid the pot for purely enjoyment purposes only?*

Well, to you both I send all my love and hope England is looking after you agreeably. For me, Africa is 100% marvellous in the way it gives me a truly agreeable lifestyle and I feel sure will do so for a while longer. Please give all my love to Guy, Kim, Ben, Jo, Sam, Gran, Grampy, Grandma, Lucinda, Simon, Bimbo, Johnny, the Brookses, Dawn, Richard, Serina, Christopher and all those other lovely folk with whom I fail to keep in touch.

I love you. Giles.

PS. Tell Ben a letter and the form are coming his way on my return to Kenya. In the meantime tell him to come down.

*Giles did, through David Stirling, get involved with the "Save the Rhino" project:

I arrived in Nairobi to find your fax waiting for me. Thank you for keeping Coutts & Co at bay. Please pay off my overdraft with Grandma's present and put £3K on deposit. I have just returned from a massive experience on Kilimanjaro – the roof of Africa. We spent 12 days on the mountain and in the process raised a good sum of money for "Save the Rhino".

There is a big change to my long term plan. I am hoping to be given some work in Northern Tanzania. The idea is to catch some wild dogs and set up a Rhino Sanctuary. That would mean I would be very close to Sam, if he goes to work at the school near Arusha. I will telephone you near Christmas and hope that Guy and Samantha may come out for New Year – so good things ahead!

I go up to Borana tomorrow, but will pop into this office to see if you have replied. Lots of love to you and Mum. Giles

Chapter XV

Capturing The African Wild Dogs

In July of 1995 Giles turned again to the business of trapping difficult animal species but this time it was for the Mkomazi Game Reserve in Tanzania. The Reserve was under the management of Tony Fitzjohn[16] who had earned his spurs in Kenya after working for almost 18 years with the legendary George Adamson of "Born Free" and "Living Free" fame. Tony along with George Adamson is a co-founder of the Tony Fitzjohn/George Adamson African Wildlife Preservation Trust.

Tony's background was unconventional to say the least; orphaned in 1945 in London he was adopted and brought up in Cockfosters. By his own admission he was a wild kid and probably destined for a reform school but attendance at a course in the Lake District brought him into contact with a former African game warden and thus his interest in the continent was sparked off. Hitchhiking to Kenya via a sea voyage to Cape Town he eventually found himself at George Adamson's camp at Kora. The two hit it off well and Tony began to learn the ways of the wild becoming a leading expert on Africa's top predators. During their time together the pair successfully reintroduced more than 30 lions and 10 leopards into the wild as they were pioneering the development and management of the Kora National Park. During this period Tony barely escaped death after a savage mauling by a lion. It was this experience of setting up camps, making airstrips and cutting hundreds of miles of bush roads while fighting running battles with ivory poachers and Somali Shifta bandits that, after George's murder, made Tony a natural for the job of taking on the challenge at Mkomazi.

The initial aim of the Mkomazi Game Reserve, supported by the George

---

16 *In November 2007 Tony Fitzjohn was appointed as an OBE for his huge contribution to wildlife preservation in Kenya. Some of the information on Tony has been taken from the website www.wildlifenow.com/tony.htm with his kind permission.*

Adamson Wildlife Preservation Trust, was to establish a protected breeding environment for one of Africa's most endangered species – the Black Rhino. The challenge was not a small one! But Tony Fitzjohn was equal to the task and all of his skills were required. Not only did he need to be an experienced wildlife manager but he needed to know the arts of bush pilot, the field engineer and the mechanic. There were roads to be built, boundaries to be marked and cut, dams to be built and maintained, anti-poaching patrols to be trained and organised and breeding programmes to be planned. All of these tasks required also the skills of the negotiator and statesman in the dealings with Africa's often turgid bureaucracy. The whole project was entirely staffed by volunteers and Tony had (and has) to travel widely in the constant and time-consuming search for funds.

He has also been active with the local communities and has provided them with a clean water supply, a dispensary and Flying Doctor service, schools and housing. This involvement with the local communities has led to positive relations and loyalty but above all it is the man's undying faith in, and his commitment to, the conservation of East Africa that has guaranteed his impressive success. At a meeting in late 2006, Tony was unstinting in his praise for the efforts of Giles Thornton during 1995. He confirmed the impressive zeal and energy, interest and commitment and the irrepressible and infectious sense of humour that Giles took to the conservation business. He also remarked on his genuine affection for the Masai and his ability to get the best from them on the hunting trips. The Mkomazi project was still young at the time that Giles became involved and it was in that year, 1995, that Fitzjohn had to decide what the first rehabilitation programme would be. He turned his attention to an animal that was scarcely equipped to endear itself to pseudo-conservationists – the African wild dog (sometimes referred to as the African hunting dog).

The Mkomazi Game Reserve is on land that had been poorly treated and managed over the years; over-grazing and poaching combined with illegal deforestation had reduced it to almost desert conditions. Fitzjohn was in the process of beginning the huge task of turning the waste land into an area suitable for the establishment of a breeding programme for the black rhino. It was to be a mammoth task. The first priority was to erect an electrified fence to contain a 45-square-kilometre sanctuary that was reckoned to be sufficient eventually to hold up to 20 black rhino. Even during those early stages, Fitzjohn, thinking as a conservationist, recognised that the African wild dog was one of the continent's most endangered species and he saw no reason why Mkomazi could not be used as a breeding ground for this neglected animal. He already knew that the dogs were notoriously difficult to breed in captivity but he wanted to try it with a view to releasing the progeny back to the wild.

The African wild dog (*Lycaon pictus*) has quite an attractive appearance. It is a medium-sized dog with a head and body length 30–40 inches and a white-tipped tail. They typically weigh 40–80 pounds. They have variable coat colours, with blotches of black, white and orange or yellow. The muzzle is always black. Their ears are large and rounded, almost bat-like, which accounts for their highly developed sense of hearing. The Latin name, *Lycaon pictus*, translates as "painted wolf-like creature" but they differ from wolves and other dogs in that they have four toes instead of five. Their lifespan is approximately 10 years in the wild.

Like wolves the dogs operate in tightly knit, highly sophisticated social groups which historically could have numbered up to a hundred animals but nowadays it is more likely to be around 10 to 15. Usually the packs will have more male than female members and it is only the Alpha female which will give birth to a litter of up to 10 pups each year. The pups will wean at about 10 to 12 weeks and meantime they are fed on food regurgitated by any member of the pack as their upbringing is a group responsibility. Whilst the males tend to stay with the same pack, the females will leave their birth group and move on to join other packs. Their normal diet is medium-sized antelopes such as impala or reedbuck but they will take larger species. Their bodies are thin and muscular with a powerful head and sharp shearing teeth. Excellent runners they do not bother to conceal themselves when they are hunting. They will select their prey, using their magnificent vision, and simply run it down to exhaustion point. Though their disembowelling of their living prey is savage, subsequent feeding is a quiet, disciplined occasion as each dog takes its turn at the carcass. The packs live in dens or burrows usually in the savannas, grasslands or open woodlands and they are at their most active at dawn and dusk. Though the wild dog is considered by the pastoral Masai to be nothing more than a killer pest, their decline in numbers has been brought about by a combination of disease, slaughter by man and the depletion of their prey. Outside Tony Fitzjohn there was little recognition of the fact that the hunting activities of the dogs actually improved the quality of the plains game by removing sick and wounded animals and scattering the remaining herds which prevented inbreeding.

That was the picture painted to Giles Thornton when he was contracted as the Field Manager and tasked to capture up to 30 almost-weaned pups for the breeding project. With the Mkomazi staff and the local Masai elders he was left to work out the best strategy for removing the pups. From the start Fitzjohn had made it clear that he did not favour the use of darts to put the adult dogs out of action. He proposed that the dens should be raided whilst the adults were out hunting. The hunting team should dig down into the dens where the pups were hidden. He hoped that the removal of the pups would lead only to temporary distress and that the dogs would then move off and mate again.

Just as had been the case with the Congo Peacock, Giles set about recruiting help amongst the tribesmen in various areas where he was seeking the dens of the wild dogs. His offers of US$50 at the time were not as avidly received in Tanzania as they had been in Zaire; here indolence took precedence over greed but nonetheless he extracted many promises of assistance. Courtesy of Tony Fitzjohn, Giles had met Cliff, a New Zealander who had a farm near Ngasumet which was an area that Giles had to check out:

I left Arusha on my motorbike with just my saddlebags. I had sent my paraglider and other stuff in the car with Cliff's men. Leaving Arusha along a hellish stretch of road that was just deep, talcum powder-like dust which dried out the chain so that it made a fearful noise. The dust continued for an hour or so and then I hit a better road and raced off due south along a gravel track – heading straight for an escarpment at the edge of the Masai Steppe. I went up the steppe and into open forest, long grass and acacia woodland. I passed the occasional 'manyatta' [small village] *and herds of cattle tended by Masai boys. They pointed me in the right direction for Ngasumet. From then on there were lots of manyattas but no people, just the incredibly open woodland in which I could easily imagine the Masai picking off the wild dogs as they cruised along in a fanned out formation at a stiff pace. As I came over a rise I could see big hills all around me some 50 miles away, but others much closer. This made me think of paragliding and I searched every hill for a launch site. Eventually I* came into a valley of cleared land. The first paddock was full of blackened sunflowers very much ready for harvesting. The cleared land was a huge area and I remembered that Cliff had told me that I would pass a farm belonging to a white man called Gerard Miller. I debated whether to go and talk with him but decided to just keep going. I charged on past another huge bean farm cut out of the steppe. A sign told me that it was the Dutch company for which Cliff was growing seed. There was a big hill beside the farm; like a massive kopje [small, conical hill]. I went on down to a mission town called Nabalela, passing straight through it and out the other side. These small places just used to be wells where the Masai brought their stock for watering. The missionaries arrived and built huge houses, churches and schools and, of course, installed pumps so that the Masai had water provided directly into troughs. Thus the missionaries snuffed out the singing that used to go with the hoisting of water in buckets up through the various levels of the well, and with it an important part of Masai culture and their day-to-day life. This happened at almost every main watering site that had a road leading to it.

I was welcomed to Ngasumet by Charlie, Cliff's Aussie manager; he was a bit fraught as he had discovered the theft of 250 empty sacks which were to be used to bag the beans. He had about 100 people pulling the beans by hand – they threw them onto large flat areas called 'tanderewas' and then a tractor was driven over them several times to break open the pods before they were thrown by hand into a tractor powered cleaner with a fan which blasted the beans out of one side and the rubbish out of the other. Charlie was running around trying to make it all happen. He did not speak much Swahili and he was ridiculously racist and the boys were running rings around him. Cliff appeared that night and when he heard about the thieving he flipped and things started to get ugly so I went for a walk. I climbed up a small hill to watch the day's end. There was a good view from such a small elevation and I could see the mountain in the North Lendanai Massif that I really wanted to climb. It had huge cliffs on one side and forest on the other. I wanted to go up that mountain, sleep at the top and fly off in the early morning – it looked perfect. We had a late dinner followed by whiskey and cigars – not bad! I thought that the New Zealander, Cliff, was as tough as old boots. He has a small fleet of aeroplanes to service the hunters in the bush, a bean farm and then, over in the west, south of Mwanza, he has just started a gold mine. He made me laugh – he drinks a great deal so I went to bed early.

Cliff left early to see another bean man, Garry Hoops, over at Nabarera but I needed to go into Ngasumet to speak to the officials in the area about the wild dogs. I needed to see the likes of the District Commissioner, the Ward Secretary, the Chairman of the Village and the Chairman's Secretary: I don't know who made up the titles but one thing is for certain – you have to see them all! A man I particularly wanted to see was a Masai called Richard Lisikoi, who was the secretary of something or other, but Tony Fitzjohn had told me that if I wanted help, then Richard was my man. I found him at the District Headquarters. He was standing outside the building talking to the DC, so I sat in the car and waited for them to stop chatting. They both walked over to me and I introduced myself, shaking hands with Richard who was a very slight man, not indulging the good things of life as, it would seem, was the DC, who was fat and sweaty like most District Commissioners. I told them about my mission to catch the African wild dogs and to transport them to Mkomazi. Richard knew about the project and seemed pleased to see me. The DC demanded a proper meeting to discuss my plans and told me to return on the following Monday morning for a briefing with all his men. The DC then pissed off and Richard and I had a decent chat. He said he was hopeful that dogs could be found especially in the area south of Ngasumet. He said that many had been seen there. I told him that I needed to find their dens so that when they had pups it would be much easier to catch them. He said that he would be visiting Cliff's 'shamba' the next day when we could talk more.

I trekked back to the village and looked for the men who were investigating the missing sacks. They had found the sacks in a shop, but the woman who owned it would say nothing. Then one of our men, Juma, who was one of the investigators, brought a Masai man over to meet me. His name was Talek; he came from an area about 20 miles to the south called Zonderages. He had a bunch of Dorobo friends who knew where the wild dogs in that area were laying up. I told him of my plans and of the TS200,00 reward for the successful identification of a den and subsequent capture. He was very happy and said he would walk to Zondereges that same day in order to find out all he could. He would be back the following Monday to correspond with my meeting with the DC in Ngasumet.

There is a sizeable hill to the north west of the shamba and I decided to ride out and climb it. The track led to another big shamba and then on towards the hill. So I burned off on my bike into open woodland with very long grass. On the way I spotted congoni, Grant's gazelle, impala and a gerenuk. It took half an hour to reach the hill. It was covered with large boulders which was fun. I had a simple climb to the top with hyrax observing my progress. At the peak I could see for miles. The shamba stood out 20 kilometres away. I could also see the Dodoma Transport shamba. In the north were the mountains and, of course, Lendanai and in the haze I could just make out the outline of the Pares and Usambaras on the other side of Mkomazi. It was so, so beautiful. I moved along the ridge and I startled a pair of mountain reedbuck, who whistled at me in alarm and belted off over the side. I suspect a leopard was watching me. Klipspringers were observing from atop of a rock but they seemed very relaxed. I sat down, smoked a fag and watched an augre buzzard soaring overhead. So, this is the Masai Steppe – well – it's good by me. This will be a fine place to hang out, do some roaming and with lots of luck I'll bag some wild dogs to satisfy my employer. As I descended on my bike I noted a great place for take-off with the paraglider – just a few bushes to be cut down – I would be returning to that place. When I got to the track I stopped to dig the thorns out of the tyres before they penetrated the inner tubes. Near to the camp there was a flash of brown on my right – BANG – the dog hit my front wheel going flat out. The bike went down and I was on the dirt track. 'Breaker', Charlie's Rhodesian Ridgeback had scored a direct hit. I picked up the bike to find a bloody great hole in the fuel tank. I was losing my cool fast and anger was rushing through me. "That fucking dog! I'm going to kill it!" Fuel poured out into the dirt. I ranted and raved and I could see the dog up at the cookhouse watching me. I rode up the hill shouting at the beast and hurled a few rocks at it and then, with the anger burned off, I was ready to think logically. There were no welders at this shamba so I took the tank off and drained it.

I took an early morning walk – the nights and morning are very cold on the Steppe. I returned to the camp, had some tea and started to write up the diary eventually arriving at this day, July 8. Wow, if it ain't my birthday. No! I'm not going to tell a soul – well – maybe tonight if I can get to that whiskey bottle. Charlie called Dodoma on the radio and found that I could get my fuel tank welded there so I filled the hole with soap and mended a puncture whilst I was waiting for Richard. He turned up at noon. He had come to sort out the problem of the thieves and to tell me where I should go looking for the dogs. He reckoned an area called Ndidu, 50 kilometres south of Ngasumet, was the right place. He had brought with him a Masai called Kiroi, who was to go with me. We arranged to go two up on the bike next Monday after the meeting with the DC. Richard was very smug – the thieves had been identified and sent off to the clink.

Next day I got my tank repaired at Dodoma Transport and in the late afternoon I headed back. As I passed through the enchanted forest I saw zebra, oryx, congoni, Grant's gazelle and also a corey bustard. But, I wanted to see a dog! Back at the camp Charlie seemed happy to see me. His nerves had been becoming a bit threadbare over the theft problem. Anyway – out came the whiskey bottle and I told him it was my birthday. We had a good laugh when he said it had been his birthday four days earlier.

Giles set off on a round trip to spread the word about his hunting project. He heard many stories about the dogs and where they may be but all the leads came to naught and he was getting a little downhearted about his lack of progress.

12 July 1995: Charlie had put a note under my water container – "Attention Giles – Dog holes! – Kiroi's Manyatta – 7.30 a.m." I had some coffee and set off along the track to Ngasumet thinking about the dogs. Up ahead an animal bounded across the road. It was a single Wild Dog. It stopped and watched me getting closer. I stopped about 15 yards from him. We watched each other. It was a big dog with a pure white tail, a black head and neck with a brown/yellow torso. The stomach had black and white patches. He was about the size of a German Shepherd. I was really chuffed; we must have looked at each other for two minutes before he set off into the long grass. When I started the bike and moved off, he stopped again and watched me pass about 50 yards from him. I thought this was a good omen and I was now convinced that the pups would be in the den. I arrived at Kiroi's boma to find Talek waiting for me and he was convinced that there were pups and dogs in the den. I put him on the back of the bike and off we went to Londereges on a windy, cloudy and cold morning.

On the way a huge kudu jumped across the road. It was probably the one I had seen a few days back. Then I saw a dog-like shape about half a mile ahead and as we drew close I could see that it was a wild dog. We stopped 10 yards away and I switched off the engine. We watched each other for about 30 seconds and then he ran in a few tight circles – no doubt we had confused him. He went off into the bush and then came back onto the road with his huge ears angled towards us. I whistled at him and he barked and jumped into the air, twisting round and bounding into the thicket *only to reappear about 20 yards further on. I moved towards him and he again ran into the bush and watched us as we passed. I was feeling thrilled and excited. This was a great start to the day.*

We passed Londereges and two miles further along the small track we met Talek's mate. Leaving the bike we set off into the bush. There was kudu dung here and there and many small game trails amongst the long, dry grass and thorn trees. After half an hour Talek said we were very close and so we crept forward. I could see mounds of red earth, which had obviously been excavated, under a bush about 10 yards ahead. I called a halt and we sat down to watch as I didn't want to scare off any inhabitants. After 15 minutes I eased forward alone. There were no sounds or dust coming from the den. I went all the way to the top – it was empty. There was one huge hole which led to a massive underground chamber with small side cavities. There was enough light penetrating the chamber for me to be able to see the interior. It was large enough for a man to lie down in. The mounds of earth had a few footprints of four-toed dogs but they were old with insect tracks over them. The dust layer which covered everything was undisturbed. It was disappointing. On the other hand there had been the dog on the road. What had happened to my 'good omen'? Talek did not seem surprised and on further investigation he confessed that he had discovered the holes the day before and he was really keen to show them to me. Africa!! Talek's mate said that he knew where there were many dens not far from us so we set off three up on the bike. We travelled about eight miles but all the holes were very old so we returned to Londereges where I was told by a number of elders that the best time to find inhabited dens with pups was during November, December or January. These elders lived in the area and spent most of their time cruising around and so they should know. I rode back to the shamba and had a beer with Charlie whilst watching the sunset and then the moonrise. The night was incredibly bright with a very large brilliant moon and a clear starry sky. I tried to work out what to do. Tony Fitzjohn was due in around 14 July and I thought that I should put it to him that we should leave and come back in December. The alternative was to use the dart gun and capture individuals.

Giles had another couple of days with the same results; lots of old dens but no sign of inhabitants. He was becoming convinced that the best option would be to return later in the year. He badly needed to lift his spirits and he knew just the thing.

I was back at the shamba by noon. Charlie had a visitor; George Angleides, another bean farmer who also does hunting safaris. I had heard the name a few times so it was good to meet the man. He was a most amusing fellow, of Greek extraction, but now a Tanzanian citizen. After lunch I had a short siesta and then I put my paraglider on my back and rode off on my bike to Ngoisuk, the hill that I had climbed three or four days back. I left the bike in a clearing and humped up the hill with a panga in my hand. I had seen a suitable place for jumping off when I was last on the hill. I had to do an hour's work clearing small bush and one tree and then my site was ready. My wind watch said that the average speed was 28 mph. On the edge and on a new hill I was a little nervous. However, I did a reverse start and I had a vertical take-off. I pressed on the accelerator bar and shot up fast and high. I peaked out at 1,000 feet above my launch site which put me 1600 feet above the motorbike. An augre buzzard came to within 15 yards to check me out. I looked over my shoulder and I could see Kilimanjaro and Mount Meru. I took several in-flight photographs, did many 360 degree tumble turns and went back up. Then I just sat there watching everything laid out in front, behind and below me on the Masai Steppe. I was so happy to be up in the sky again. After one and a half hours of soaring it was time to land. The light was fading so I twirled down and swooped over the big Tortilla Acacias and hooked into the glade where my bike was. Back at the shamba I found out that one of the Masai watchmen had spotted me flying, although the hill is almost 10 miles from the shamba. We had a laugh – he had no idea how I managed it.

15 July provided a beautiful dawn. I filled the bike with petrol and cruised off, heading for Lendenai. I arrived at Ormote, where there is a huge rock and a deep water pool. There were four lion cubs curiously watching my arrival. I stopped and switched off the engine immediately. They thought about running, but decided against it, either crouching or sitting on their haunches. Then they just looked at me. They were about five or six months old with huge oversized paws. Now, where was the mother? She was the one I had to be careful about. We sat and watched each other for about five minutes. I made silly noises at them, which made them come a bit closer. They were about 20 yards away from me now. Where was the mother? It was time to move on. I started the bike and moved towards the cubs scattering them. Then, suddenly, there was mum! What a big beast she was, with a very long body, a huge snarling head and all her teeth on display. The tail was swishing and the adrenalin rushed through my veins as I headed off into the bush to circle round her. Anyway she decided not to make mincemeat out of me and I got by. She looked a formidable creature at 10 feet! A mile further on I came up behind the big male who had finished watering and was padding away to a good spot for a snooze. He had a dark brown mane and a heavy body. He did not hang around and darted into the thicket. The poor chap had probably been hunted in his time and now had a deep-rooted fear of the internal combustion engine.

On the way to Seke, Giles stopped at some Masai manyattas to enquire about the dogs and he was again treated to visits to various empty dens. Though one showed signs of recent visits there were no puppy footprints.

There is a gap in the diaries but in a letter home dated 6th November 1995, Giles makes further reference to the project. In early August he made the six-hour bike ride to meet up with his younger brother, Sam, who was taking part in a project in Moshi and so by inference the conclusion to the hunting dog operation came around late September of that year.

The wild dog capture was an amazing experience. It turned out to be 100% successful in every way. I spent a great deal of time with the Masai in the area. They are excellent folk, however savage and barbaric their life style may appear to be. They took me in and trusted me and thus helped me a great deal in my quest. There is no way in which I could have been so successful without them.

It was the cattle herders who knew where the dogs were denning. They push their cattle into the thickets looking for a bite to eat and they stumble on the tracks of the dogs. I soon began to find the spoors of dogs on cattle paths and amongst car tracks. Within two weeks we had found two dens with pups. All this was done riding on my motorbike. I picked up the Masai boys, put them on the back and off we went down a pathway to check out the dens. There is no way it could have been done in a Land Rover, unless you were prepared to walk for miles into the bush from the vehicle. Then it was a case of watching and waiting. Out of the six dens that we found I chose the three which were the best ones to dig up. We only wanted 25–30 pups. I spent the next four weeks sitting up trees or on cliff ledges looking down at the dogs, counting the pups and watching them grow up. It was amazing to observe the interactions when the main adult group came back with food to regurgitate for the young. There was much playing, cuffing and greeting of the hierarchy.

At last it was time to pounce. The pups were about two months old and ready for weaning. Each morning at dawn, when the pack had left for the hunt, the sister of the Alpha female would stay to guard the den. However, at about ten o'clock she would go for a scout around the area and that is when we moved in. Five Masai and I armed with spades, hoes and picks went to work. It was a digging frenzy and then there were eight pups in the box. The box was tied onto the back of the motorbike, the boys jumped on and away we went on the one-hour ride back to the holding pen near a bush airstrip. The next morning we tackled another den with 13 pups and the morning after a den in a cave from which we took four female pups leaving the rest to stay in the cave until mum returned. Remarkably all the pups remained quiet and calm during capture. They were cool and started eating a milk and mincemeat diet almost immediately.

Then began a three-week intensive induction course in human interaction. The radio was playing 12 hours a day; plenty of talking, playing cards, backgammon and chess were the orders of the day. Next we made them come and get their food from our hands or a big bowl held between our legs. Then there were games (more like fighting) with a piece of rawhide – you on the one end and eight dogs on the other. After this we laid up in the mid-day sun together with them in the shade. They tamed down pretty quickly. Tame pups are less prone to stress and are much easier to handle of course. It was now time to bundle them into boxes again for the 40-minute flight to the Mkomazi Game Reserve. There they were put into their new big bomas with huge underground dens and trees for shade. They had at least one acre for each group in which to roam. It's their home now and it forms the basis of Tony Fitzjohn's breeding programme. Their progeny will be released into the wild when mature enough to cope.

Tony hopes to release the dogs at Mkomazi, Serengeti, Manyara and Tarangiri National Parks. All very good stuff! The only irony is that down in southern Tanzania on the Masai Steppe there are plenty of wild dogs, even here in the Selous I have seen two individual packs in the small area in which I have been walking. When talking to hunters from the southern Selous and other hunting blocks, they all report large numbers of African hunting dogs. Anyway, that's a problem for the scientists.

59. Preparing to ride on the updraft over the edge of the cliff

60. A view along the cliff from the paraglider

61. Posing in a photo shoot for the Boden catalogue

62. Emma Campbell and Giles, New Year Safari, Chulu Hills

*63. Simon
Dugdale*

64. Stopping for refreshments with Emma in Tanzania, while on a return trip from Katavi

65. Jonathan Salonka and Kani in the Chyulus, 2006

66. William Kupe at Borana, 2006

67. Jackson Sakimba at Ol Donyo Wuas, October 2006

68. Has the WD40 released the bolt?

69. With Danny McCallum's clients, September 1998

70. October 1998

71. Borne by his four brothers to the Funeral Pyre at Borana, Laikipia

72. The Funeral Pyre

73. The conclusion of the Funeral Service

74. His father at Giles's memorial rock, Borana

Chapter XVI

With The Bonhams In The Selous

In early November 1995, Giles worked again for Richard Bonham in the Selous Game Reserve. This fascinating tract of land became one of Giles's favourite places in Africa. He got on very well with Richard Bonham who was already an iconic personality as a hunter, guide, conservationist and safari organiser. Bonham had been the first to lease land in the Selous and was a firm believer in walking safaris for which the area is perfect. He had built his safari lodge on the great Rufiji River about 10 miles downstream of Steiglers Gorge which is a large and beautiful natural phenomenon 100 metres deep and 100 metres wide. At the lodge, Sand Rivers, the Rufiji is about one kilometre wide offering a spectacular view over the rocks and sand bars with their resident hippos and crocodiles.

The river was beginning to erode the banks close to the tents and one of Giles's jobs was to build rock walls to contain that situation, build more water tanks and cut new game trails. Occasionally he would be asked to guide clients on the game walks but this was a task he avoided where possible:

Mark and Millie are running the lodge side of things. They are going slowly mad as one does if one has to deal with clients all hours of the day. Mark and Millie are good people and we have many laughs behind the scenes. I find it hard not to be unbelievably rude to people that I don't like and don't want to be with. They piss me off and they are stupid. So, I stay clear of that show as much as possible. I just do my thing with the men unless Mark, the manager, is in a real spot and needs help.

In mid-November Giles planned to leave the Selous. He was long overdue some sky diving and paragliding sessions. He would initially go to the Chyulu Hills. The Chyulu Mountain range is in southern Kenya, close to the Tanzanian border and it is the newest mountain range in the world having been created by volcanic activity only 500 years ago. Richard Bonham has a lodge in the hills called Ol Donyo Wuas, which Brian and Verity visited in 2006. They met several of Giles's friends there, including Jackson Sakimba, who had been employed by Bonham when the lodge was being built and then stayed on to become his top man. They also met two guides, Jonathan Salonka and Kani, who were full of stories about Giles. They told them about the time Giles came back from the UK loaded with old motorbike tyres, which were invaluable to the locals for making sandals. Giles loved the place, because it has perfect sites for paragliding:

I'll go back down to the Chyulus to paraglide and jump for two days. Then it will be off to Malindi on the coast for the "free-fall boogie" – 10 days of big blue skies. 200 mph and smiling faces, monster posing, landing on the beach in front of the hotels and restaurants at lunch time or evening beer time. I just can't wait – I need my free-falling so badly.

Another year has flown by – faster than fast itself. I shall be off to Borana again for Christmas and the New Year. I'll be doing a bit of culling and ranching there for Michael. I have not decided whether it will be the Alps for March and April or maybe I shall go back to Ethiopia on a far more vigorous and far afield safari. If I do go to Ethiopia this next time it will be for a good two to three months. I will travel well north up into Eritrea and the Dhalak Islands – there's so much to see up there.

1995 seems to have had more work than play than the average year. Still it was excellent to visit England and then France in the spring. Since returning to Africa I have been flat out – first catching the dogs, then looking after them at Mkomazi. After that I went down to the Selous to be the gang foreman. Still I can do with the cash. Then there was Sam Thornton [younger brother]*, who did his time up in the Pare Mountains with Bantu man, doing his shamba eating and living. He was high up and away from the Great Plains and bush of Africa. Still he was able to see some of it from the windows of another hell bus, going from one Bantu metropolis to another. I hate myself for not having dragged him away from that African 'Coronation Street' and showing him the Africa that I love. However, when the time came that he could get out I was six hours away, doing 10 hours a day looking for, catching and then tending the hunting dogs. Still, he might come back.*

Chapter XVII

The Second Motorcycle Safari

Giles made it to England in time to be the best man at his brother Ben's marriage to Emma Moss in July 1996 and he stayed on until brother Guy's marriage to Samantha Barker in September. After the newlyweds departed to India on their honeymoon, Giles and Michael Dyer spent a busy week preparing their bikes for another epic journey. Six months ago they had planned to ride from England to Kenya. For the European part of the journey they would be accompanied by Michael's wife, Nicky. The initial leg, passing south and east through France, was uneventful and they were soon over the Alps and turning south into Italy.

They circumnavigated Genoa and turned into the coast further south where they enjoyed a night in a luxury hotel overlooking the Ligurian Sea. On again – south to Siena and into the small town of Buencomento where they spent a few days being hosted by Jasper and Camilla Guinness before continuing south. They climbed onto the Apennine spine, moved on through Campobasso and down to the flatlands of Molise and Puglia. They got their first view of the Adriatic Sea at Barletta. Giles would have loved to have spent more time exploring the old fortress towns that had changed little since the Crusaders had built them.

Thoughts of Italy? Many, many more people live in Italy than I expected. I guess that's contraception and Catholicism. Also there are police everywhere whether civil, military, local, state or provincial – they are everywhere. It did feel like a fascist state to me.

Thoughts on Greece? Dirty, wasted EEC money. Don't know how to build roads. Some very friendly but also some hellish people. I loved it!

From the border crossing point at Ipsala on the River Evros, the onward journey to Tekirdağ and Istanbul is unprepossessing but once through the dirty industrial outskirts and into the ancient architecture of Old Constantinople, the scenery improves dramatically. Mosques, palaces, fortresses and old stone houses are divided by narrow, shady cobbled roads alive with street markets, carpet shops, restaurants and coffee shops. The Grand Bazaar is an incredible place. The atmosphere is alive and it is fascinating just to observe all the different racial trends shown in the varying faces of the vendors and passers-by. During their time in the old city, Giles gave Michael and Nicky as much space as he could – their time together was drawing to a close:

Sunday 13 October: The last breakfast together. The sunshine was beautiful as we looked over the Bosporus from the rooftop café. We packed up the bikes and I let Mike and Nicky make their goodbyes. Then we were off down to the ferry. Nicky was flying that day to London and then onto Nairobi. We got onto the ferry for Asia and I could tell that Michael was gutted at leaving Nicky so I gave him some space and I carried on acting the fool with the Turks.

The journey through Turkey and into Syria was uneventful but very enjoyable:

We headed south on the great Damascus highway. Nearly every car, lorry and bus sounded their horns and the occupants waved and smiled. At Hims we turned west because we knew there was an old castle (Krak des Chevaliers) somewhere in the vicinity. After half an hour we saw a huge castle up on a hill to our north and we wheeled off in that direction. We parked by a small café and had some tea before walking up to the place. It is a huge construction, built in the 12th Century by the Crusaders. It is in great condition. In its time it housed 4,000 troops. We walked around the outer wall first with its 13 towers and magnificent main entrance. Then there was the inner moat separating the central construction. There were huge rooms, chapels, bedrooms, stables, baths, courtyards, latrines, ovens, kitchens, stores and guard's quarters all of which we saw. It is a phenomenal castle in such a good state that you can picture the goings on 800 years ago. We got out and walked to the nearest hill from which we watched the castle turn from red to grey in the fading sun. We returned to the castle the next day to take some shots in the early morning light and then we set off for Palmyra. Palmyra (Talmud to the Arabs) is an oasis in the middle of the desert. There are ruins covering many acres consisting of huge buildings and columns rising into the desert sky; surrounding these are large cultivations of date palms and olives. We carried on out into the evening light and looked back to marvel at the red and orange colouring of the ruins – we got to the top of a rise just in time to watch the sun go down. I had some whiskey in my hip flask and it tasted like nectar. We got out our bed rolls and watched the colours change. Down in the valleys the Bedouin were herding their sheep into the camp leaving little dust trails in the air.

Waking in the desert is a fabulous experience. The light in the east is blood red and to the west there is just blackness. I got up and rolled everything up – I wanted to be back down in the ancient city when the sun hit. I roared off down the hill leaving Mick gathering himself up. The sun hit the castle and then another hill with other fortresses all bathed in vivid reds and oranges as the sun climbed rapidly. Mick and I met up and we got stuck into a breakfast of tea and omelette after which we blasted up the hill to the Citadel for an awesome view of Talmud. We motored on towards Damascus through the arid desert passing phosphate mines, salt trading posts and military encampments. We passed Sab Abas and hit the tarmac road. It was dead straight and we rode side-saddle as we thundered west. The Iraqi border is only 60 kilometres away. When we got onto the main Damascus – Palmyra highway the smog appeared and thickened as we passed through the industrial areas and went into the city in our search for the Orient Palace Hotel. It was an old French hotel – a relic of the days when the city was under French government after World War I. It was a grand place that had seen better times but the old charm was still there. We were invited to wheel the bikes through the grand lobby and into the ball room where we were told to leave them – some garage!

Both Michael and Giles were happy to leave Damascus. They were more at home in the open spaces. Michael was struck down with a dose of the 'Syrian Quick Step' which made travelling the next leg of the journey less than pleasant but the trip to the border with Jordan was made in good time. Giles planned to return to England on 25th October for his youngest brother, Jolyon's wedding to Sarah Nichols, on the following day. Leaving his bike in Jordan during the visit presented some paperwork problems and he had been given a contact, Mohammed, to help him with the customs officials in Amman. Giles made contact by telephone and arranged to meet Mohammed the next day in the city.

After finding a better hotel for Michael's lonely sojourn they drove two-up to the airport and Giles was off on his journey home.

I got a bottle of whiskey for Dad and hopped onto the plane. We went via Berlin and I had a laugh with some English squaddies who had been diving in Aqaba. We landed at 4.30 p.m., and as I had only hand baggage I roared through customs and was into the main terminal where I phoned Ben and Guy and arranged to meet at Samantha's house. I used the underground to Earl's Court and walked down those grey London streets to the house in Hollywood Road. We had a laugh, then Guy came and we took off for Suffolk, a three hour drive to Aldburgh where we met up with the family and I got wrecked with Sam and crashed out. Welcome to England.

In the morning I went over to Mum and Dad's house. Clean up and then on with the togs and off to the church for some ushering of family and friends. There was a fine sermon and many tears in the congregation. The reception was at the Aldburgh Yacht Club a fine venue for it and then I ploughed into all the relations and did some awesome PR work which was good fun; hearing all and telling all. The speeches were good and Jo gave a great one. They left on a boat up the River Ald and we let off some flares and sounded aerosol fog horns. 200 yards away the boat broke down! Fingers were pointed at the Thornton Bros but we were not guilty...

Sunday 27 October: Ben and Emma were off to London early so – no worries. We left Aldburgh at 6.15 a.m., on a wet grey East Anglian morning: I picked up my kit for Jordan (new tyres etc) and then off to Heathrow where I managed to get everything checked in without having to pay any extra. I had a direct five hour flight and when I arrived at the Syrian Customs, I asked whether it was possible to leave a bike at the airport when going out of the country temporarily instead of depositing it at Central Customs. They told me that they had a special facility for tourists who came into Jordan in their own vehicles and then had to fly out again for short periods. I was now furious with that wanker, the shipping agent, who had made me go through all the rigmarole before I left. So, when Michael and Mohammed came to pick me up, I told them about it and we agreed not to have anything to do with him again for our onward journey.

They were soon back on the open road and loving every minute of it. They took in the wonderful site of ancient Petra (illegally camping overnight within the hallowed area). The next day they reached Rift Wall with its panoramic views into Petra, the surrounding rock formations and the Rift Valley way down below. Michael's bike had developed an oil leak which they treated with silicone but they knew it would need proper attention before too long. At Wadi Rum they gave more first aid treatment to Michael's machine before settling in to enjoy the most spectacular sunset and moonrise imaginable.

Their pace was leisurely as they enjoyed the freedom of the open road and the hospitality of the Bedouin travellers. At Aqaba they found the boat to Sinai was scheduled for the next day at noon so they decided to try their luck at getting into Israel with a view to driving through Eilat and on into Egypt.

Mossad was there to greet us. There were long questions as to the who, when, what, where, why and everything before they let us through into passport control. There we found out that a Kenyan citizen needs a visa even for the 30-minute drive through Eilat. So we turned and went back into Jordan where the laughing officials fortunately gave us back our documents and stamped us back into the country. Then it was back to Aqaba to buy tickets for tomorrow's boat.

Chapter XVIII

Return To The Dark Continent

Crossing the Gulf of Aqaba was a pleasant experience and Giles chilled out leaving Michael to go through the tortuous entry formalities. There would be no boat for a month so the answer was to go to Suez or Cairo. Here they managed to get their bikes onboard a boat bound for Assab whilst they flew. On 14th November they were ready to move on. They headed north to Massawa so that they could experience crossing, or at least driving alongside, the Danakil Depression.

The Danakil Depression (known as Death Valley) is one of the most unwelcoming places on earth. It consists of desert flatlands and isolated mountain groups with the occasional valley dotted with thorny acacias. There are infrequent oases such as that at Beylul. Inland, towards the Ethiopian Highlands, the Depression sinks to a depth of 120 metres below sea level and it is one of the hottest places in the world with temperatures reaching up to 145°F in the sun. Thousands of years ago the Depression was part of the Red Sea when the earth's crust collapsed and it flooded. The relentless, blazing sun gradually evaporated the inland sea leaving enormous salt flats and saline lakes. The area is sparsely populated by the Afar tribes who make the majority of their limited income from salt mining. There is no rain for three-quarters of the year and what water does get into the area is quickly swallowed up by the saline lakes. The wind is savage, dry and scorching – it brings no relief. Crossing the Depression on motorcycles is not for the faint-hearted and the bikers hugged the coastline for the first part of their journey.

By 9.00 a.m., we were off, we had just said goodbye to Bryan and his mates and now we were heading north, rather ironically since Kenya is to the south west.

The wind is strong from the south and as we enter the desert we go straight into a dust storm so with the wind behind us we are as hot as hell; there was no airflow as we were travelling at the same speed as the wind. The track was clear but rutted, corrugated and rocky. The heat was so intense and I just drank and drank – we were carrying 12 litres of water but we knew where more good water could be found.

We came down to the sea again and into doum palms. This was the village of Beylul. There were lots of wells and camels being loaded with skin water bags. We saw some amazing Afar girls all in brightly coloured cloth. Then the track headed west and inland towards the mountains. Everywhere there was grey rock, grey sand and grey gravel – a million years ago it must have been a volcanic hellhole... the desert formations were stunning as we entered the foothills. We began to see machines of war, mainly Russian tanks, armoured personnel carriers, trucks and a huge burned out helicopter – all from the Mengistu-Eritrean war of some five years ago. The tanks looked so sinister – inside everything was twisted and broken or melted from a huge explosion and fire. Outside it all looked as though it could have happened yesterday. There were even empty shell cases still lying around. The helicopter was a charred pool of aluminium with the tail rotor some 20 yards away. Great photo opportunities.

We climbed on into the mountains passing the small village of Gehara where we saw more camels being loaded with water. The containers are whole goat skins tied at legs, head and tail making them look quite disgusting – like bloated carcasses. The people were friendly and pointed us in the right direction. The mountains were high above us at 5,285 and 7,277 feet but we used a pass between them at 2,000 feet along a well maintained track. In late afternoon we arrived at Afombo, a large village with a school and an army post. We ate some meat and drank some coke and talked English to some young army lads. The area is a very beautiful luggah [dry river bed] and there are lots of acacias and that is where we spent our third night.

The dawn light was stunning and the desert looked very like the NFD in Kenya. We got a brew of tea going and we were joined by an Afar lad – his timing was perfect and we gave him our spare mug and a brew. We were away very early. The track followed more luggahs and we stopped in the village of Dulabiy which has a sweet water well. The local army squad was having a tea break and they invited us to join them and pored over the map as we chatted. We filled up with water and went on into the desert passing lots of Afar huts. It was extremely beautiful and still relatively cool due to the altitude. We saw the odd gazelle which were of a type I didn't recognize. Then we had to descend and found ourselves getting hotter and

155

hotter. *Suddenly we were into a full sand desert and the bikes needed all that low torque which is so awesome on those KTMs. The wind strengthened and the dust got thicker until visibility dropped to less than 50 yards. We rode close together. We knew the sea was nearby as we could smell it – also there was a lot of coral on the tracks. Visibility dropped to 20 yards and the track was disappearing fast but luckily we hit the T-junction and knew that Tio was only 10 kilometres away. So we headed on in the virtual white-out of swirling sand in a 40 mph wind. Tio was a shanty town and the dust was so thick that you could not see the sea. We reckoned that it was more fun to ride a bike in a sand storm than to sit in it so we roared off into the void. The void being the Danakil depression. Right back into the Great Rift Valley that we had last seen in Jordan. We could see nothing except the faint outline of the track but the going was quite good.*

Then suddenly it was bright blue sky overhead and we could see for miles while behind us was a wall of dust 100 feet high. This was the Front. We stopped for a cigarette but the storm began to catch us up so we raced ahead of it into the dry, stony desert. There were some outcrops of hills in the west but otherwise it was flat patches of foul, foul dust two feet deep which kept testing us. I went blasting into one and I was thrown off in a huge cloud of choking dust. With a following wind I was sprawled in two-feet-deep particles – it was swirling all around me and I could see nothing. Dust in my eyes, nose, ears, mouth and clothes – what a state. Anyway, in a lull I got organised again, washed my face and had a ciggy with Michael. Then the storm caught up with a vengeance and overtook us. We set off in a fury of wind and sand following our route only because it seemed that there was a four-wheeled vehicle ahead of us somewhere that had left deep tracks. The going was good as we raced through that surreal world of 50 yard vision, no horizon, no colour – just those tracks ahead to follow, follow, follow...

Then we were out of the storm again and leaving the now 200 feet high wall of dust behind us. We collected water at an Afar camp and soon we were passing the village of Mersa Fatma – we went on for another 15 kilometres. It was getting dark and the sky was clouding over so when we spotted some acacia trees off the road, we decided to stay there for the night. It was calm and still and very, very hot. Darkness came quickly due to the cloud cover and Michael had the problem of an explosion of cream in his bag – it covered everything and he was not happy. I cooked up some herrings, beans and a tomato paste and we got our heads down. The temperature increased and then it began to drizzle with rain. I fell asleep there in the open and the rain evaporated on contact with my skin and clothes. Then a huge wind hit us. It was so strong that it blew my bike over and we were up and running about with torches grabbing our kit that was trying to escape across the desert.

That was a hellish night with the wind filling us up with sand and a fine dust as it thrashed down the Danakil and out to sea. Michael could not find his tobacco and his temper began to kindle and then we had trouble starting his bike. When we set off he fell in deep sand and without a fag Michael Dyer was in an extremely unamused state of mind. However, the morning became beautiful even with the strong wind and we entered a more mountainous area leaving the dust behind. I saw an ostrich charge off in front of us – a male black and white beauty. There was much amusement when I took a tumble in some dust. The road was now right beside the sea as we passed through a mangrove swamp where it was as slippery as hell. Then we hit the solid lava and it was stunning cruising with the sea alongside – it was just like Lake Rudolph – blue ocean, black lava rock and a strong wind. Back into the dust again as we entered the village of Foro which is by a huge dam that seemed to contain only silt. We had some lunch and then went to look for Ally who was a Peace Corps volunteer who Debs had told us about. We found her wooden hut and stuck our heads inside to say hello. She was 24 years old, blue-eyed and pretty. She was just into a three-year hit of teaching English in Foro, a village so hot that in the months July to August your brain boils. She was very happy to see us and we chatted for an hour or so before moving off to the north again.

We cruised into classic NFD country with the valley full of bush and acacia trees with 800 feet high hills on either side of us. We got to Massawa in the late afternoon and Michael was keen for a beach hotel so we headed out and found a funny Russian-built box of a building. The management was friendly and there was air conditioning and lots of water. After a shower I felt really good. A dinner of fresh fish and pasta with many beers and then I was asleep on my feet as I walked up the stairs.

On Sunday 17th November Giles and Michael made their way up the mountains into Asmara, the capital city of Eritrea. The drive up was beautiful as they climbed up to 7,500 feet through terraced cultivations in the cool, dry mountain air. At Asmara they found the house of Rusty and Debbie where they fed well and were able to wash their clothes and service the bikes. Their intention was to stay in the mountains and go to Keren to visit the British War Cemetery where Debbie had seen a grave with the name Dyer on it. This was Michael's uncle, a pilot, who had been killed somewhere near the Sudan in the early 1940s. They found the grave: M.R.C. Dyer, Royal Air Force, Died 1941. This was a moving moment for Michael.

From Keren the miles were eaten up as they pressed on through Nakfa where the Eritreans had held off the advance of the Ethiopians before breaking them completely and chasing them back to Assab. The surrounding beauty was marred by the debris of war. They met more Afar tribesmen and, as they moved north, they began to encounter the Tigray men with their camels. It was a tranquil drive and they were at peace with the world as they moved through Akordat, Barentu, Mendegera, Kishdik and on to the Ethiopian border post in the village of Rama. After immigration procedures they were speeding on to Aksum:

Michael and I sit and have a picnic and a chill out. The afternoon was spent mending inner tubes and checking over the bikes. In the evening, with a young lad as guide, we went up to the Orthodox Monastery. It was very dilapidated and the monks were ancient. They showed us an old Bible written in some language called Chiz which is supposedly the father of Amharic. We climbed up to a chapel perched right on the top and we had a fine evening view of the world around us, especially the mountains we had circumnavigated. Going back down to the town at last light we passed the church which is supposed to hold the so-called "Ark of the Covenant" – there were some peculiar obelisks outside. Then it was back through the cobbled streets to supper and bed. In the morning I went to the obelisks again to take some pictures and I was immediately accosted by stick-wielding security guards who were shouting aggressively telling me to go into the museum and pay for the pictures I had taken. They threatened to remove the film from my camera. My engine was still running so I calmly told them that there was no sign saying 'museum' nor was there a sign that said 'no photographs'. When they lunged for my camera I took off and waved them goodbye.

Farewell to Aksum and on into the Tigray flanking the Simĕn Mountains as they cruised south. They had to descend 6,000 feet in order to cross the Tekeze River before climbing back up again to continue south. The countryside now was comparatively heavily populated and they weaved between the thatched 'rondavel' style houses, horsemen, barefoot nomads and the riot of livestock that wandered at will. Fuel was scarce and so they headed for the large town of Gonder which would be relatively well supplied. From Gonder they visited Bahir Dar on Lake Tana close to the source of the Blue Nile:

We started out at first light as we wanted to get to the Blue Nile Falls before the package holiday mass arrived. We packed and loaded and left Bahir Dar and followed the dead-end track for 30 kilometres to a small village where we had breakfast. We arranged for a young lad to guard our bikes and clobber and we set off to the ancient footbridge which was built so many centuries ago by one of the Ethiopian Emperors. This single bridge opened up the North West corner of Ethiopia and it crosses the Nile at a thin gorge just down from the falls. The width is only 30 yards and it is made of rock with holes through to let the water drain away when the river is particularly high. We crossed the bridge and headed upstream where we saw the first cataract and the gorge below through the swirling spray. The footpath goes on to allow the traveller to see all of the falls and, as there had been some heavy rain, the volume of water was high. We got soaked in spray and peering over the edge was mesmerising but great fun. A small lad told us to walk upstream where we would be able to get a papyrus raft to take us across to the village where we left the bikes. Sure enough this was possible and we were soon reunited with our kit. We paid our security lad and set off quickly for Addis Ababa.

I knew Addis quite well from a year ago and from cruising with Enzo a few weeks ago and we went straight to his house. That day he had a harem of three girls and an Italian mate and we arrived just as lunch was ready. Food at Enzo's house was superb and just what we needed. We gave our dirty clothes to the girls, bought some oil and steam cleaned the bikes in preparation for a full servicing the next day.

Michael and Giles spent some time in Addis Ababa enjoying Enzo's hospitality but on Friday 29th November it was time to continue:

We reached Lake Lagana and stopped in at a hotel that Enzo had recommended. It was government owned but it was good. After lunch and a siesta we carried on south to Lake Abijaha, a soda lake and so-called Game Reserve. There was no game but plenty of cattle and goats and it was a beautiful area.

Eight days were spent completing the Ethiopian section of the safari and along the way there was the opportunity to renew acquaintances with many of their old friends. From a previous visit Giles remembered some hot springs near Lake Abaya and a pleasant time was spent there luxuriating in the hot water. They passed through the tribal lands of the Afar, Tigray, Konzo, Mursi and Caro and in passing Giles made a hit with many of the different tribesmen and women by doling out the beautiful ostrich feathers that he had bought in Damascus. On Thursday 5th December they camped on the high ground above the Omo Wenz River that feeds into Kenya's Lake Turkana.

Friday 6 December: Morning on our high place was just magic. Oryx, Grant's gazelle and tiang were all in sight. The dense thorn down in the Omo was full of birdsong mainly yellow neck and francolin sounding off. We set off south to Omerati, the last village in Ethiopia, where there used to be a huge cotton plantation but that had gone bust. We snaked our way through the thick bush seeing plenty of lesser bustard and other game. Then the game thinned out as we got closer to Omerati and we drove on down a dried up irrigation ditch into town. The police pulled us in straight away. They were relaxed but a bit menacing and they scanned our passports intently – they spent 25 minutes on each document. Just keep cool – there is nothing we can do. We were asked if we had permits to travel in the south and we protested that no-one had told us anything about that and he let us go. We went into the hotel for our last food and water on Ethiopian soil and then got the hell out of there – 15 miles out of Omerati there is a turning to the south down a dirt track that leads into Kenya. Hardly any traffic is seen on that trail because it is an illegal way to leave Ethiopia but who's going to stop us now.

We pass through Dasanich country and Lake Turkana comes into view and as we cross the Kenya cut line a cheer comes up from Michael's helmet. A few miles further on we approached the Ileret Police Post up on a hill some eight kilometres to our front. We travelled up a tiny luggah and went east for a few miles coming to rest under a big thorn tree that had roots in the water beneath the sand. We topped up with fuel – got the whisky out and sat there watching the sun set. The mossies came in by the thousand and the nets were put up in record time and we carried on chatting in our individual domes.

Up early in the morning and as I was grabbing my stuff I got stung by a scorpion much to the amusement of Michael. He then got me to put a spark plug on my finger and zapped me across the desert. Michael laughed, I swallowed some Ponstan and Brufen and then we were off to the Police Post. The police boys recognized me from a year ago and even the head man, Julius, knew me. He had been at that post for over four years and it really is miles from anywhere. The end of the road in Kenya but the beginning of the road for us. We had tea and chupattis in his shambolic, falling down Police Post and Julius was especially helpful since we left him with some Time and Newsweek magazines. We took a small track which followed the lake shoreline towards Koobi Fora which we reached in the late morning. Koobi Fora was built by old man Leakey and added to by his son, Richard, while they wandered around the area looking for hominids and other fossilized remains. Now it is empty but there is a band of caretakers who look after the houses and people who come to stay for a while. Peter was the boss and Marle the cook. They welcomed us with tea and showed us into a house with a shower while they prepared some food. We had a good stew with chupattis and then a siesta until the sun weakened at 4.00 p.m.

We were half expecting Martin Dyer to fly in from Kisima either that evening or the next morning – we were not sure which because it had been arranged by telephone from Addis Ababa. In the evening I went off for a stroll, Michael wanted to stay put in case Martin turned up. There is a spit of land that juts out about four kilometres into the lake and that is where I was headed. I was three quarters of the way along the spit when I heard an aeroplane. The sun was low in the west and the light was great. I saw the bird, Y DER, fly low over Kubi Fora, bank, and head for the main strip. I thought that Martin must have brought a lot of people if he was using the Saratoga and not the Cessna 185. I kept on with my evening goal of reaching the end of the spit. Grey herons seemed to be having a fine feast on the tiny tilapia that boiled in the shallows. Crocodiles dived off their sand bars when they detected my intrusion. Plovers, dippers and cormorants had a huge red ball of sun illuminating them as it sank over the horizon. North Island looked ridiculously close. It was time to return to Kubi and see who had turned up in Y DER bird. What a great surprise it was when in the fading light I saw Llewellyn and Jack running over to meet me. We had a great laugh. There were Nicky, Martin and Sebastian (Sophie's brother), lots of beer, food and stories. Champagne and beer, full of fillet steak and laughing so much.

Sunday 8 December: I woke just as the glow in the east was starting and, as we had arranged the night before, I went with Martin and Sebastian out onto the spit again. The light over the lake and North Island was sublime. The birds were returning from their overnight roosts inland and the crocodiles were surfacing to warm up. We got to the end of the spit just in time for sunrise. Hippos began to bob in the lake but the heat was coming and we scurried back to Kobi to enjoy the breakfast that Nicky was cooking. We had delicious bacon, eggs, tea, coffee and chattered away – how good it was to have people that I knew so well coming back into my life. Everyone was so happy just to be there with each other. It was decided that Martin and the others would fly back home with nearly all our luggage; Nicky would then be in Namaniac to meet us the next day in the late afternoon. We would roar down to Loyangalani today and the next day move on to Namaniac for the rendezvous.

We loaded the plane, refuelled the bikes and paid the bill. After take off Michael and I roared off on our now lightweight bikes for the 200 kilometres journey to Loyangalani. We saw lots of beautiful game on the way but we just kept on – we stopped only once at the junction where the road splits. It was a lovely place on top of some undulating hills and we drank water and smoked a cigarette or two. Right at sunset we got to that magical bit of Turkana where the El Molo people live. There was not a breath of wind – the lake was a millpond and there was such a beautiful sunset. We should have slept there but – no – it was on into Loyangalani which we reached just as it got dark. There was a disappointment – no cold beer so we boxed on again using headlights until we found a place by the lake to spend the night. We splashed in the cool waters to clean off and then it was corned beef and baked beans (cooled in the lake) for supper.

I had a lovely scene to confront me when I woke up. A flat front tyre. I mended it and off we went and immediately I got another flat. Oh dear. Is it going to be one of those days? We mended it and cruised on into South Horr for tea and breakfast, filled up our water bottles and then hacked out of the Horr Valley. Heading across the Baragoi plain we came up to a car parked on the side of the road and found Yov and Emma waiting for the Turkana bus that brings them their mail and vegetables etc. We had a long chat and I explained that we were meeting Nicky at Namaniac.

Into Baragoi to put some petrol into the tanks, drink some sodas and then off south to Barsaloi and into the Seya Luggah for a rest under a thorn tree. It was mid-afternoon so we went up to Wamba and into the village for tea and chupattis before pointing ourselves towards Namaniac. We were only a little early when we met up with Nicky, Alex, Lulu, Jack and Jospat. We cruised into the town and then on to the area of Sabachi. There were not many Samburu around and hardly any game except for signs of a lot of elephant traffic.

Well Nicky wanted Jack and Llewellyn really involved in some way with our trip from England and so we spent three days pottering around the Namaniac, Wamba, Barsalinga, Kipsing, Ngare Ndare areas and up to Borana. The kids rode on the bikes and had fun. The car carried all our baggage but what was on Michael's mind (and mine) was 'Let's get to Borana and finish this trip and get into some farming and find out what's been going on.' However, we had to do a three night's safari for Nicky and the kids and that was fine – just not quite what I wanted at that time. But the countryside is beautiful and green after some good rain and there are clear, big views. But, I'll be chuffed when I get off this bike at Borana.

Chapter XIX

The Call Of The Selous
With Emma Campbell And Simon Dugdale

Giles spent the next three months in and around Borana. He worked at whatever tasks Michael set him. There was plenty of time for paragliding and he was earning enough cash to fund his next safari which was to be a two-month jaunt down to Namibia with some friends to enjoy the desert biking and, of course, more paragliding.

They left in April of 1997 but it was to be a painful experience for Giles as he dislocated his shoulder and had to leave his bike behind when he returned to Borana. Back at Borana he took on light duties whilst his injury healed. He spent a lot of time with Kupe doing the rounds of the local villages, keeping an eye open for the poachers. By this time another love had entered his life in the form of Emma Campbell; over the years it was an attachment that had grown ever stronger. Emma shared Giles's passion for motorcycles and rough safaris and accompanied him whenever she could.

At Borana he met up once more with an old friend, Simon Dugdale, whom he had first encountered in Tanzania. Simon later recalled that first meeting:

"I met up with Giles at a time when I had spent many weeks in the bush and I was suffering from various infected cuts and scrapes. Giles gave me a double dose of various unguents and took me off to Richard Bonham's camp to recover. Prior to that I think he'd been working for Danny McCallum for about three months. We became good friends. Travelling with Giles was good – we were totally different in character and, surprisingly, this made for an easy relationship. If Giles wanted to do something different and I did not, then we just did our own things without any rancour. Over a couple of years we met up quite frequently. Giles's plans for any meetings were quite precise in an offhand kind of way. It may be something along the lines of 'I'll meet you at the first tea shop on the left of the main road in Ongobongo village at 11.45 hours in six weeks' time.' He would always be there at the appointed hour.

"On this particular occasion we planned a safari for the three of us to go down to Mozambique. Giles and I would first meet up in Lilongwe and drive from there to Mozambique to be joined by Emma who would be flying in. I remember that Giles planned the journey in great detail and he took copies of various maps from Tony Dyer's collection – this included one by Ionedes which purported to show the Selous in great detail."

Giles's first problem was that his bike was still in Namibia so he had to fly down and then make the long, arduous journey to Lilongwe alone. He tackled the venture with his usual aplomb – he chose to take a route which took him along the Caprivi Strip which branches out from Namibia's north-eastern quarter. He followed this along the border with Botswana then on into Zambia on reasonable roads to the rendezvous point at Lilongwe.

They headed south in order to circumnavigate the huge Lake Malawi and then swung north up towards Niassa. Niassa which is a vast area of millions of acres, is as inhospitable as the NFD. It is a world within a world containing bleak mountains, desert, scrub and forests. It is very sparsely populated and the route that the party took was the only thing that could vaguely be described as a road which crosses the country west to east before it emerges at the bustling coastal town of Pemba. The surface of the road is dreadful and the state of the hundreds of rotting wooden bridges crossing the many rivers and gorges is appalling. The Rough Guide gives stark advice to the traveller: "If your vehicle breaks down on this road then you should build a house, take a wife and be prepared to stay there for the next 30 years!"

Simon Dugdale remarked about an irritating problem:

"Giles had a lousy bike. The fuel system was such that every time the bike fell over – and this was frequently in such rough terrain – the carburettor would flood. This required Giles to go through the time-consuming procedure of hand-pumping the fuel system to clear the carburettor and then waiting for the fumes to evaporate and start the machine again. If that didn't work the first time the whole procedure had to begin again. Every stop for a flooded carburettor would mean at least a frustrating 10-minute delay."

Simon recalled other experiences: "We didn't stay long at Pemba. It was a dirty town and it seemed to be full of bearded, rough South Africans on the look out for anything which would make them some money. We went north and found a beautiful small port and beach resort at Mocimboa da Praia. It was an idyllic place to rest for a few days. There was a well constructed 'hippy' beach where there were surfboards and water skis and decent huts to sleep in. We gorged ourselves on the biggest lobsters we had ever seen. According to the fishermen they had to be caught with spear guns because they were so big they just tore apart the lobster pots.

"After two or three days we took a boat to the police post at the mouth of the River Ruvumos in the south of Tanzania. We then had to ride through the estuary swamps which was very hard work. The bikes had loads of about a quarter of a ton. This was made up of large quantities of water and fuel – our personal baggage was very sparse. We made it to Mtwara where Emma left us to fly back to Nairobi. The standard of cooking then deteriorated rapidly! I can still remember well the first meal that Giles prepared after Emma's departure. He simply poured some hot water over cous-cous and added a few vitamin tablets. When I cooked I have to say that I produced a very passable meal."

They were now travelling towards the Selous in complete isolation. Occasionally they would break out onto roads for short periods of time but even these had potholes that could be a hundred metres long and very deep. This was also aggressive lion country and the few villages that they did pass all had stockades of 10 feet high sharpened wooden stakes surrounding them. The presence of the lions was a sobering thought whenever they settled down for a night's sleep.

When they reached the boundaries of the Selous they pondered their route. Being a Game Reserve there was a ban on travelling by motorcycle within the whole of the area. They made a pre-dawn entry on their forbidden machines to find that navigation was slow and difficult causing many arguments but they did agree on one thing – they had been totally lost for several days. They were making their way slowly northwards with the aim of finding Richard Bonham's safari camp on the Rufiji River. They were completely amazed when they broke out of the bush and saw Bonham's camp on the opposite bank. Richard immediately sent a boat across to ferry them and their bikes across the river but as soon as they off-loaded they were put under house arrest by Minja, the resident ranger, for having transgressed the law about motorcycles in the Selous Game Reserve. This was serious business but help was at hand. When Minja reported to the Minister of Tourism in Dar es Salaam, Richard Bonham's friend, Bim Theobald, was able to intervene on their behalf and succeeded, over a period of four to five days, in getting the punishment, set at US$600 reduced to US$150.

Simon related an amusing tale of an event that happened when they arrived at Bonham's camp:

"Whilst Giles had been working on the construction of the camp he had shot a large quantity of crocodiles and, knowing that their skulls might be needed as gifts for friends, he had buried a number of them. When he left Bonham's employ some time later he left behind the crude map that he drew of the skulls' locations. I had always wanted a crocodile skull so Giles told me that he'd dig one up but the map had disappeared. We heard stories about one of the Game Wardens who had spent some time furtively digging along the edge of the river so we went to take a look. Sure enough there were little holes scattered around the site. Giles didn't find any of the skulls but we had a good laugh as we realised that the Game Warden obviously thought that he was going to find something of value like elephant tusk or rhino horn. He must have been quite disgusted and it would have been very amusing to witness his chagrin.

"Before we left the area Giles wanted to take another trip down the Ruturu River to see the famous Ruturu Falls. Close to the site we found a lovely pool – on the bank was a huge crocodile but to my astonishment this did not deter Giles or Emma (who had rejoined us) from stripping off and enjoying a swim.

"Giles had a fund of funny stories and I liked the one he told me about when he was working at Borana and he wanted Charlie Dyer to join him on a quick visit to Nairobi. Charlie wasn't interested so Giles set off on his bike. Rounding a bend he almost fell off his machine in amazement. There to the side of the road were about a dozen scantily dressed girls! Pirelli was shooting sequences for one of their famous nude calendars. Giles revelled in this stroke of good fortune and he even managed to make US$300 by allowing his bike to be used in one of the shots. He rubbed Charlie's nose in it for months afterwards. He also recounted the time that he and Emma had visited Danny McCallum's place where one of his clients had just shot a lion. In time honoured tradition the testicles had been fried in breadcrumbs and given to the client who, on finding out what they were, refused the 'treat'. The balls were eagerly eaten by Giles and Emma much to the client's disgust."

The adventurers parted company once they reached Nairobi; Emma and Simon had to get back to work and Giles was keen to return to Borana. It was September 1997 and their safari had lasted a little over three months.

For most of that year Giles worked for the Dyers and Gilfrid Powys. He took occasional breaks to go on motorcycle safaris with Emma. In May he set off on the motorbike with his paraglider and some friends for Namibia. On this occasion his gymnastics did not save him from a heavy fall, which broke his collar bone. This entailed a very painful journey in a Land Rover to Windhoek where the shoulder was repaired and a subsequent return journey to Namibia to collect the motorbike. He also made another solitary journey to Mozambique, but there are no diary entries to describe either of these adventures. In fact since meeting Emma, Giles's diary (and other correspondence) took a much less prominent place in his life as he sought to spend more and more time with her. Emma commented later that she thought that Giles had stopped maintaining his diaries because, in her, he had finally found someone he could talk to.

By now he had been in Africa for about six years – had it changed him? Emma was the person closest to him:

"He was an alpha male and as such he collected other alpha males around him – men with the same romantic vision as himself. Many of those people had done the same things as Giles but they had matured and set off their experiences against designing a future for themselves. Giles lived totally in the present and it was impossible for him to project or contemplate the future. He did not want children of his own – that would have been too much of a responsibility.

"I remember on the trip in Namibia we stopped for a break and with some sticks we found we started fencing which used to be one of my sports. It called to mind the dying words of Petruccio in Romeo and Juliet and I taught Giles the speech "Curse both houses..." He may well have done that before he died – cursed the black and white "houses".

"Giles was a very good communicator – he called me most days and if he said we would meet somewhere at a particular time – he would always be there. He could be very selfish – not with material things but if he wanted to do something then you were expected to go along with it even if it did not suit your own plans. For instance he was very down when he broke his collar bone – Simon Dugdale had to leave him to get back to work so Giles sent for me. But if one got angry with him it would not last long because he would beguile one with that smile of his."

When Emma was asked why she had used the phrase "Enyway a jump is a jump" on the service sheet for Giles's funeral, she said that it related to the death of Emma McCune (referred to on page 67) and it was recorded in his parachute log book. Emma McCune had been a close friend of Giles and he was terribly upset. To express his feelings of loss he made a special parachute jump shouting her name as he left the aircraft. Emma thought that in some cryptic fashion Giles was indicating that Emma's death was simply a jump to another plane which is why she thought it apt for the funeral service sheet.

In July 1998 Giles was offered more work with Danny McCallum who wanted him to help with setting up a safari trail, some construction work and some fencing. He did not see Emma for about three months and when they got together in early October they planned a restful break on Kenya's holiday coast.

On 19th October 1998 Giles, Emma and her children took a half-term holiday at Was, a small town close to Mombasa which boasted a beautiful beach. On their second night in a small cottage a commotion outside caused Giles to step out and investigate. He came face to face with five or six men bent on robbery. True to his nature Giles, conscious of the occupants of the cottage, and declaring that there was no money on the premises tried to talk the robbers into leaving. They were having none of it and at a signal from the apparent leader of the gang, Giles was shot.

Immediately after the event Emma, on finding the badly wounded Giles, did her best to save him by making a high-speed drive to the ferry and getting him across to the hospital. Sadly it was too late. Giles had lost too much blood and despite the best efforts of the hospital staff he soon slipped into oblivion.

The murder remains unsolved.

Chapter XX

This Is Africa!

Brian and Verity's home, Priors Mesne, nestles comfortably in a fold of a ridge that backs onto the leafy splendour of Gloucestershire's Forest of Dean. To the front is an expansive view of the wooded deer park and green fields; the eye is drawn down over the gently rolling hills and out across the estuary of the River Severn. It is a peaceful house and a few minutes spent gazing over this panorama from the bedroom window made the beginning of each day a real pleasure for Brian and Verity. In the late autumn of 1998, however, their idyll was shattered. In Brian's own words:

"When the telephone rings at four in the morning, you jump out of your dreams, look at the clock and fear the worst. This happened to Verity and me on the morning of 21st October. The caller was Emma Campbell, who told us that our third son, Giles, had been murdered during a botched attempted robbery at a house on the coast in Kenya. To be told of the loss of one's own child is like having a black and suffocating cloud descend on you shutting out rational thought. The lovely view from our bedroom window which usually inspires us at the start of each day appeared as a blank canvas.

"It was not long before more calls came in from Africa and we began to wonder at the speed with which news travels. I had to make sure that Giles's five siblings and the rest of the family were told the devastating news before they heard it from elsewhere. We spent most of that morning in a highly emotional state, telling friends and relations the dreadful account of Giles's murder. In the afternoon the press started calling, hungry for any detail that might have allowed them to castigate Africa or to dredge up some story which might hark back to "white mischief". We helped them as best we could but when they failed to find a salacious background to the tale their interest soon faded.

"Giles had lived with Emma Campbell for several years and she told us that if he died in Africa he wanted to be cremated way out in the bush. He had never expressed any particular wish to us and had left no will, so, despite some misgivings, we agreed to abide by his wishes. Our doubts were soon dispelled when Michael Dyer, who lives on and runs a ranch, called Borana, on the northern side of Mount Kenya, told us that all the arrangements were in hand. The cremation was to take place on 28th October, '…could we arrange to come out on the 27th and stay at Larraguy?' This is a lovely house, which at that time belonged to the Cecil family, and is situated on top of the escarpment of the ranch. Verity and I were both still dazed and decided to give the Dyers, who had been amongst Giles's closest friends, a free hand.

"We arrived at Nairobi International Airport with our four sons Guy, Ben, Jo and Sam; our daughter, Kim and her husband, Geoffrey Wheating, Verity's cousin, Bimbo Stancioff and Jimmy Millard (a friend of Ben and Giles). Inés Sastre, a stunningly beautiful past girlfriend of Giles made up the party. Sally Higgin, a great friend of Verity's sister, joined us at Wilson Airport for the one-hour flight to Borana.

"We were weary after the night flight from Heathrow, but before going to Larraguy to relax, Michael Dyer proposed that we see Giles before he was placed in his coffin. He was lying on a bed in their house dressed in his usual leather bush jacket, looking serene. We kissed his cold forehead, hung on to each other and tried to overcome the overwhelming sense of loss and sadness that engulfed us.

"From there Michael took us to the place where the funeral service and cremation were to take place. It was to be on the top of a hill, about a mile from Michael and Nicky's house. The views in every direction were spectacular; the brooding, snow-capped crags of Mount Kenya loomed upwards in the distance and in the other direction lay miles of the open African bush that Giles had loved so much.

"The next morning, having woken from our comfortable beds at Larraguy, a hearty breakfast was served on the terrace in the Cecils' beautiful house with views stretching for miles. We watched the game in the surrounding bush and, after a swim in the pool, went back to Nicky and Michael's house.

"The body of our son, Giles, was placed in a simple wooden coffin with wooden rails as handles; messages and feathers were placed beside him, the lid was screwed down and his bush hat placed on top. Guy, Ben, Jo, Sam and I carried the coffin to a waiting Land Rover and the whole party then drove out to the hill. There we were met by the officiating minister, The Reverend Tim Daikin along with a Hindu expert in cremation. Again, we carried the coffin and laid it on a steel frame so that it was about a foot above the ground. Having felt quite nervous about the whole process and worried that it could all go wrong, my confidence returned, though in the back of my mind I remained concerned that we had had no control over the arrangements.

"The next task was to build the funeral pyre under, over and around the coffin under the expert supervision of the Hindu official. A few of Giles's friends had begun to arrive already. They came on foot, by bicycle, by motor bike, car and aeroplane; some even by paraglider. They brought feathers of every description and threaded them between the logs of the pyre. (Giles had a fascination with feathers and had been an avid collector.)

"Lunch was served back at Larraguy and afterwards we prepared ourselves for the funeral. On passing Michael and Nicky's house I was taken aback by the sight of the large number of aeroplanes that were parked on the airstrip and I began to wonder just how many people were coming to Giles's funeral.

"At the hill banners had been erected in a semi-circle and a large throng of people were standing waiting to pay their respects.

"The funeral service was one of the most uplifting, even exhilarating ceremonies I have ever experienced. Apart from the extraordinary place in which we were assembled, I was very moved by the words that were spoken both in prayer and eulogy, the hymns that were sung and the very large numbers of both black and white people about us; but it was the wild animals, especially the elephants, that were watching from the hills nearby, which brought a very special aura to the proceedings. In particular it was the address given by Tim Daikin that was especially poignant. A relevant part of his words are quoted here:

"...Giles was not from Kenya, but, like so many before him, he found his home here. He would as often mix with local people as he would with his own kind. And he had the constitution, practical ability and inclination to spend long periods in the bush, particularly in desert places with nomadic people.

"Of course, Giles's nomadic freedom was exasperating to both his family and friends. But he will be long remembered by the many who knew him for even a short while, for he lived life to the full in an unselfconscious way. He truly loved women (and felt free to kiss them in a rather public way), and his boyishness enabled him to relate freely to children, and yet he also had the respect of men – 'real' men who knew what it meant to eke out a living, farming in Kenya. His love of the bush also made him a natural friend of many others – he seemed to belong to the bush and knew how to survive.

"Giles had his own way of relating to the opportunities which Kenya offered him. He was a man of the air. His parachuting exploits were nothing if not unusual, and he was known for jumping out of aircraft without too much notice! Yet though he had a free spirit he was not a person who disregarded commitment. He was both hard working and very loyal and also did some extravagantly kind things.

"He had what we used to call personality – now charisma – and he was very generous with himself. He thus created an emotional link with people which meant that many felt attached to him. He had a deep sense of right and wrong and a clear understanding of how people should be respected. Our hearts go out to his parents, family and friends, and particularly to Emma, who shared Giles's last few years and was with him, and tried to save him, on the night that he died. Emma, we can't make sense of this terrible tragedy, but in you we know Giles found a kindred spirit and someone to love..."

Brian continued: "Members of our family joined us to set light to the pyre with tapers. The rising hot air freed the feathers to soar upwards to catch the gentle breeze; when it was well alight we all departed to a wake in the nearby hills. Stories of Giles's exploits were being recounted by all and sundry well into the small hours. Indeed many of his friends chose to sleep beneath the stars that night. Tony Dyer, Michael's father and a friend of Giles, was later to say that this was one of the biggest funeral attendances in Kenya in living memory.

"Later, in November, a Service of Thanksgiving took place at St. Paul's, Knightsbridge. Giles's many friends in England were joined by just as many who came from Africa and I came to realise that our son had possessed a most unusual combination of talents and personality. He had a gift for communicating his enthusiasm and energy to all around him. There was a certain amount in his own diaries, journals and letters which shed some light on his exploits and attractive nature. In researching this book, which was conceived as a memorial to our son, I, like I suspect many fathers in my position, have been able to discover much more about him and it has helped Verity and me to come to terms with our tragic loss."

Epilogue

The Last Word

Giles's last written communication was addressed to his Grandmother on hearing of the death of his grandfather, Ken Thornton, at the age of 89:

Dear Gran,

I have been in touch with Mum and Dad over the last six months and tried to follow how poor Grampy went through his last months. I felt for you so very much, I was thinking that you probably have not spent a night apart for many years. I felt so sad that I would not see him, talk to him, and get all that sarcastic story time or that hard advice, which he would deliver concerning my rather infrequent visits. The plus of the whole matter is: I never saw him go down, I never saw him in his sickness, I never saw him when he knew he was going to die; that was the plus. All I have in my mind is good: Grampy on form, off walking with me in the forest behind Woodside, whistling his dogs in, also, for me, a great part of Grampy is at Hampton, shooting with Richard. He just loved working his dogs and you, turning up at lunchtime with soup, beer and boiled egg sandwiches. I remember those weddings of my Thornton brothers in 1996 – Grampy looking so, so elegant, so good looking. The man knew how to dress. Your generation were so smart, so swish, so... what I want to be!

Especially out here in Africa: the amount of times I think, "How good it would be to have been born two generations ago!" Then Africa was pristine. The people who were here were genuine. There were no impostors and frauds that seem to litter East Africa these days. In those days the game and the bush were untouched, unspoiled and largely unexplored: something I am searching for all the time. There are pockets of great country to be found, but you have to travel great distances to find them and you pass through much of destroyed Africa, overcrowded and overpopulated mess. I suppose that's what they call 'development'. At the time you came to Africa with Grampy and went on safari with Digby Tatham-Walter, you were in the nick of time.

You saw a beautiful place and you had great people to guide you – how lucky you were! East Africa is still very beautiful and it is still has a huge grip over me, but it is half the experience, which you saw and enjoyed. The untouched country disappears under the weight of humanity day by day. The game is shot to feed the masses; the trees and bush are cleared for firewood by small farmers to eke out a living on marginal land, which they should never be on. They manage to reap a harvest once in five years if they are lucky,

I am painting a bad picture. Of course not all of East Africa is doomed. There are National Parks and privately owned land where game abounds and there are vast stretches of pristine bush, but you have to pay to go there and join hundreds of cars and minibuses, all doing the same thing: polluting your vision and your mind. What I crave and seek is untouched, unspoilt, unknown Africa, where you can go and never be bothered or harassed, where there's game to watch, views to take in and you can just become part of the scenery.

If I had been born at the turn of the century, the only things I would miss are my motorbike and my paraglider. Then again, I would be happy to give up both in order to be in Africa at that time. Paragliding has given me such experiences here. The whole glider folds up into a rucksack, which I carry on my back. Then I climb a mountain and launch myself from the top over Africa. I'm airborne, with no engine noise, just the wind to carry me up and across the great horizons. The phenomenon is so strong, the sight of the wildlife below on the ground, the various birds of prey soaring up there with you, the freedom to go where you please – as long as the wind permits: it just beggars description.

This year I have started work with Jane Tatham-Walter's son-in-law, Danny McCallum. As you surely know, he is a white hunter in Tanzania. He is a marvellous man who has been hunting since he was 19 years old. He is now 55 and has had so much experience. He has spent a great deal of time in the bush and will teach me much in the art of hunting big game. At the moment I am way out in the middle of nowhere at his hunting camp. There is plenty of game in some species such as buffalo, hartebeest, zebra, sable, roen and reedbuck. But elephant and the great predators such as lion and leopard are hard to find, though you hear them at night. The rhino have long gone. He was too easy to hunt and had such a valuable horn on his nose – he was doomed.

The client hunters arrive for two week safaris, shoot their trophies and depart. As this is my first year involved as an apprentice, I have started at the bottom. My job is cutting tracks through the bush, locating the herds of game and assisting with the placing of bait to attract the big cats. Danny is a professional and I am his apprentice. This arrangement will continue until October 1998 when the season ends. We pack up and I will return to Kenya to farm where I live and work for a man called Michael Dyer. It is then that I take out my paraglider and launch into the sky again with all the passion of a lost love!

Gran, I hope very much to be coming to England around March or April next year or maybe earlier. I will be coming to see you armed with my photos and stories. It will be different and without a doubt it will be difficult. In the absence of Grampy, his voice and his presence that were just part of Woodside, it just won't be the same. But you will be there. You are the person I will be coming to see, Ange Pange, and I look forward to it very much.

Gran I'm sorry you have heard, seen or read so little of me. It's one of those regrets of life, which too many people suffer from. No excuses allowed, I'm just a bad communicator and in the end it's my loss. It really does not take too much time to sit down and write every now and then.

I send you tonnes of love, a big kiss and a long hug. I hope all is well at Woodside.

I love you – Giles